PRIMARY COMMODITIES
IN INTERNATIONAL TRADE

By the same author

The World's Coffee. London, H.M.S.O., 1963

PRIMARY COMMODITIES IN INTERNATIONAL TRADE

BY

J.W.F. ROWE

Fellow of Pembroke College

and sometime Lecturer in Economics

in the University of Cambridge

CAMBRIDGE

AT THE UNIVERSITY PRESS

1965

PUBLISHED BY
THE SYNDICS OF THE CAMBRIDGE UNIVERSITY PRESS

Bentley House, 200 Euston Road, London, N.W.1
American Branch: 32 East 57th Street, New York, N.Y. 10022
West African Office: P.O. Box 33, Ibadan, Nigeria

©

CAMBRIDGE UNIVERSITY PRESS
1965

Printed in Great Britain at the University Printing House, Cambridge
(Brooke Crutchley, University Printer)

LIBRARY OF CONGRESS CATALOGUE
CARD NUMBER: 65-18930

TO MY WIFE

PREFACE

This book is fundamentally based on lectures given at Cambridge during the 1950's, but it is by no means a mere transcription. It is intended primarily to serve the needs of undergraduate students. I hope that post-graduate students and teachers of economics may find at least some chapters of interest, especially perhaps the appendix to chapter 5, and the later chapters of part IV on commodity control schemes. It must be emphasised that, as its title declares, the book deals with primary commodities in international trade, and not directly with the problems of 'underdeveloped countries' dependent on exports of primary products, though these are of course incidentally considered, and much of parts III and IV is relevant. Within its appointed realm, I have sought to make the book a comprehensive study within a reasonable length; but this has only been possible by selecting certain aspects and features for more intensive study than others, and my selection may disappoint some readers who will criticise the book as superficial here and unnecessarily detailed there. In particular, some readers may feel that the historical treatment has been overdone, but it is my own conviction that only by historical studies can one obtain that 'feel' of the production and marketing problems of the primary industries which is so essential to their full understanding, and that a realistic grasp of the problems of commodity control can only be obtained by studying the gradual evolution and changing character of actual control schemes.

It is to my mind curious that comparatively little attention even today appears to be paid by British economists to the primary industries, despite Britain's vital interests as an importer of foodstuffs and raw materials, and as a producer for export of many of them throughout the world: not to mention the part which British merchants play in the international marketing of primary commodities. In the U.S.A. economists appear to have been scarcely more interested, at any rate recently, than those in Britain. Much basic material has been provided by government departments both in Britain and the U.S.A., and of course by the United Nations Organisation and the Food and Agriculture Organisation. To my knowledge, however, no general study of this subject from an international or world-wide point of view has been published in English since the last war; and even reasonably up-to-date books on particular primary commodities are few. Whatever its defects, I trust my book will help to fill this large gap, and in particular I hope it may be a useful complementary study to the far more abundant recent literature on 'underdeveloped countries'.

In the course of my investigations of primary industries I have received unstinted help from a very large number of persons—producers, merchants, processors and manufacturers, politicians, civil servants and economists—not only in Britain, but also in a not inconsiderable number of producing countries which I have been able to visit during the last thirty years or so. To them I owe much, especially in helping me to acquire first-hand knowledge of the organisation of primary production and marketing, and a realistic approach to commodity problems. In the actual making of this book, however, I have incurred particular obligations to some of my colleagues, especially to Mr C. W. Guillebaud and Professor A. J. Youngson, who have both read almost the whole manuscript, and also to Professor E. A. G. Robinson and Mr M. V. Posner, who have read a substantial part of it. Their criticisms and suggestions have been most valuable, and while I alone, of course, am responsible for the final product, I wish to record my most grateful thanks to all four of them for their interest in this project and their labours to improve its outcome.

J. W. F. R.

Pembroke College
Cambridge
May 1965

CONTENTS

Preface   *page* vii

List of Tables   xi

PART I   THE PRODUCTION OF PRIMARY COMMODITIES

1 The principal primary commodities in international
   trade and their sources of supply   1

2 The structure and organisation of production   13

PART II   THE ORGANISATION OF MARKETING

3 The principal consuming markets   28

4 The physical processes of marketing   32

5 The determination of prices   43

   Appendix: The economics of private merchanting
   versus government bulk trading   56

6 The behaviour of prices   66

PART III   GENERAL TRENDS AND FLUCTUATIONS OF
           INTERNATIONAL TRADE SINCE WORLD WAR I

7 The inter-war period   77

8 The period 1939–50   91

9 The period 1950–64   101

PART IV   COMMODITY CONTROL SCHEMES

10 Evolution and development of commodity control
    schemes to 1929   120

11 The crisis of 1930 and government interventions   129

12 The new control schemes of the 1930's   136

ix

CONTENTS

13 Control schemes since 1945   *page* 155

14 The mechanics of commodity control   184

    Appendix: Crop-equalisation schemes versus the
    merchant regime   205

15 The recent progress and future prospects of commodity
    control   209

Index   221

LIST OF TABLES

I   The principal primary commodities in international trade and the value and volume of their exports, 1959–61   *page* 5

II   The principal exporters of primary products outside Europe   7

III   The principal consuming markets importing primary products from overseas   30

IV   Commodity prices and the Korean War   102

V   The principal exports of primary products in 1934–8, 1948–52 and 1959–61   113

PART I

THE PRODUCTION OF PRIMARY COMMODITIES

---

1. THE PRINCIPAL PRIMARY COMMODITIES IN INTERNATIONAL TRADE AND THEIR SOURCES OF SUPPLY

If asked to define the primary industries, most people would reply that they are the industries which supply foodstuffs and raw materials as contrasted with those which supply manufactures. As a rough guide, this will pass, but the contrast suggests that primary products are either just grown and harvested or dug out of the ground, and sold in those forms. This is in many cases far from the truth: even grain crops have to be threshed, and cotton has to be ginned to separate the seed from the lint; sugar cane and beet are processed, often in very large-scale plants crammed with machinery; the processing of tea is undertaken in what are commonly called 'estate factories'; and in some countries the same is true of coffee. Similarly, natural rubber comes from the tree in semi-liquid form, most of which must be consolidated into thin sheets; sisal is harvested as huge fleshy leaves which must be decorticated, usually by mechanical power. Metallic minerals have to be smelted and refined, processes which are often undertaken either at the mines or in the producing countries, and usually before the metals are first sold. Moreover, the processing or manufacturing may well make a vast difference to the quality, and therefore the price, of the products. Almost all primary products are really semi-manufactured, though the extent of the manufacturing varies greatly; and even with any one there is often considerable variation in the extent of the processing or manufacturing which the producers undertake, or which is undertaken in the different producing countries. Sometimes the producer sells to the processor, and sometimes he does the processing himself; but the form in which the commodity is first exchanged internationally is more or less standardised. A better definition of primary industries therefore is that they are those industries which supply foodstuffs and raw materials by agriculture or mining in the form in which they are first exchanged internationally. Agriculture of course includes both vegetable and animal products, while vegetable products here cover both ordinary crops and also arboreal or tree crops such as rubber, sisal and copra. Mining covers every method of mining minerals, both from the surface and underground.

All countries produce some primary commodities, but no country is completely self-sufficient. Some countries have a surplus supply of one or more primary commodities, and the surplus is exported in order to finance the import of other primary products or manufactures. In a similar way, industrially advanced countries export mainly manufactures in order to finance their deficiencies in primary products. Thus the volume and value of the world's primary products are vastly greater than the volume and value of primary products which are traded internationally, though in a few cases almost the whole world production is exported by the producing countries: tin, for example, is a primary commodity of which the producing countries use hardly any themselves. This study is confined to primary commodities in international trade. It must, however, be borne in mind that home consumption of some primary products within a producing country may far exceed exports, even though these may be a large proportion of total world exports. Of this, the place of wheat and cotton in the economy of the U.S.A. is an obvious example. On the other hand, for some commodities there may be no home consumption at all, even though the country is a relatively large exporter.

At the beginning of the 1960's the statisticians of the United Nations and the Food and Agriculture Organisation estimated the annual value of world exports of primary products at about 55 billion U.S. dollars (average 1959–61), and the value of total world exports, primary products and manufactures, at about 124–125 billion dollars: thus primary products account for about 44–45% of total world exports. Of the world exports of primary products, agriculture (including forestry) provided 70% and mining 30%. A division between foodstuffs (including animal feeding stuffs) and raw materials is more useful for most purposes, and this shows foodstuffs as 40% of the total exports of primary products, and raw materials 60%. Of the raw materials, 50% were minerals and metals, and 50% were of agricultural origin. All these proportions are to be treated as approximate only, but they do give an indication of the relative orders of magnitude of the different parts of the picture.

What then are the principal primary commodities in international trade? There are a very large number which are traded internationally though the values of world exports of many of them are very small relative to the obviously important ones. Even the less important commodities remain of considerable importance to particular exporting and importing countries; for example, cereals other than wheat, rice and maize, or various spices. Then there are a number which in statistical summaries are often shown under a single heading, but which are really groups of commodities varying greatly in kind and quality, and with corresponding variations in price. Thus the heading 'fruit' covers all the diverse kinds of fruit in various states, fresh, dried or preserved: 'fish' is a heterogeneous group of very different sizes and sorts, and so is 'hides and skins': 'wines' includes some of quality which are many times the value of others. As groups these headings may show considerable total export values. The grouping may, however, conceal such great differences that if they are treated as single commodities in comparison with other particular commodities, then the result may appear contrary to common sense and common knowledge. Of course this is all a matter of degrees of diversity. It might be argued that wheat and cotton and wool, and many other primary commodities, vary so much in type and quality that they ought not to be talked about as single commodities: but they do come, as it were, from common stocks, and the characteristics which they have in common are more than their differences. A line has to be drawn somewhere, and the groups mentioned above will be considered as coming below it and are therefore excluded. Again there are other products which, mainly because of the costs of transportation, have regional rather than world-wide trade: for example, the timber which is exported by the Scandinavian countries is mostly marketed in the U.K. and western Europe. Canada's exports of timber go to the U.S.A., and the same is broadly true of wood pulp. Similarly, most of the exports of bauxite, other than intra-European trade, are from Jamaica and the Guianas to the U.S.A. and Canada. In recent years the trade in coal has become more and more regional rather than world-wide, as it was before World War I. Iron ore is, so to speak, a border-line case: there is the large trade amongst European countries and between them and the U.K. (including the production of North Africa), and there is another regional trade from

3

Venezuela, Brazil, Chile and Peru, all to the U.S.A. It may well be argued that this distinction between regional and world-wide trade has little significance, and certainly it is all a matter of degree; but, in order to reduce the list of the principal primary products of international trade to manageable proportions, these commodities will not be treated. It should however be remembered that these regional trades are of considerable value and involve considerable tonnages.

This study must seek a representative list of commodities which are commonly considered to be the staple primary commodities of world-wide trade. It will not matter that the list contains various anomalies, as long as it is representative. Thus the value of the world exports of some items on the list will be small in comparison with the obviously important ones, but to omit, say, tin, lead and zinc would be absurd. Notwithstanding what has been said above about groupings of products, groups such as oils and fats, meat, dairy produce and hard fibres must be included, though some breakdown will be given later. Also, in spite of what has been said above about regional trades, tea, with its regional production and one overwhelmingly important though far-distant market (the U.K.), will be included: to do otherwise would contravene common usage and common sense. The list is probably more open to criticism as to what it omits than what it includes, but to make it longer would probably not make it more satisfactory. Nevertheless, the omissions explained above should not be forgotten.

Table I therefore shows a selected representative list of the principal primary products in international trade of a world-wide or inter-ocean character. Against each entry is set the average value of world exports in the three years 1959–61, the percentage which that forms of the value of total world exports of all primary products, and the tonnage of the exports. The values and tonnages are drawn from U.N. and F.A.O. sources;[1] but the difficulties of compilation are obviously so great that the figures shown here are best regarded as little more than indications of the relative orders of magnitude of the world exports of the various commodities and groups of commodities. The percentages should be treated with a similar caution. Nevertheless, the figures given are a great deal better than no such figures, and will serve well enough for the present purpose.

The next step in this study must be to ascertain the principal

---

[1] See *U.N. Commodity Survey 1962*, and *F.A.O. Trade in Agricultural Commodities in the U.N. Development Decade*, vol. 2, part IV (1964).

TABLE I. *The principal primary commodities in international trade and the value and volume of their exports 1959–61*

Commodity	Value of world exports (million U.S. dollars average 1959–61)	Percent of value of total world exports of primary products	Volume of exports (million tons)
1. Petroleum, crude	5,280	9·5	375
2. Meat	2,769	5·0	—[2]
3. Wheat and flour	2,603	4·7	39·5
4. Fats and oils	2,510	4·5	—[2]
5. Cotton	2,270	4·1	3·6
6. Coffee	1,878	3·4	2·6
7. Copper[1]	1,550	2·8	2·5
8. Wool	1,545	2·8	0·9[3]
9. Sugar	1,498	2·7	17·5
10. Rubber	1,460	2·6	2·2
11. Dairy products	1,141	2·0	—[2]
12. Tobacco	940	1·7	0·7
13. Rice	694	1·3	6·6
14. Maize	632	1·1	12·0
15. Tea	616	1·1	0·5
16. Cocoa	521	0·9	0·9
17. Tin[1]	392	0·7	0·2
18. Jute and hard fibres	318	0·6	1·4
19. Zinc[1]	278	0·5	1·8
20. Lead[1]	207	0·4	1·2
Total of above	29,102	52·4	—
Total world exports of all primary products	55,507	100·0	—

[1] Excluding U.S.S.R., China, and other centrally planned economies.
[2] Kinds and qualities too heterogeneous to be added together.
[3] Clean basis.

sources of the international supply of the commodities listed in table I: in other words, what are the chief exporting countries? Now the U.K.'s domestic exports of primary commodities are insignificant, and the exports from the countries of continental Europe (including the U.S.S.R.), though in some cases relatively important, are almost exclusively to other European countries and the U.K. Europe can therefore be reasonably treated as a region, and as such may be disregarded as an exporter of primary commodities. This will greatly simplify the answer to the foregoing question, which then becomes 'What are the principal exporting countries outside

Europe?', for this, with few exceptions, will mean countries exporting overseas. A mere list of countries exporting each product will, however, be unsatisfactory, for even among the chief or main or important countries the amounts normally exported may differ very widely, and any classification of these countries as major or minor exporters, or on similar lines, is bound to be misleading. The only satisfactory course is to put against each country a representative figure for the volume of its exports, even though this requires a table with many figures. There is no other way of ascertaining their relative importance as exporters with any reasonable accuracy. Though the relative values of the exports of different countries may differ from the relative tonnages exported, owing to differences in the quality of the product, volume measurements are the only simple uniform standard of comparison. In table II, the figures against each country are approximate averages of the volume of their exports in the three years 1959–61, or, in special cases as marked, figures which are deemed to be still more representative. Readers will not, of course, try to carry any of these figures in their heads. A glance will suffice to show which country or countries are the chief exporters, and roughly in what proportions, and will produce a far clearer general impression than the use of adjectives.

Table II therefore shows the principal exporters outside Europe of the primary products listed in table I, with average or representative figures for the volume of their exports from 1959 to 1961. All figures are thousands of tons unless otherwise stated, and are based on the *F.A.O. Trade Yearbooks*, or the *Statistical Summary of the Mineral Industry, 1957–62* (Overseas Geological Surveys, H.M.S.O.), or the Commonwealth Economic Committee's review *Non-Ferrous Metals 1963* (H.M.S.O.), with one exception as noted.

6

TABLE II. *The principal exporters of primary products outside Europe*

(All figures are averages for 1959–61 in thousand tons, unless otherwise stated.)

(1) PETROLEUM PRODUCTS[1] (MILLION TONS)

	Crude	Fuel oil	Motor spirit	Gas oil	Diesel oil
Kuwait	81	6	—	1·8	—
Saudi Arabia	62	5	0·8	—	1·5
Iraq	45	—	—	—	—
Iran	44	6	3·3	1·1	0·6
Quatar	8	—	—	—	—
Total Middle East	240	17	4·1	2·9	2·1
Venezuela	114	30	2·3	3·7	2·7

[1] Exports 1962 only, as a steady and rapid increase is occurring every year in nearly all these countries.

(2) MEAT

	Beef (fresh, chilled or frozen)	Mutton and lamb
Argentina	321[1]	33
Australia	190[1]	67
New Zealand	101[1]	342
Uruguay	39	—

[1] Average 1959–62.

Note. Overseas trade in pig-meat and poultry is very small. Meat is also exported in various dried, salted, smoked or otherwise prepared forms, some in tins and some not, mainly from Brazil, Uruguay, Paraguay, Australia, Canada, and the U.S.A.

(3) WHEAT AND FLOUR (MILLION TONS)

U.S.A.	15·4	Argentina	2·2[1]
Canada	8·9	Australia	3·4[2]

[1] Average 1959–62 owing to very small crop in 1961.
[2] Average of rapidly rising exports (1962 was 6·3).

7

TABLE II (*cont.*)

(4) FATS AND OILS

Total exports of the principal kinds of fats and oils show the composition of this group. The first figure after the chief exporters of each kind shows the exports of seed, followed in parentheses by its oil equivalent: and the figure after the + sign shows the exports of oil. Thus the Philippine Republic exported 884 of copra, the oil equivalent of which is (557), and 66 of coconut oil. The conversion factors used are copra 63 % oil, soya beans 16 % oil, groundnuts 42 % oil, palm kernels 45 % oil.

	World exports in terms of oil	Chief exporters
Copra and coconut oil	1150	Philippine Republic 884 (557)+66; Indonesia 230 (145)+0; Ceylon 43 (27)+73; Malaya 0+44
Soya beans and oil	1184	U.S.A. 3667 (587)+385; China 1044 (167)+34
Palm oil	572	Nigeria 182; Congo Republic 168; Indonesia 110; Malaya 84
Palm kernels and oil	385	Nigeria 427 (192)+0
Cotton seed and oil	291	U.S.A. 6+201
Linseed and oil	426	Argentina 54+197
Lard	360	U.S.A. 278
Inedible fats (tallow, etc.)	915	U.S.A. 748

In addition, world exports of fish oils 240, and of whale oil 494.

Note. The above figures are based on statistics in annual addresses by Mr J. C. A. Faure (Unilever Ltd) to the International Association of Seed Crushers congresses.

(5) COTTON

U.S.A.	1330	Uganda	63
Mexico	342	Other Africa	201
United Arab Republic	330	Brazil	64
Sudan[1]	137	Peru	109
Turkey		52	

[1] Average 1959–62 as more representative.

8

TABLE II (*cont.*)

(6) COFFEE

Brazil	1030
Colombia	360
Other Central and South America	503 of which Mexico 84, El Salvador 86, Guatemala 81, Costa Rica 47
Africa	633 of which Ivory Coast 132, Uganda 104, Angola 98

(7) COPPER

	Unrefined	Refined unwrought
Rhodesia (Zambia)	156	380
Chile	273	213
Peru	158[1]	28
Congo Republic[2] (est.)	110	176
Canada	—	228

[1] Average 1960–2 as very large increase from 1960 compared with previous year.
[2] I.e. Katanga mines.

Small quantities of ores, concentrates, etc., are also exported by these and other countries.

(8) WOOL

Australia	610 mainly merino
New Zealand	246 mainly crossbred
South Africa	120 mainly merino
Argentina	140 mainly crossbred
Uruguay	47 mainly crossbred

PRODUCTION OF PRIMARY COMMODITIES

TABLE II (*cont.*)

(9) SUGAR

Cuba	5445	Until 1961 received limited tariff preference from U.S.A.	
Dominican Republic	844		
Peru	523		

		Australia	780
		British West Indies	700
(A) Philippine Republic 1067	(B)	Mauritius[1]	505
		British Guiana	297
		South Africa	270
		Fiji	181

(C) Formosa 753   Reunion 185   Mozambique 113

(A) Philippine Republic has preferential rate in U.S. tariff.
(B) These countries have a preferential rate in U.K. tariff.
(C) Formosa exports mainly to Japan, Reunion to France, and Mozambique to Portugal.

[1] Average 1959 and 1961 only, as severe hurricane damage in 1960.

(10) RUBBER (NATURAL)

Malaya   693 (exports minus imports)
Indonesia 664 (including estimated unrecorded shipments)
Thailand 175
Ceylon   96
Africa   130 (mainly from Nigeria, Liberia and Congo Republic)

(11) DAIRY PRODUCTS

	Butter	Cheese	Eggs
New Zealand	175	85	—
Australia	74	17	—

Note. As an exception to the exclusion of European exporters from this table, the following figures are added

Denmark	119	78	85
Netherlands	37	107	183
Switzerland	—	31	—

TABLE II *(cont.)*

---

(12) TOBACCO (UNMANUFACTURED)

U.S.A.	221	Rhodesia[1]	87
Turkey	71	India	42
Bulgaria	66	Brazil	37
Greece	61	Cuba	24

[1] Including Nyasaland (Malawi).

---

(13) RICE (MILLION TONS)

Burma 1·7   Thailand 1·3   U.S.A. 0·8

---

(14) MAIZE (MILLION TONS)

U.S.A.	6·2
Argentina	2·5 (average 1959–62, as exports were much reduced in 1961)
South Africa	0·8 (average 1959–62, as exports were rapidly increasing; 1962 was 2·1)

---

(15) TEA

India	205
Ceylon	184
Indonesia	32
Africa	41 (mainly Rhodesia and Nyasaland (Malawi), Kenya and Mozambique)

---

(16) COCOA BEANS

Ghana	325
Nigeria	163
Other Africa	181 (mainly Ivory Coast and Cameroon)
Brazil	103
Ecuador	32

Also small exports from some Central American countries and West Indies.

TABLE II (*cont.*)

---

(17) TIN

Production of ore in terms of metal content[1]

Malaya	56	Bolivia	20
Indonesia	19	Nigeria	8
Thailand	13	Congo Republic	7
China (est. exports)	18		

[1] These production figures are used instead of exports, for though the whole output of these countries (except China) is exported, the export statistics are affected by the location of smelting plants, e.g. Malaya exports 78 because some ores produced in Indonesia, Thailand, etc., are smelted in Malaya. The figures are averages for 1960–2 as organised restriction was in operation in 1959.

===

(18) JUTE AND HARD FIBRES

Jute
Pakistan	724
Thailand	81

Sisal and other agave fibres
Tanganyika	209	Indonesia	15
Kenya	56	Brazil	117
Angola	57	Mexico	35
Mozambique	29		

Manilla fibre
Philippine Republic	94

===

(19) ZINC

	Ores and concentrates (zinc content)	Metal (unwrought)
Canada	164	177
Australia	155	36
Mexico	188	32
Peru	144	26
Congo Republic	47	50
Algeria and Morocco	87	—

Note. The U.S.A. and western Europe are large producers as well as importers of concentrates.

TABLE II (*cont.*)

(20) LEAD

	Ores and concentrates (lead content)	Metal (unwrought)
Australia	63	185
Canada	52	91
Mexico	—	153
Peru	60	63
Morocco	63	26
South-west Africa	62	—

Note. The U.S.A. and western Europe are large producers as well as importers of concentrates and metal.

2. THE STRUCTURE AND ORGANISATION OF PRODUCTION

The previous chapter has provided a summary account of the relative importance in international trade of the principal primary commodities or groups of allied commodities and of the more important exporting countries. The next stage must be to inquire how these primary commodities are produced, and how processed into the form in which they are internationally marketed, by what size and sort of business units, or by what sort of businessmen, and by what sort of labour. It is generally known that the structure and organisation of the primary industries are enormously varied, and, often, so are those of the same industry in different countries and even within one country. Some primary commodities are mainly produced by peasant smallholders, for example oilseeds or cocoa; some by relatively large farmers, for example wheat or dairy products; some by relatively small joint-stock companies, for example tea or sisal; and some by very large joint-stock companies, for example copper. But there are also many primary commodities which are produced by business units of widely varying sorts, for example cotton by smallholders and also by large plantation companies, wool by small farmers and the great pastoral companies, coffee by smallholders, substantial farmers and very large family concerns. These variations are often to be found within one producing country. Hence generalisations are extremely difficult and are apt to be misleading. A comprehensive survey would necessitate individual studies of the structure and organisation of each industry. This would be an impossible task for any individual investigator, and would far exceed a book of manage-able size. Moreover, much of the detail would be of little general interest to the ordinary student of economics. Nevertheless, despite the inherent risks, it seems worth while to attempt a brief survey over a wide field of primary production. Even if this means little more than arranging and codifying general knowledge, it will direct attention to a few leading ideas and general principles. Such a survey is indeed justified if only as a fundamentally necessary prelude to further study of the primary industries.

The petroleum industry, and especially the international trade in its products, is known to be dominated by a few very large inter-national concerns. When the industry began to develop in the U.S.A., large numbers of independent small concerns produced crude oil, because the amount of capital required to drill and operate a well was not great. The transporting of the oil to refineries did, however, demand considerable capital, as did the refineries, which were characterised by high overhead costs and comparatively low running costs. In marketing, as well as in certain stages of production, the economics of large scale were soon evident. Once the process of concentration had got under way, companies which had developed large refining and marketing interests might find themselves short of crude oil supplies unless they integrated backwards, while the generally inelastic demand for petroleum products tended to pro-mote integration forwards. Research of all kinds, and exploration for new supplies, also demanded large capital resources. Without going into further detail, it may be said that there are powerful forces in this industry making for very large-scale concerns vertically integrated all the way from crude production to the final sale of the processed products. Thus today in the U.S.A. some twenty such concerns[1] cover a very large proportion of the whole industry, though there are many more relatively small companies engaged mainly in the production of crude oil or in specialised operations. Outside the U.S.A., the industry is still more intensely concentrated and integrated. The development of the industry in the Middle East could only be accomplished by very large concerns commanding the

---

[1] According to *Oil Companies and Governments* by J. E. Hartshorn (Faber, 1962) on which the present author has drawn freely for this summary. The book is a most interesting study of the modern politico-economic problems of the industry.

capital resources for the costly exploration and exploitation of the very large concessions which were negotiated with the countries concerned, and for refining, transport and marketing. The same was true on a smaller scale in Venezuela and the Caribbean. The development of the oil industry outside the U.S.A., and outside the U.S.S.R., is virtually in the hands of five of the largest American concerns together with the Royal Dutch Shell Company, the British Petroleum Company, and a French company which does not compare in size with most of the others. There are also many independent companies in the refining and marketing stages, while many tankers are chartered from shipping companies in addition to those which are owned by the big oil concerns themselves. These eight international concerns co-operate together, especially in the Middle East. Thus, all of them are shareholders in one company which operates the Iranian industry, five are shareholders in one company in Iraq and four in Saudi Arabia. In this way the degree of concentration is in a sense increased. There is also some joint organisation in refining and marketing, for example between Royal Dutch Shell and B.P. Not all these concerns are equally strong in all the various stages; there are great differences between them, and a measure of competition exists. There is, however, no doubt that together they form an enormous oligopoly, and, as is usual under such circumstances, competition is mainly in quality of products and of services, rather than in price, though discounts and rebates, some open and some hidden, are said to play a part.

The structure of the petroleum industry is indeed a special and individual case, but this very brief summary must suffice here. Next it will be convenient to survey the non-ferrous metal industries, because their structure and organisation are rather more homogeneous than those of the agricultural industries, in that the producing units are mostly of a definitely capitalistic nature. This is because underground mining usually involves considerable capital expenditure, and the same is broadly true of open-cast mines on the surface. Most mining operations are more economically conducted on a very large scale; in consequence joint-stock company organisation has long been usual. The tin-mining industries of Malaya, Indonesia and Nigeria, as contrasted with Bolivia's underground tin mining, mostly work alluvial deposits quite close to the surface. Even the use of tin dredges for working such deposits involves considerable capital and therefore joint-stock company organisation, though in Malaya

Chinese partnerships, with only small amounts of capital and excavating the tin-bearing soil largely by hand, still account for a significant total output. Most mining companies were originally formed to deal with one and only one property. Until the beginning of this century there were a large number of relatively small companies, though even then a few very large companies existed in the copper, lead and zinc industries. Gradually these numerous nominally independent companies have combined to form big, sometimes very big, groups. This has happened formally by the creation of holding companiés as in the copper industry almost all over the world; or less formally by the appointment of common directors, or by the exchange of shares; or less formally still, though quite effectively, as the result of the influence of the firms of mining engineers which originally did much to promote the companies and continued to serve them in various ways: such influence has, for example, been a powerful factor promoting common policies and combination in Malaya's tin-dredging industry. The tendency to horizontal combination has come about in order to facilitate the raising of more capital for expansion and for financial reasons generally, in order to lessen risks by spreading them, in order to secure greater bargaining power with smelters and merchants, and for greater ease and economy in exercising adequate control over often far-away properties. Vertical combination to cover smelting and even refining at or near the mines has gone a long way in the copper, lead and zinc industries. It has gone less far in the tin industry because the high value of tin concentrates permits transport, because the individual mines are relatively small, and because tin smelting is technically a very difficult process. The real extent of common control varies greatly, and is often difficult to determine. It may be confined to general policy or it may extend, so to speak, to daily operation. In some cases it varies from time to time with changing general or special conditions. But there is no doubt that, generally speaking, what may be termed the units of control are very much larger, and therefore fewer, than the nominally separate units of actual production, i.e. the nominally independent companies. Hence, the adoption of a common policy for a large section of any of these mining industries, or even for the industry as a whole, is in practice very much easier than might be supposed in view of the multiplicity of nominally independent producing units.

As illustrating the extent to which horizontal and vertical combination, and the concentration of production, can develop, the structure of the copper industry may be very summarily outlined. In the copper industry throughout the world, smelting is normally undertaken at the mines,[1] primarily because of the low copper content of the ores (even Rhodesia's ores only average about 3 %), while the association of refining with smelting has many advantages, especially since the advent of the electrolytic process. Hence horizontal combination is, so to speak, reinforced by vertical combination, and the world's copper industry is now controlled by a very few, very large, concerns. The U.S.A. is, and has been since the last century, by far the largest producer of primary copper, but consumes the whole production. The principal exporters are now Rhodesia, Chile, Canada, Congo Republic and Peru.[2] The copper industry of the U.S.A. is dominated by three very large concerns—Kennecott, Phelps Dodge and Anaconda—which between them now produce some three-quarters of the U.S. mine output, and control 94 % of the smelting capacity. They also control a very large proportion of the refining capacity, sufficient to deal also with most of the unrefined exports of Chile and Peru. These concerns have so concentrated their mine production that five mines now produce half the U.S. output, and ten mines produce about three-quarters. Two of these 'Big Three' have developed the greater part of the copper industry of Chile, where only three mines account for 90 % of the country's output of around 500,000 tons of primary copper. Similarly, two American-owned companies virtually control Peru's much smaller industry. In Canada the International Nickel Company's mines provide about 30 % of the national production, but there are several other more or less independent companies, for copper is now mined in the west as well as in Quebec. The more recently developed, but now very large, Rhodesian industry, producing over 500,000 tons of primary copper, is almost entirely in the hands of two large concerns— the Anglo-American Corporation and the Rhodesian Selection Trust—in both of which American capital has large holdings, while the former owns a substantial amount of the latter's capital. The actual mines are also few and large. Each concern owns three, apart from undeveloped properties. Finally, the mines in the Congo Republic, with a production of over 200,000 tons, are all owned by the Union Minière du Haut-Katanga. The world's copper industry is thus very highly centralised. This does not however integrate the

---

[1] Hence the absence of any considerable world trade in ores and concentrates.
[2] For statistics see chapter 1, table II, page 9.

different views of the main producing and exporting concerns, still less those of the governments of the countries in which they operate, especially where copper exports form a large proportion of the total exports as in Chile, Rhodesia and the Congo Republic. Lead and zinc are often found in the same ores, and in these industries horizontal combination and concentration have resulted in some large concerns; but vertical combination is less developed, and there is a substantial export trade in lead ores and concentrates, and a still larger one proportionally in zinc concentrates, for smelting in non-producing countries.

Turning to agriculture, attention may first be given to the products of the temperate regions, which are mainly cereals and animal products. Wheat is grown in nearly every country which consumes wheat, usually as part of a mixed farming, sometimes by very small peasant holdings, sometimes by much larger units. But the supplies of wheat which are traded overseas come in the main from farms of relatively large acreage which specialise in wheat growing. Of the four big exporters, this is least true in certain parts of the U.S.A., for there the tendency towards mixed farming is strong, and has gone further than in Canada or Australia or Argentina, though all these countries are moving in the direction of more mixed farming. Mixed farming usually means smaller farms, though mechanisation is tending to increase the optimum size, and also the amount of capital and credit required. These and other obvious factors result in great differences in the size of farms. In the main the farms in the wheat-exporting countries are one-man businesses or small partnerships, but the acreage of the farms varies very greatly, from a few hundred up to several thousand acres. In Argentina there are still many large farms more or less specialising in wheat. The large farm usually scores by greater and more economical use of machinery and mechanical transport: the smaller farm by more careful farming and higher yields. The average yield per acre, however, especially on the large farms, is in all the exporting countries still much below that in England or western Europe—it is still extensive rather than intensive cultivation. With modern mechanisation, labour employed per acre is very small, and labour costs and total costs per unit of product are very much lower than in Europe. Yet even in these matters there are wide variations, and generalisations of any value are almost impossible, apart from the broad statement that the range of variations is very great in almost all respects. This also applies to barley and oats, though there is not usually the same degree of specialisation as in wheat; these are much more truly products of mixed farming. Maize must be grown in the warmer parts of the temperate regions, and now that Argentina has so largely reduced its exports, the southern U.S.A. is the principal overseas exporter. Again, all that can be said is that there is great variety in the size of farms and in the degree of specialisation in this crop.

As with cereals, practically every country in the temperate zones produces home supplies of the main animal products—beef, mutton and pig-meat, butter, cheese and eggs, wool, and hides and skins. Many sub-tropical and tropical countries produce some at least of these products. Usually these home supplies are produced on mixed farms of no great size, but the supplies which are traded overseas come in the main from larger and more specialised farms. This is least true of pig-meat, butter and cheese, but the main supplies of beef, mutton and wool, and therefore of hides and skins, come from the large ranches of Argentina and Uruguay, from the extensive cattle and sheep ranges of the great pastoral companies in Australia, South Africa and New Zealand, or from large, more or less specialised farms in those countries. Thus with these products the joint-stock company plays a considerable part, though many large farms and ranches are one-man or family businesses, built up gradually to their present size over several generations. In general, production is extensive and not intensive, and is on a large scale measured by acreage, though the amount of labour employed is relatively small. The amount of capital used tends to vary greatly, for fixed capital may be required on a fairly large scale for the provision of water supplies and fencing and for housing the workers. The rapid building up of flocks and herds may also require a good deal of working capital. The processing of the animals into meat in exportable form is performed by large specialist concerns, mostly joint-stock companies but sometimes co-operatives owned by the farmers. Here the advantages of very large-scale plant and operations are considerable, limited only in practice by the costs of transporting the animals to the factory; but this has little or no direct influence on the size of the farms. The processing and packing of dairy products are simpler, and the economies of large scale are much more limited: hence the plants are more commonly owned and run by co-operative societies of the farmers. As with cereal farming, however, there is almost infinite variety, and little more can profitably be said by way of generalisation.

For the agricultural products of tropical and sub-tropical areas, rather fuller treatment seems desirable because these industries may be less generally familiar than farming in the temperate zones. Broadly speaking, there are two very different types of producing unit—the plantation or estate of fairly large size and employing a good deal of hired labour, and the smallholding of the peasant proprietor. Some industries are dominated by the one or the other type, and some exhibit both types in operation in different countries, or even within one country. Typical of the plantation industries are tea, sisal and tobacco, though there is also an appreciable production of these crops by smallholders. Typical of the peasant smallholding industries are rice, vegetable oilseeds (such as copra, palm oil, palm kernels and groundnuts), cocoa and jute; but again the units of production are not exclusively of this type. Typical of the mixed plantation and smallholding industries are cotton, coffee, sugar and rubber. Such a varied picture obviously invites inquiry as to why some industries are dominated by one type of producing unit rather than the other, and how it comes about that in the 'mixed' industries both types exist side by side, instead of one type ousting the other; for the mixture is no transitional short-period phenomenon.

The typical plantation industries may be considered first. Outside of China, the production of tea used to be almost entirely in the hands of mainly European-owned joint-stock companies. It was Europeans who first introduced the cultivation of tea to India, Ceylon and the Netherlands East Indies (now Indonesia), which remain the biggest producers. As organised by Europeans in relatively large units, a good deal of capital was usually involved in the opening up of suitable sites for plantations, and often for housing the local workers and the European staff. Further capital was required for the initial planting and the care and maintenance of the bushes until big enough for plucking to begin, and for the buildings—commonly referred to as the estate factory—for the preparation or 'manufacture' of the leaves into the tea of commerce. Consequently, the joint-stock company was the usual form of organisation. Fundamentally, however, no great amount of capital is necessary: smallholders can plant up patches by investing their own labour, and small 'factories' can be established by co-operative societies with some government or 'outside' financial help, just as co-operative coffee pulperies have been established in Kenya and elsewhere. But the preparation of tea does involve a certain amount of technical knowledge and skill and, above all, never-failing care and attention. This, coupled with the proper cultivation and plucking of the bushes, has so far given the estate an advantage over the peasant smallholder, though smallholders have been taking up tea in East Africa at an increasing rate in recent years. It is these factors, and not primarily the length of the gestation period, i.e. the 4–5 years between planting and production, which so far keeps tea mainly an estate industry, for roughly the same gestation period for coffee, and the still longer gestation period for rubber, has not prevented the rise of very large smallholders' industries.

It is much the same with tobacco. The drying and preparation of the leaf is the keystone of successful production, and the greater part of the tobacco which is traded internationally is produced by men of European descent, whether actually in Europe or in the U.S.A. or in Southern Rhodesia. The scale of the tobacco-producing units is usually much smaller than for tea, and the joint-stock company is relatively rare: the one-man or family farm of moderate size is typical.

The factors determining the structure and organisation of the sisal industry are, however, quite different. Until recently, power-driven machinery was necessary for tearing the fibre out of the leaves, while the size and weight of the leaves made mechanical means of transport, on the scale required by the machinery, economical as compared with even very cheap labour. The industry was therefore developed in East Africa and the Netherlands East Indies in joint-stock company form, some companies being large and owning several estates, and some really only one-man businesses or partnerships in company form. In East Africa, African farmers have in many areas planted sisal hedges round their holdings, and a small output now comes from this source, the leaves being sold to the nearest estate for processing. In recent years, however, a small hand machine for tearing out the fibre has been developed, and the new sisal industry which has been built up in Brazil since World War II is a smallholders' industry. The future of this Brazilian industry, however, is not too well assured, and there is little reason to suppose that the dominance of the plantation industry in Africa will be seriously diminished in the foreseeable future.

Turning to the typical smallholding industries, rice in the big exporting countries of Burma and Thailand is grown by peasant proprietors and their families by the methods and in the circumstances which centuries have made traditional.[1] Vegetable oilseeds, like copra, palm oil and palm kernels, once the trees are planted, involve continuous harvesting rather than cultivation, and the preparation processes are not too difficult. When the demand for copra became considerable towards the end of the last century owing to the development of margarine manufacture, a number of coconut plantations were established by Europeans in the Far East and the Pacific. The local people soon discovered how profitable the copra business had become, and how relatively simple the production was, and before long most of the plantations[2] found themselves unable to compete with the native smallholders, for the advantages of large-scale production were not sufficient to outweigh the cheaper costs of family labour. There are a number of oil-palm plantations in Africa and the Far East, but smallholders dominate the industry. Similarly, the production of groundnuts on a large scale does not result in sufficient economies to cover the overheads involved, as a recent notorious experiment in Africa by the British government clearly showed. The production of groundnuts continues to be a smallholders' industry. Jute in India and Pakistan, and cocoa in West Africa, have always been peasant industries. In Brazil, however, there are cocoa plantations employing hired labour, and this may be a relic from the time of slavery.

Finally, there are at least four very important industries—coffee, cotton, sugar and rubber—which exhibit both types of producing units, or really all sizes from smallholdings to large farms and big plantations.

The cultivation of coffee trees, and the preparation of the coffee whether by the wet or the dry process,[3] can be done on a very small scale, involving very little equipment but much labour, at much the same cost as it can be done on a very large scale, using machinery and mechanised transport. Thus in Brazil, which still supplies 40 % of the world's coffee and used to supply 80 %, there are estates with

---

[1] On the other hand, in the U.S.A., which has become an exporter since World War II, though on a relatively small scale compared with Burma and Thailand, rice is produced by modern methods of mechanised farming.

[2] Exceptionally the old-established copra industry of the Seychelles remains a small estate industry because the European settlers in these previously uninhabited islands planted up almost all the suitable land with slave and later freed-slave labour. The quality of the product is high.

[3] The wet process involves the wet pulping and fermentation of the berries (or, as they are usually called, 'cherries'), subsequent drying, and a final milling to remove the parchment covering: the dry process means drying the berries in the sun, and subsequently rubbing off the husk by machinery (hulling). The wet process results in superior quality.

a million and more trees, and there are very large numbers of one-man or family holdings of two or three thousand trees or even less. The estates dry their crops on vast concrete or asphalt terraces, and usually do their own hulling. Small-scale cultivators dry their crops on areas of hard-beaten earth, and sell to an independent hullery. In Colombia, the world's second largest producer, almost the whole crop is produced by peasant smallholders, each man preparing his own small contribution by the wet process, or arranging for this to be done by a slightly larger neighbour. In Central America, estates predominate, though there are many smallholders who sell their crops to the estates for preparation, which is all by the wet process. There are, however, fewer large estates than in Brazil because the mountainous terrain does not conduce to very large-scale plantations and because of a different historical and social tradition. The situation in Africa is still more varied. There is a substantial European estate industry in Kenya, and a much smaller one in Tanganyika, while estates predominate in the Portuguese colonies. Many small European estates are to be found scattered over the former Belgian Congo and French colonies. In Kenya there is also a rapidly growing African smallholders' industry, and an old-established one in Tanganyika, while in Uganda coffee is almost entirely a smallholders' industry. With the many smallholders in the former Belgian and French colonies, much more than half the total African production comes from native smallholders. In Africa the days of estate production may well be numbered, and the larger estates in Brazil and certain countries in Central America may be split up as the result of political and social changes; but the world's coffee industry seems likely to remain a mixture of all kinds and sizes of producing units, unless and until the balance of economic advantage swings decidedly in one direction or another as the result of technical progress in cultivation or preparation. There are at present no signs of such developments.

The cotton industry also is a mixture of large and small producing units, though most of the world's production comes from the latter. There are some large cotton plantations in the U.S.A.; Brazil's cotton is mostly grown on former coffee estates, and interplanted with coffee on others; in the Sudan cotton growing was started by British companies; and there are many medium-sized plantations in the former French and Belgian colonies in Africa. In Egypt, India and Uganda, production is almost entirely by peasant proprietors, and smallholders are dominant in the U.S.A. and Mexico. In all the other producing countries there are smallholdings as well as plantations. Comparing the two types of producing units, the essential points are: first, that cotton is an annual crop and its cultivation does not necessitate large-scale capitalistic operations; secondly, that the picking is a simple unskilled job, but demands very much larger supplies of labour per acre than the cultivation, and so the peasant proprietor with his reserve of unpaid family labour behind him scores heavily in this respect; and, thirdly, that though the separation of the seed from the lint must be done by power-driven machinery, yet the product as picked is light and easily transported to local ginneries, and there is little advantage in a ginning plant above a relatively small size. The large plantation in the U.S.A. scores by mechanical ploughing and by more scientific cultivation. Furthermore, the gradual perfecting of mechanical picking machines has in recent years been tending to neutralise the smallholder's advantage, by reducing the plantation's difficulties in securing temporary labour for this operation, though only at considerable capital cost. The large plantation can run its own ginnery, but will not get much economy thereby compared with the costs of an independent ginnery serving a district of smallholders. In Brazil, cotton was developed by the older coffee plantations owing to the great and prolonged over-production and consequent low price of coffee in the 1930's. The families of the labourers could be drawn in for the picking of the cotton just as they had been for the picking of coffee. In the Sudan irrigation was necessary, and companies were formed to provide and exploit the necessarily large-scale schemes. In the former French and Belgian colonies in Africa, cotton production was originally introduced and developed in plantation form by European settlers with the aid of some preference in the home tariffs, but it was soon taken up by African smallholders. Taking the world as a whole, smallholding production has always been, and still is, quantitatively far more important than plantation production, though not in certain areas, and by no means so exclusively that cotton can really be classed with the smallholding industries. In recent years mechanisation has been tilting the balance against the small producer, and there may be changes in such countries as the U.S.A.; but it will surely be a long time before the advantages of large-scale production become so great as to bring about decisive changes in the economic and social structure of the cotton industries of Egypt, India and tropical Africa.

With cane sugar, which is almost exclusively the sugar traded overseas, the grinding of the cane and the extraction of the sugar can only be done economically by machinery and plant involving heavy capital expenditure. The economies of large scale are really only limited by the cost of transporting the cane to the factory. The same is of course true of beet sugar, and the two are broadly alike in that the mills or factories are usually owned by joint-stock companies which buy their beet or cane supplies from independent farmers. Cane sugar is mostly grown by small peasant proprietors as their only or predominant cash crop, but in Cuba some of the big American mills themselves used to grow a substantial proportion of their requirements by large-scale mechanised farming, mainly in order to ensure supplies but also as a check on the costs of cane production. In some other countries, too, the companies which operate the mills grow their own cane, but there are usually definite overriding reasons in each case. Thus, in Hawaii, Queensland, and Natal, irrigation schemes are often necessary, and expert management is required to cover the heavy costs by securing the highest possible yields. In the once large but now deceased plantation sugar industry of Java, the mills grew their own cane because the Dutch government's regulations for the use of land for sugar growing made necessary the most intensive cultivation. In Cuba and also in Peru, as well as in certain other exporting countries, there are cane farms of quite substantial size employing wage-earning labour, but, taking the cane sugar exporting countries as a whole, smallholding production undoubtedly predominates.

Last, but by no means least, of the four great 'mixed' industries is natural rubber. Its production was introduced and developed in the Far East about the beginning of this century by Europeans, and so in plantation joint-stock company form. Up to about 1930 plantations were the dominant form of producing unit, though they varied greatly in size. There was a native smallholding industry with an appreciable total output in Malaya, and some similar production in the Netherlands East Indies, but the output of the estates was very much larger. During the latter half of the 1920's, however, the natives of the Netherlands East Indies were planting rubber trees on their abandoned rice plots[1] on a very large scale, and since World War II

---

[1] In Sumatra and Borneo the local people plant dry rice for one or two years, after which the soil becomes exhausted for rice production, and then they make another clearing, and abandon the former plot for ten or more years.

smallholders have produced more rubber than the estates. The situation is similar to that already noted in other industries. Rubber can be produced in a very simple manner on a small scale: the farmer pushes in seed with his thumb, and provided he prevents the seedlings being choked by weed growth, they will grow; tapping is a simple operation if conservation of bark does not much matter; the latex can be coagulated in petrol tins cut in half; and sheets can be roughly rolled out in a hand mangle. Rubber can also be produced on a large scale in a much more scientific manner and with the aid of considerable capital; the yield per tree will be much higher than the smallholder obtains, but he plants many more trees per acre, and the yield per acre was until recently not so different. A price which is reckoned remunerative by estates is also reckoned remunerative by the smallholder: the price has usually to fall very low before the latter stops tapping. The estates have considerably reduced their costs since the last war, especially by developing high-yielding trees, but also in other ways, including combination of several estates under one management and the consequent reduction of overheads. Nevertheless, smallholders, particularly in Indonesia, still find rubber production a worthwhile occupation, as they too have adopted better techniques. There are, then, no such economies in large-scale capitalistic production of rubber as to give it any great advantage over small-scale production in the economic conditions of the Far East: there has so far been a sort of equilibrium between the two methods, and this may last for a very long time, since not all kinds of invention, and technical and scientific progress, are to the exclusive advantage of the estate. In many respects where the estates gain a lead, the smallholder can very soon follow.

Summing up this survey, it is only too obvious that the structure and organisation of the primary industries vary enormously, even more widely than those of manufacturing industries, though both are subject to the same fundamental influences. The factor which runs as a continuous thread throughout these complex pictures of structure and organisation is the principle that up to a point a larger scale of operations results in lower total costs of production. With some primary products the limit is reached at a very small scale; with others it is uncertain whether the largest existing units have yet reached it; and with still others costs may be much the same for large-scale and very small-scale producers, though higher for those of intermediate sizes. Producers are perpetually searching for the optimum scale, and while many may not yet have reached it, some may well have overshot it. All this results in great variations in the size and character of the units of production in different industries, and within the same industry; but in the latter case the variations are vastly increased as between different countries, and even in different areas of the same country, by the influence of local conditions of land topography, land tenure, climate, labour supplies, the availability of skilled entrepreneurs, the social structure of the local community and its history, as well as the general economics and financial development of the country, or of different producing areas within it. Viewed in this light, the wide extent to which the units of production in so many primary industries vary in size and character, not only in different countries, but even within the same country, becomes less surprising, as does the spectacle of large farms and estates surrounded by tiny smallholdings which are their direct competitors. It is indeed more surprising to find that sometimes the pattern of structure and organisation in any one primary industry is reasonably homogeneous.

PART II

THE ORGANISATION OF MARKETING

3. THE PRINCIPAL CONSUMING MARKETS

As was explained in chapter 1, international trade in some commodities is mainly regional rather than world-wide, and for that reason they were excluded from the list of the principal primary products in table I (page 5). Before considering the principal markets for the commodities on this list, it will be as well to add a little more to what was said in chapter 1 about this regional trading, for it must not be allowed to slip too far into the background even if commodities on the list occupy the forefront of the stage.

In Europe there are of course two virtually separate regions, the Soviet block, and western Europe including the U.K. in this respect, but only in this respect. Trade between the U.S.S.R. and what is usually called eastern Europe is varied and of considerable volume. It takes place on such special terms that it demands a detailed specialised study, such as will not be attempted here. In the Western European region, many countries, including the U.K., import timber and wood pulp from Sweden and Finland; Germany exports coal to France, Italy and the Netherlands; Sweden, France, North Africa and Spain export iron ore to the U.K., West Germany, Belgium, Italy, etc.; Denmark and the Netherlands export dairy products to West Germany and the U.K. and, similarly, though on a much smaller scale, meat; Turkey and Greece export tobacco; and so on. Western Europe, as distinct in this respect from the U.K., is nearly self-sufficient in bauxite and in lead and zinc, if supplies from North Africa are included, but some countries export to others and there is much intra-European trade. Outside Europe, there are some other cases of large regional trade: Canada exports timber, wood pulp and iron ore to the U.S.A.; Jamaica and the Guianas bauxite to the U.S.A. and Canada; even the export of iron ore from South American countries to the U.S.A. is really a regional trade.

On the other side of the world, there is a regional trade from Manchuria to Japan in coal and iron ore, and in soya-beans, while Japan still draws most of its sugar supplies from Taiwan (Formosa). Most of the exports of rice from Burma and Thailand go to other Asian countries, notably Indonesia, Pakistan, Hong Kong, Ceylon, India, Malaya and Japan. Thus in total all this regional trading adds up to a large value, and is very important to the countries concerned, even if it is not so interesting and important to the student of economics as the world-wide trade in the staple primary commodities.

Turning to these staple commodities as listed in chapter 1, the picture of their principal markets is, in the broad outlines which will suffice for the present study, remarkably simple. The international overseas supplies of most of these commodities are predominantly consumed in one or more of three large markets, namely Western Europe, the U.K., and the U.S.A.; though Japan is also an important market for some of them, and on a smaller scale Canada, Australia and New Zealand; and on a smaller scale still South Africa. Of the three large markets, the U.S.A. is the biggest importer of coffee, sugar, sisal and lead; the U.K. is the biggest importer of meat, dairy products, tea and zinc; and western Europe as a whole is the biggest importer of all the rest, namely petroleum, wheat, cotton, vegetable oilseeds and oils, wool, rubber, copper, tobacco, cocoa, tin, jute and maize. Western Europe is also an important market for coffee, and on a smaller scale sugar; the U.S.A. is also an important market for petroleum, wool, rubber, cocoa, tin and zinc; and the U.K. is either the chief or at least an important market for almost all these commodities except coffee. Of importing countries in the rest of the world, Japan is much the most important generally, and particularly as a market for petroleum, wheat, cotton, wool, sugar, rubber, rice, maize, jute and hard fibres. Canada is a market of some importance for petroleum, as are Australia and New Zealand; and these import a variety of primary products in considerable amounts, as does South Africa on a still more limited and less significant scale.

The picture of world trade in the principal primary products is thus relatively straightforward in its main outlines. But the previous paragraph is rather a catalogue, and in order to introduce some precision and more detail, table III shows the net imports (imports minus exports) of each commodity by the principal importing countries or regions. The figures show in thousands of tons the approximate volume of their average imports in 1959–61, unless otherwise noted. The table is thus a companion to Table II in chapter 1 (page 7) which showed the principal exporters, and is based on the same statistical sources.

TABLE III. *The principal consuming markets importing primary products from overseas*

(All figures are averages of net imports 1959–61 in thousand tons unless otherwise stated.)

	Western Europe	U.K.	U.S.A.	Japan	Canada	Australia and New Zealand
(1) Petroleum, crude[1] 1962 (million tons)	136[2]	52	64	39	7	13
(2) Meat						
Beef	27	335	224	5	—	—
Mutton and lamb	—	367	24	15	12	—
(3) Wheat and flour (million tons)	5·1	4·5	—	2·6	—	—
		(Also India 3·6, Brazil 1·9)				
(4) Fats and oils[3]	—	—	—	—	—	—
(5) Cotton	1267	257	—	701	77	19
		(Also India 120; Hong Kong 95; Korea 52; Taiwan 39)				
(6) Coffee	870	53	1353	11	66	12
		(Also Algeria 29; Argentina 27; South Africa 11)				

[1] Refined petroleum products are too numerous to be included in this table, and cannot be sensibly grouped together: hence only net imports of crude are shown, and for the year 1962 only as consumption is steadily and rapidly rising in all countries.

[2] E.E.C. countries only (i.e. West Germany, France, Italy, Belgium, Luxembourg, Netherlands).

[3] Vegetable oilseeds and oils. The U.S.A., though a large exporter of soft oils (soya-beans and oil, and cotton seed and oil), is short of hard oils, and imports substantial quantities of copra and coconut oil, and of palm kernel oil. Japan imported over 1 million tons of soya-beans. Otherwise, western Europe and the U.K. are by far the largest markets for all the other oilseeds and oils; and the relatively small remainders are imported in small quantities by numerous other countries throughout the world; and the same is broadly true of lard and other animal fats, though Japan imports on an appreciable scale. Similarly, western Europe and the U.K. account for over two-thirds of the total world imports of linseed, and more still of linseed oil, Japan taking a large slice of the remainder.

TABLE III (*cont.*)

	Western Europe	U.K.	U.S.A.	Japan	Canada	Australia and New Zealand
(7) Copper[1]						
Unrefined	294[2]	116	253	—	—	—
Refined unwrought	614	310	—	57	—	—
			(Also India, refined 46)			
(8) Wool	465	287	157	203	6	—
(9) Sugar (million tons)	1·1	1·9	4·1	1·2	0·6	—
		(Also Iran 0·4; Morocco 0·3; Algeria 0·2; Iraq 0·2)				
(10) Rubber	492	156	459	184	38	43
		(Also Argentina 26; Brazil 18; South Africa 19)				
(11) Dairy products						
Butter	—	414	—	—	—	—
Cheese	25	133	78	2	—	—
		(Also Algeria, butter 8; cheese, 19; Venezuela, cheese 10)				
(12) Tobacco	197	151	—	2	—	20
(13) Rice	211	94	—	193	33	—
		(Also Indonesia 877; Pakistan 585; Hong Kong 549; Ceylon 525; Malaya 500; India 460)				
(14) Maize (million tons)	4·8	3·1	—	1·4	0·4	—
(15) Tea	36	226	50	—	20	34
		(Also Iraq 22; United Arab Republic 21; South Africa 14)				
(16) Cocoa beans	379	86	264	11	15	14
		(Also South Africa 35)				
(17) Tin: consumption[3] of primary tin	53	21	49	12	4	4
(18) Jute and hard fibres						
Jute	316	126	47	52	2	8
		(Also South Africa 25)				
Sisal, etc.	247	76	85	29	30	28
Manilla fibre	21	15	30	26	2	—
(19) Zinc[4] unwrought	—[5]	172	80	23	—	—
(20) Lead[4] unwrought	107	168	221	23	—	—

[1] Small quantities of ores, concentrates, etc., are also imported by western Europe, U.S.A. and Japan.

[2] Of which Belgium–Luxembourg took one half, if Congo Republic (Katanga) blister exports are assumed to have gone there.

[3] As estimated by Commonwealth Economic Committee. None of these consuming countries produces appreciable quantities of tin ore.

[4] The principal importers of ores, concentrates, etc., from overseas are the U.S.A., Japan, Belgium–Luxembourg, West Germany and the U.K.

[5] Western Europe is roughly self-sufficient.

4. THE PHYSICAL PROCESSES OF MARKETING

In chapter 2 an attempt was made to survey the structure and organisation of primary production. Now an attempt must be made to do the same for the marketing of that production. The marketing process really covers the whole business of transferring supplies of the commodity from the producing units, whether these be individuals or small or large corporate companies, to the processors or manufacturers in consuming countries. Marketing thus involves physical processes of collection from the actual producers, transport within the producing country to the ports, ocean shipment, stock-holding, and distribution in the consuming countries; these processes are often most complicated and necessitate suitable financial arrangements all along the line. Moreover, with most primary products the ownership of a particular lot or consignment will change hands during these physical processes, and with some it may change several times. This involves the determination of the price at which each exchange takes place, and so necessitates a study of how prices are made in the large number of markets for individual commodities all over the world, and of how they are kept in proper relationship with one another. The marketing of primary products is thus an intricate mechanism. Though it varies in detail with different commodities, the main structure and principles of marketing are much the same for all. To a much greater extent than for the structure and organisation of production, it is possible to generalise concerning the physical processes of marketing and the financing involved, and also concerning the determination of prices and their co-ordination in different markets and at different stages of the marketing process. This is not to say that the description and analysis now to be undertaken will provide a blueprint for the marketing of all primary products, still less for that of individual products. It should, however, provide some fundamental general ideas, and a rough sketch-map which will be a reliable and useful basic guide in the detailed study of the actual marketing organisation for any particular commodity.

This chapter will deal with the physical processes of marketing, leaving consideration of the determination of prices all along the line until the next chapter. The vast bulk of international trade in primary products involves, as has been shown above, ocean shipment. This necessitates suitable ports with modern plant and equipment for berthing, loading and unloading large ships. Few countries have any large number of natural harbours—the U.K. for its size is more favoured than most—and the establishment of the very costly installations required for a modern port will tend to be concentrated in one or a very few of the best natural harbours. Thus the supply of primary products tends to pass through one or a very few ports in each producing country, and again through one or very few ports in the principal consuming countries, or serving groups of adjacent consuming countries. Hence the marketing process tends to be composed of three successive stages—the drawing in of supplies from the various producing units to the main port or ports in the producing country, secondly the shipment of these supplies to the ports near the chief areas of consumption, and thirdly the distribution of these supplies from the ports in consuming areas to the processors or manufacturers who require supplies. The physical flow may thus be depicted in a very simple diagram which will be essentially in the following form:

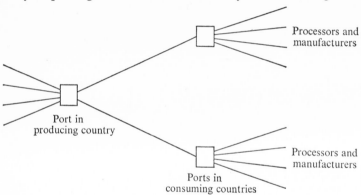

This diagram shows one port in each producing country shipping to two ports serving consuming countries or areas, because usually production is more concentrated than consumption. By multiplying the number of ports in each producing country and the number of producing countries each with one or more ports, and by multiplying the number of ports of arrival, the diagram can be made much more complicated and more nearly representative of the trade in any particular commodity. Its essential form will remain the same. With ocean shipment there is bound to be a sequence of the three stages, namely collection, shipment and distribution, simply because well-equipped ports are relatively few in number. Moreover, the same is essentially true of regional trade, for if there is no shipment by sea the railway will take its place, and trunk railway lines between adjacent countries are for obvious reasons usually few.

These three stages will now be considered in more detail. It is obvious that the business of collecting from the individual producing units, and concentrating the whole supply at the nearest port, will vary in difficulty and complexity with the size, and therefore the number, of the individual producing units. Small and numerous producing units will be considered first, and then larger units. If the producers are smallholders, they cannot usually arrange economical transport for their little lots of produce and consign them for sale individually at the port market. There is also the fact that most small-holders want cash for their produce at the earliest possible moment. There are two possible solutions: either they must sell to a local merchant, or they must form a producers' co-operative society which will bulk their individual lots, undertake any initial processing, arrange transport to the big market of their district or to the nearest port market, and sell there. Historically the co-operative society, except in a few countries like Denmark, is a recent development, dating in the main from the inter-war period; and though it has spread widely and rapidly since World War II, the local-merchant system is probably still more common than producers' co-operation, taking the world as a whole. The local merchants may be independent dealers, often combining their buying of primary produce with running a local shop; or they may be agents of larger merchant firms or of independent processors. The smallholders sell outright to such local merchants, and they in turn sell at the national or port market of the country. This sort of merchanting organisation for the collection of supplies is found in areas where cotton, rubber, coffee, cocoa or oilseeds, etc., are produced by smallholders who have not developed co-operative marketing. Some countries where the producers are small and numerous have set up government-controlled marketing boards as the sole legal buyers and sellers of a commodity. The boards fix the prices at which they will buy from local merchants or initial processors, and sell at the best prices they can get in the national or port markets. There are such boards, for example, for cocoa, oil-seeds, and other products in Ghana and Nigeria, and for cotton and coffee in Uganda. In the controlled part of the Uganda coffee industry, to describe one example in a little more detail, there were

34

in 1962 at least 300,000 farmers, and some 1200 licensed up-country buyers of sun-dried coffee berries (kiboko) required to sell to licensed hulleries for processing at a legal minimum price. The hulleries in turn must sell at a predetermined higher price, covering their costs and profit, to the Uganda Coffee Marketing Board. This normally sells by auction in Kampala to the representatives of the large exporting merchant houses, who ultimately ship the coffee from Mombasa. These marketing boards thus set, in one way or another, minimum prices to the growers, and so reduce exploitation of the producers by local merchants. On the other hand, in Ghana and Nigeria as well as in Uganda the official buying prices have at times been kept far below parity with the prices at which the boards were able to sell, sometimes deliberately in order to avoid inflation, sometimes as the result of too cautious estimates of future market prices. Consequently, most of these boards accumulated large funds, so large that at times they have been raided by the governments for national development purposes instead of being wholly used for the benefit of the producers collectively, as for example to finance price stabilisation schemes (i.e. to maintain the producers' price above parity with the market price when this falls below a certain level), or to finance research or irrigation schemes for the industry concerned. In effect, therefore, the producers have been specially taxed for the benefit of the country as a whole; and from their point of view this must be set against any advantage in price which may have resulted from centralised control as compared with the unfettered operations of local merchants.

Turning to producers' co-operation, the general system is to form societies on a local basis and for these to become members of a union of societies. The individual members of the local societies usually deliver their produce themselves to a local depot, and receive a pre-determined cash payment, commonly around two-thirds of the current price at the big market of their region or country. The local societies collect from these depots, and transport the produce to one or more warehouses owned by the union, which then bulks, processes where necessary or arranges this, transports to the national or port market and sells the produce. Any excess of revenue over expenditure by the union, i.e. profit, is shared out amongst its member societies, which similarly share it out amongst their individual members according to the quantities they have delivered, less whatever the union or each local society may decide to retain as capital.

This is the usual structure and working of the system, with variations to suit different commodities. Producers' co-operation has been rapidly developing, especially since World War II, in Africa and many other parts of the world, and is even beginning in some Latin-American countries. Incidentally, co-operation of this kind is not confined to produce for export. The great advantage of such co-operative marketing is that it cuts out the local merchant, who is apt to give the small producer less than a fair price, because the producer's information about prices in the big market of his area is inadequate or out of date, or because of the producer's imperative desire or need for cash, or sometimes simply because the local merchant has few, if any, competitors. Producers' co-operation thus avoids the problems of determining local up-country prices, which is usually a great gain from the small producer's point of view; but it does not reduce the actual physical processes of collecting and concentrating the produce of large numbers of smallholders, its initial processing if any, and its transport to the port. The financial results of co-operation depend greatly on the skill and integrity with which the officials of the societies and the unions conduct their business, and particularly the actual selling unless this is done by public auction. The history of many local societies and of unions in certain parts of the world shows a record in respect of integrity which leaves much to be desired.

The complicated organisation of the collection process where the producers are small and numerous becomes progressively simpler as the size of the producing units increases, and their numbers become relatively fewer. The large rubber, tea and coffee estates commonly sell direct at the big national or port markets of their country or region. For rubber and tea the selling is often done by agency companies who act for a number of independent producing companies, and then some of the produce may even be consigned to markets in importing countries and first sold there. Similarly, most of Tanganyika's sisal is first sold in London: it may incidentally be mentioned that after World War II many of the sisal estates formed a central selling organisation, the Tanganyika Sisal Merchanting Association (commonly known as TASMA),[1] which now handles a little over half the total crop. The large coffee estates in Brazil, however, sell direct in the port markets; in the Central American coffee countries

[1] On this and all other aspects of this industry, see *An Economic Survey of the Sisal Industry of Tanganyika,* by C. W. Guillebaud (Nisbet, 1958; new edition pending).

the estates, which are mostly of medium size, sell their crops as picked to processors (beneficios) who, after preparing the coffee, sell to exporting merchants. Wool farmers in Australia, New Zealand, South Africa and the Argentine are usually producing on a large scale, and the business is dominated by big pastoral companies or large family businesses. The greater part of the wool clips of these countries is consigned from the farms direct to the ports, and first sold there, though the smaller farmers often sell to up-country itinerant independent merchants, or the itinerant representatives of the large exporting merchant firms. Meat demands considerable processing which is best done on a large scale, and the farmers sell to the processors, and they in turn to exporters. Most mining is in the hands of large joint-stock companies, and as most metals are refined to certain standards and so can be sold by description, the producers may first sell by description either direct to large consumers or to merchants in consuming centres. The same is broadly true of tin, lead, and zinc, though there are great variations, for smelting is sometimes undertaken by the producers and sometimes by independent smelters; and sometimes smelters buy concentrates from the producers outright, and sometimes smelt on commission. In all these cases, however, the collection stage is essentially a physical process, and does not involve changes in ownership and therefore the making of prices to the actual producers, as it does where the producers are small and numerous.

As a general summary it may be said that where the producing units are few, large and so financially strong that they do not need to turn their produce into cash at the earliest possible moment, this first stage of the marketing process tends to be a purely physical process of transport and concentration at the ports. But where the producers are many, small and financially weak, then unless they are organised co-operatively and so in effect become large selling units, this first stage is likely to involve the intervention of various middlemen and merchants. The resultant buying and selling will involve the making of prices at various stages before the produce reaches the nearest port and is bought by exporting merchants.

The second stage of the marketing process is the shipment of the commodity from the main port or ports in the producing countries to the main ports serving the consuming countries. This is purely a physical process and, as such, a relatively straightforward business.

The structure, organisation and operation of the world's shipping industry, however, is extremely complicated and intricate, involving many technical as well as economic problems, and demands specialised study. It constitutes a separate subject and no attempt will be made here to describe even its outstanding features, for such a summary would be liable to be misleading. It will therefore be assumed that somehow the produce is transported from the producing countries to the ports serving consuming countries. Nothing more will be said about this second stage except that the goods will of course be insured during transit, and that copies of the bills of lading will provide the exporting merchant, in one form or another, with the means of financing at least a large proportion of the value of his shipments during their voyages.

With the arrival of the produce at the ports serving the principal consuming countries, the third stage of the marketing process begins, namely the distribution of the produce to the wholesale distributors, processors and manufacturers who want to buy supplies, i.e. the first consuming units. At this point the merchant must step into the picture, even if he has not already done so as exporter from the producing countries, for the consuming units are usually numerous and at any one time require the commodity in quantities which are relatively small compared to the shipments. Moreover, someone must hold reserve stocks, and in the case of agricultural crops harvested at one period of the year someone must hold seasonal stocks and spread the supply evenly over the year. Stock-holding of either sort is not a function which individual producers or individual consuming units can perform efficiently if only because of the financial problems involved. Stock-holding is essentially a function of the merchant, though clearly processors and manufacturers vary their purchasing, and therefore the stocks they hold, for speculative reasons. Consequently, there is nearly always a market at the large ports in consuming countries where importing merchants buy from the exporting merchants in producing countries (though sometimes a large merchant firm will combine both exporting and importing functions), or direct from large producers, and sell to the consuming units. If the country in which such a port market is situated is a very large consumer of the commodity, and especially if it is conveniently situated to a number of other smaller consuming countries, then that market tends to become the chief market at the consuming end for a wide region.

All shipments will tend to be consigned to that port and sold there, and merchants from the other consuming countries will tend to buy their supplies there, subsequently selling them at what may be described as sub-consuming or satellite markets in their own countries. Thus London obtained its commercial pre-eminence as the result of its geographical situation from the point of view of ocean shipping, its proximity to the ports of western Europe, and its early development as a financial centre, especially for investment in primary producing industries abroad and for the financing of trade in their products. London was, up to 1939, and still is in a lesser degree, the chief or dominant consuming market for western Europe as well as the U.K. in a large number of raw materials. Examples are the non-ferrous metals, wool, rubber and hard fibres, as well as various foodstuffs such as tea, cocoa, and even to some extent coffee (though the actual consumption of coffee in the U.K. was, and still is, very small). Continental merchants buy in London large supplies of such commodities for the principal markets on the continent, like Le Havre, Amsterdam and Hamburg, which in their turn supply other markets nearer still to the actual consuming units. Liverpool early established the supremacy of its wheat and cotton markets for similar obvious reasons; and, though there was less entrepôt trade than in the big London markets, Liverpool prices had a dominating influence on European continental markets. Similarly, the dominant consuming markets in the U.S.A. for coffee, sugar, tin, rubber, hard fibres, etc., are in New York, though there are other smaller markets for these products in the interior of this large consuming country. Thus the third stage of the marketing process is one of decentralisation and distribution at the consuming end, corresponding to the concentration of supplies at the producing end. Just as with most commodities there is at least one big market in each exporting country, so there is at least one big market for each large consuming region, the former being served by, and the latter serving, a number of smaller satellite markets. Though markets in exporting countries may be absent for some commodities, there is always a big market for each large consuming region.

This account of the structure and organisation of the physical processes of marketing would be incomplete without some account of how and where stocks are held. Because of the effect which the size and location of stocks have on prices, this is a necessary prelude to the study in the next chapter of the determination of prices and their co-ordination throughout the whole marketing process. How-ever homogeneous stocks of a commodity may be physically, they are not homogeneous from the economic or even commercial point of view. Merchants of all kinds, processors and manufacturers must always hold a minimum of supplies in order that their business may proceed smoothly and efficiently, just as retailers must have stocks of finished goods, and even housewives stocks of foodstuffs. Such stocks are commonly referred to as stocks of convenience, and they will of course vary in total amount with the current rate of absorption or consumption of the commodity. The ratio of stocks of convenience to current absorption is not, however, a constant for all time. It is normally subject to a decreasing long-period trend due to the quicken-ing of modern communications and transport. Thus the continual spread of the telephone and wireless speeds up communication, just as the telegraph and cable services did in an earlier age. Moreover, more and more freight tends to be carried by liner services which are much speedier than the ordinary tramp steamer, and both tend to increase in speed. Similarly the passage of crops from the farm to the rail-point is much faster by motor vehicles than by animal or human transport. Recently the use of mechanical aids in warehousing has saved time as well as costs. On the other hand, the ratio also tends to be affected, sometimes over quite short periods of time, by changes in the business community's view of the relative merits of 'hand to mouth' buying and a 'cast-iron' or impregnable stock position. This will of course tend to vary with the community's optimism or pessimism regarding future trade prospects, and its forecast of the future supplies and price of the commodity in question, and shades off into conscious deliberate speculation; and where the stocks increase above the current level of stocks of convenience, the excess consti-tutes speculative stocks, which may or may not be justifiable, depend-ing on the accuracy of the speculator's forecast. Then, too, with agricultural crops produced at one period of the year, seasonal stocks must be held to enable consumption to proceed regularly throughout the year. Thus the volume of the existing stocks of a commodity, and its fluctuations, require careful interpretation if correct conclusions are to be drawn as to whether the current total indicates conditions of equilibrium, or of shortage, or of excess supply.

Such interpretation is all the more difficult because in fact only part of the total stocks of a commodity existing in the world are usually known. The stocks which are recorded and published constitute the 'visible supply', or visible stocks, and the rest are termed invisible: and the proportions are not by any means the same for all commodities because the extent of the recordings varies greatly. Individual producers may sometimes hold stocks on their farms, plantations or mines, but if they do, these are rarely recorded unless this is taking place as part of a collective scheme controlling output or deliveries. Normally, however, producers sell their output as soon as possible to a middleman or merchant, or through their own co-operative society, because they want to get cash for it as quickly as possible. Any stocks which individual producers do hold will rarely be 'visible', and the first item of the visible supply is usually stocks held by merchants and exporters in large public or semi-public warehouses, situated sometimes at important rail centres in the interior, but most commonly at the ports in the producing countries. These stocks are usually recorded and published at regular intervals. The second item in the visible supply is usually the quantity 'in transit' or 'afloat', and since with many commodities the producing and consuming areas are long distances apart, for example, rubber or tea or tin, the amount may be very considerable, perhaps the equivalent of three months' absorption or even more. These 'in transit' or 'afloat' statistics are very important for the making of prices, for they indicate changes in the rate of supply to consuming markets in the near future. The third item in the visible supply is the stocks in public warehouses at the ports of arrival and at the chief centres of distribution in consuming areas. Again, these are usually recorded and published regularly, for example, monthly. These three items commonly compose the visible supply. With a few commodities stocks held by the larger processors and manufacturers are wholly or partly recorded, and included in the visible supply, which, as has been said above, has no universal definition. Usually, however, stocks return to invisibility when they are sold by the importing merchants. In the aggregate the invisible stocks held by smaller merchants and by processors and manufacturers may be quite considerable relative to the visible supply or the current rate of absorption, and they may fluctuate considerably. Estimates of the volume of the invisible stocks of a commodity often appear in trade publications, but these are really guesses and, as history has often shown, may be quite erroneous and misleading.

The costs of holding stocks are of two kinds: physical and financial. The former depend on the capital sunk in the land and warehouse buildings and their upkeep, together with the expenses of operation, which will be mainly wages: if the buildings are not weatherproof or suitably designed for their purpose, some or all of the produce may deteriorate in quality, and the consequent loss in value must also be reckoned as a physical cost. If stocks are held on farms or up-country, the physical costs are likely to be much lower than in large towns or ports, provided that there is not much loss in quality. Rent of the land or its equivalent, building costs and operating costs are all likely to be much lower. On the other hand, the financial costs will almost certainly be much higher, for banks will not as a rule make loans against stocks unless they are held in public warehouses where the produce is weighed and inspected under proper conditions by independent authorities. Such public warehouses are sometimes located at large up-country rail centres, but mostly at the ports of producing and consuming countries. The physical costs, that is, the warehouse charges, may be relatively high, but the financial costs will be smaller, and this will be specially so if the ports have large organised markets for the commodity (for reasons which will be explained in the next chapter) or are large financial centres where merchants can obtain loans at the cheapest possible rates from merchant banks which specialise in this business. Whether the bulk of the stocks of a commodity will be held at the ports of exporting countries or at those of importing countries will depend mainly on the relative general financial and commercial development at the two ends, and on the relative levels of current rates of interest. Usually the physical costs of storage are much lower at ports like Singapore, Calcutta, Mombasa or Santos than in congested cities like London, Liverpool, Hamburg or New York. On the other hand, the banking systems and general financial development at these cities are likely to result in cheaper financial costs of storage, that is, cheaper terms for loans, unless the current rates of interest in exporting countries are much lower than in the importing countries; while stocks in importing countries are of course ready for sale to consuming units, whereas shipment from the producing countries may take an appreciable time. Thus the distribution of stocks will be according to the total costs and the relative convenience of holding them at either end.

5. THE DETERMINATION OF PRICES

The last chapter reached two generalised conclusions. First, that there is likely to be in each exporting country one big market, usually at the main port, which is served by a large number of middlemen and merchants, and often by smaller satellite markets in the producing areas up-country. Secondly, that there is almost certain to be at least one big market for each main consuming region, where importing merchants, and sometimes very large individual producing units, sell to first users, or to other merchants who supply smaller satellite consuming markets spread over the region. It must now be explained how the big markets act as price-leaders, and how the intermediate transactions of middlemen and merchants are co-ordinated with the prices at which the producers sell and with the prices at which the first users buy. The local merchants who buy from small producers on their farms, or at the nearest country village or town, will nowadays get to know within a very short time, as the result of the development of the telegraph, the telephone and, more recently, wireless broadcasting, how prices are moving in the big market which they serve. Even if he lives in a remote district, such a merchant will probably learn each evening or at the latest on the following morning how prices have moved in the big market during the day. It is part of his business to estimate the costs of bulking, handling and transporting his purchases to the big market, and therefore he knows that if he buys at a certain margin below the big-market price, his buying price will be in line with the big-market price. In effect, therefore, he uses the big-market price of the day before, less the local differential, as a basic price for his daily operations. He makes his actual bids for particular lots of the produce according to their precise quality, and according to the conditions in his local market and his own need to obtain supplies, but always bearing in mind his basic price. The producers from whom he is buying will similarly use the latest available information concerning prices in the big market as their basic guide in selling. Thus dealings up-country and in up-country satellite markets are geared to the big market of the producing country.

Similarly, in the satellite markets of a big consuming market and in all subsequent transactions, the sellers and buyers use the prices in the big market as their basic guide *plus* a differential for transport, handling, insurance, etc., from the big market to the satellite market or to the place of delivery. These dealings are therefore geared to the big consuming market. Finally, since dealings in the big exporting markets and in the big importing markets are reported to each other, often inside a matter of minutes, prices in all the big markets for a commodity all over the world tend to become uniform—uniform, that is, when allowances are made for varying qualities or grades, and for the different freight differentials and handling costs incurred by the time the produce reaches each market. For most important primary products, therefore, it is possible to speak of a world market and a world price. Under modern conditions of rapid communication the markets all over the world work together as a co-ordinated system, strengthened by relatively rapid transportation which facilitates the switching of actual physical supplies between the main consuming areas if the need arises. These phrases—a world market and a world price—sound both simple and satisfying. It is as well to remember that for many commodities they are only given meaning as the result of the intricate operation of an immensely complicated system.

How, then, are these world prices made at the big markets? The answer to this question is no simple one, and a historical approach is perhaps the most informative way of tackling the problem. A hundred years or so ago, before the advent of the telegraph and the telephone, the price in any particular market reflected the state of demand in that market, and the state of supply, including foreseeable supply, to that market. In other words it reflected demand and supply within the geographical area with which that market was concerned, for supply and demand in that area were only affected very slowly, and as it were haltingly, by the conditions in other markets. The price was determined by the merchants and dealers in each market as part of, and in the course of, their ordinary business. Since the merchants could keep themselves reasonably well informed about their own market area conditions, they were reasonably competent price-makers for that area, though prices in other market areas might differ considerably. Moreover, it was part of the ordinary business of such merchants to bear the risk of changes in the values of commodities whilst they were being marketed. The introduction of modern rapid communications, however, meant the emergence of a world market, and the making of a world price which had to reflect demand and supply conditions over the world as a whole, both immediately and in the foreseeable future. This meant an additional burden for the merchants. World price-making was much more difficult than making prices in one particular market, and under certain conditions it became profitable to specialise in this art. Some merchants found that they could make a better living by applying their time and brains to correcting deviations of the price in particular markets from the world price, and differences in the absolute level of that world price from what they considered it ought to be. If by careful study such a man discovers that the price in a particular market is above or below the world price, he can make a profit by buying in the cheaper market and selling in the dearer. The detection of such disparities between markets is largely a matter of ascertainable facts, and therefore relatively easy; but whether the level of the world price is too high or too low, taking into account present conditions and any changes in the foreseeable future, is a matter of opinion, guesswork and speculation. Since this is as difficult as the detection of price disparities between markets is easy, merchants who specialised in price-making made that their main business, and largely or wholly ceased to undertake the physical processes of marketing. This earned them the title of professional speculators, though there is much to be said in favour of dubbing them merchant speculators, because that does indicate their evolution, and links them with the whole business of marketing in which they play such a very important role.

The merchant speculator who corrects price disparities between markets by what are termed arbitrage dealings makes a profit. He also performs an economic function by maintaining one basic price the world over, so that all producers of similar qualities of a commodity receive that basic price, all first users are able to get supplies at the same basic price, and final consumers should benefit accordingly. The speculator who forms the opinion that the world price ought to be higher than it is at the moment, and that therefore in due course it will rise, makes a profit, if his view is correct, by buying now and selling later. At the same time his purchase performs the economic function of helping to raise the world price immediately, and so setting in motion tendencies to stimulate supply and reduce demand immediately, whereas without his purchase there would have been a more violent adjustment in the future. If the speculator's opinion is wrong, he loses money, and so pays a personal penalty for having misjudged the working of economic forces. Similarly a speculator who forms the opinion that the world price is higher than it ought to be, and that therefore it will in due course fall, will try and make a selling contract with a delivery date some time ahead when,

45

if his opinion is right, the price will have fallen, and so he will be able to make a purchase at a lower price to fulfil his selling contract. If his opinion is correct, he makes a profit, and performs the economic function of helping to adjust the price correctly and more smoothly, because earlier, than would otherwise have happened. If his opinion is wrong, he loses money as before. Thus, if on balance speculators help to keep the price nearer to its proper level than would be the case without their specialisation on price-making, they perform a valuable economic function, and their operations are not just gambling. As this chapter proceeds, further study will be made of this matter.

These merchant speculators, as specialists in price-making, naturally tended to emerge at the largest and most important exporting and importing markets. Their operations still further increased the importance of these markets by adding to the volume of transactions. As turnover grew, it became worth while in the case of certain commodities to devise special rules and methods of trading. These rules greatly facilitated operations, particularly in making selling contracts with a future delivery date, which are the means by which a speculator seeks to correct a price which he considers to be too high. Some big practical difficulties are involved in such transactions. Unless the terms are standardised, it would take time to arrange all the necessary details of such a contract, and the buyer in such a contract must have confidence in the integrity and financial standing of the seller. Such difficulties can be overcome by establishing an organised market in the charge of a corporate body which will lay down conditions of entry for members, formulate a standardised contract, and generally control all dealings. There is a more fundamental difficulty in that the buyer in a contract for future delivery must be certain of the seller's ability to fulfil his contract. Likewise the seller, unless he is dishonest, must feel similarly assured as to the availability of supplies in the future. This means that the commodity must be susceptible to accurate grading as to quality, and that warehouse or such-like receipts, corresponding to the grade specified in the contract, will be available when the seller has to buy to fulfil that contract. Only then can the commodity be confidently and safely bought and sold by description. Since many primary products cannot be accurately graded in this way, organised markets with dealings in contracts for future delivery do not develop for all commodities. Moreover, there are still two other conditions which must be reasonably well satisfied if speculation by means of future delivery contracts is to be a tolerably safe and sound proposition for the speculator. One is that the supply of the commodity must not be too quickly and readily adjustable in response to changes in the price. Speculation would obviously be too risky if a change in price rapidly brought about a large increase or decrease in supply. The other condition is that there must be no considerable measure of monopolistic control of production or supplies; for if there is, speculation simply becomes a gamble on what the monopolist is going to do.

These three major conditions must be at least reasonably well satisfied if an organised futures market is to develop, and though few in number they are hard conditions. For this reason organised speculation has always been limited to certain commodities, though amongst them are some of the most important. Wheat and cotton can both be very accurately graded, and both are harvested once a year only, so that when the seeding time is passed the supply from each producing country cannot be altered for a twelvemonth, no matter what happens to the price. Up to the beginning of World War II both these commodities were tolerably free from any monopolistic control, though the position has since changed. Up to 1939 the dominant futures markets for wheat were Chicago and Liverpool, with Winnipeg a smaller third. For cotton the markets were Liverpool and New York, with New Orleans a less important third. In these markets the world price level was really set, though for both commodities there were several other futures markets with contracts for the particular kinds of wheat or cotton produced, or mainly consumed, in each market area. Examples were the cotton markets in Alexandria and Bombay. The chief non-ferrous metals also satisfy the three conditions. They satisfy the condition concerning grading even better than cotton or wheat, for, with metals, chemical formulas can be used. They satisfy the second condition, inflexibility of supply, much less well, and even before 1939 there was at times some degree of monopolistic control over supplies. The metal exchanges in London and New York have always been the most important futures markets, but again there are also special minor ones, such as Singapore for tin. Futures markets also developed for rubber in New York and London; for sugar in New York and Liverpool; for coffee in New York and on a smaller scale Le Havre, and recently for East African coffees in London; and for cocoa in London and New York. Recently, too, a futures market for wool tops has been established in London as well as Antwerp, and there is now a futures contract for raw (greasy) wool, though it is of limited scope owing to the difficulties of grading wool. Mainly for this same reason, though sometimes also because of the inadequate fulfilment of the other two conditions, no futures markets have developed for primary commodities such as petroleum, or vegetable oilseeds and oils, or meat or dairy produce, timber and wood pulp, tobacco, tea, hard fibres, hides and skins, etc. For all these commodities, however, there are one or two dominant markets which set the general level of their prices. The absence of an organised futures market does not mean that there is no speculation in these commodities, but simply that it will be more limited because less highly organised.

For a limited number of commodities, therefore, organised futures markets have evolved using standardised contracts[1] for delivery at future dates, for example, for each month up to perhaps as much as a year ahead. Such a futures market has evolved primarily in order to facilitate speculation for a fall in the price, to correct what the speculator believes to be an unduly high price. Once the futures market has evolved, the speculator who believes the price to be unduly low will no longer need to buy the actual physical commodity and incur the costs and trouble of storing it until the price rises, nor to engage in the tricky and complicated business of negotiating a purchase for delivery at a date in the future at which he reckons he can sell profitably. All he need do is to buy a standardised contract for future delivery and then sell it when he wishes. Consequently, when an organised futures market develops, it becomes the market where at least the great bulk of any speculative transactions takes place and where, therefore, the price level is set. The ordinary market for more or less immediate delivery contracts, say 7–14 days, known commonly as the 'spot' market, becomes almost exclusively confined to what may loosely be termed genuine trade transactions, that is, transferences of the actual physical commodity. There must however be no misunderstanding of the qualifying phrases in the previous sentence. There is nothing to prevent speculation in a spot market. Speculation is more difficult, especially for a fall in the price, but where no organised futures market evolves, then such speculation as

---

[1] These standardised contracts are in terms of an imaginary standard grade of the commodity, and to fulfil them a small number of actual grades are specified as constituting good delivery, these actual grades differing little from each other and so commanding very nearly the same prices; or, where actual grading is not so fine, a schedule of premiums and discounts for delivery of grades above or below the imaginary standard grade is laid down. A standard unit of quantity is also prescribed, and the time and conditions of delivery are stereotyped, so that given the delivery month only the number of units and the price have to be settled by the contracting parties.

does take place—and limited speculation is common with nearly all commodities—is effected through the ordinary spot market and its machinery. Similarly, a futures market is not confined to purely speculative transactions, for on all futures contracts actual delivery of the commodity is enforceable. This is indeed the lynchpin of the whole organisation, for it is this enforceability of actual delivery which makes a futures market a genuine price-fixing market, and not a mere casino, because it automatically keeps prices in the spot market and futures prices in line. For if the price in the spot market is higher than futures prices by more than the relevant carrying costs, then a sure profit could be made by enforcing delivery of the actual commodity against a purchasing contract in the futures market, and then selling the delivery in the spot market. Similarly, if futures prices were higher than the price in the spot market, it would be profitable to sell in the futures market and at the same time buy in the spot market and, when the delivery date of the futures contract arrived, fulfil it by tendering what had been bought in the spot market. Usually of course a speculator will match a futures buying contract by making a selling contract for a more distant delivery date, and vice versa. The vast bulk of the contracts on a futures market are matched pairs, so that the speculator only receives, or pays, the margin between the buying and selling prices of all his pairs of contracts, these margins being sorted out by a kind of clearing-house mechanism. But there is nothing to prevent a single contract being made and physical delivery being enforced. It may be that the producer, or a merchant who has bought the commodity from him, will decide to sell it in the futures market for delivery some time ahead rather than in the spot market. It may be that a processor or manufacturer, or a merchant supplying them, will decide to buy supplies in the futures market for delivery some time ahead, rather than wait and buy in the spot market. The enforceability of all futures contracts thus keeps prices in the two markets in line with one another. It also ensures that price changes in the futures market will be reflected by changes in the spot price, while if the prices do diverge they will speedily be brought back into line.

As has been explained above, organised futures markets developed, where the necessary conditions were satisfied, primarily in order to facilitate the price-making activities of merchant speculators, enabling them to correct, with maximum ease and speed, divergences in either direction from what they think the price ought to be. This may be termed the directive or regulating function of speculation, the function of directing or regulating the price to the proper level, not only in the futures market but also in the spot market, as has been explained in the preceding paragraph; so also in all the markets and for all the transactions in that commodity all over the world, for all the prices are co-ordinated, as was explained at the beginning of this chapter. Even this is not the whole story, for once a futures market evolves from an important spot market, another whole class of transactions becomes possible. These are transactions aimed not at regulating the price by offering the speculator a profit if his opinion is more correct than that of his fellow speculators, but at the avoidance of loss by merchants and first users through a fall in price while they are holding physical stocks of the commodity. This they can do by shifting the risks of such loss on to the professional speculators, who are ready to accept the risks because they reckon that they possess greater specialised skill in forecasting the future course of prices, and so will be able to make a profit as, so to speak, the merchants' insurance agents. This is known as 'hedging'. Though it sounds a mysterious business, and though the detail of different methods of hedging varies greatly, yet the essential principle is comparatively simple and straightforward, namely the making of an equal but opposite transaction in the futures market for every genuine trade transaction. Suppose a merchant has made a purchase in a far-off producing country, and wishes to insure himself against loss through a fall in the price during the two or three months which will elapse before the produce reaches his market and can be sold. As soon as the merchant buys the produce, he sells a futures contract for delivery three or four months ahead. When he eventually sells the produce, he buys a futures contract for the same delivery month as his previous futures contract to sell. He has thus made two equal but opposite pairs of transactions, one pair in spot markets, his purchase and sale of the actual produce, and an equal but opposite pair in the futures market. Provided prices in the two markets move similarly, as in general they should, then if they have fallen, he will lose on his spot transactions, but he will gain the same amount on his transactions in the futures market. The position will be reversed if prices have risen. He has achieved his object of insuring against a fall in the price on his actual produce or trade transactions, the premium being that he foregoes the chance of a profit if prices rise. In effect he hands this chance over to the professional speculator who bought his selling contract in the futures market, and so transfers to him the risk of loss. The speculator of course reckons that over his transactions as a whole he will make a profit, but he may be wrong in any individual transaction, and therefore on that he may lose. Thus by making such hedging transactions possible, the futures market performs a risk-bearing function as well as its price-regulating function.

It seems unnecessary to examine here the varying technicalities of different hedging contracts. It should, however, be observed that the perfect hedge, that is, the profit on the pair of spot transactions exactly equalling the loss on the futures pair or vice versa, is a rare chance, if only because the movement of the two prices is unlikely to be exactly the same, especially if the grade of the actual produce is markedly different from the grade or grades of the standardised futures contract. But the divergences are normally small, and therefore any gains or losses on a hedging operation will normally be small. On a large number of hedging operations, such as a merchant would make in six months or a year, his gains and losses would very closely cancel out. Up to 1939 hedging was widely and regularly practised by merchants during the physical movement of wheat, cotton, the non-ferrous metals and other commodities for which active futures markets had evolved. Banks, indeed, normally advanced a larger percentage of the current value of a consignment if it was hedged, and this in effect resulted in hedging wherever possible. Futures markets were thus performing a useful economic function by enabling the merchant to do a larger amount of business on a given capital, and so reducing his costs and ultimately benefiting the consumer. There was also up to 1939 an appreciable amount of hedging by first users, for example, by millers of wheat or spinners of cotton. Here the probable degree of protection would be less than for the merchant, because the price of flour or of cotton yarn is less likely to follow closely the variations in the futures price of wheat or cotton than the spot price of wheat or cotton is to follow the futures price, which is the relevant correlation for a merchant's hedge.

Since 1939, as will shortly be explained more fully, the whole sphere of organised futures markets has been narrowed. For this and other reasons the practical possibilities of hedging, as well as in some cases the need for it, have been reduced. There is little doubt, however, that organised futures markets which are working with reasonable efficiency, as many are still, do perform a useful economic function by automatically providing means for the transference of the risks of falling prices from ordinary merchants to the merchant speculators. As specialists in the art of price determination and forecasting the merchant speculators are better equipped to carry such risks. Moreover this risk-bearing function of organised futures markets reacts on the efficiency of its price-regulating function. The addition of hedging transactions means a more active market with a greater total of transactions, and thus a greater and more continuous flow of guesses at the correct level of the world price. For, in practice, transactions with the object of price regulation and hedging transactions are of course inextricably mixed up in the whole volume of transactions on the market. A speculator who buys because he thinks the price is too low may be buying from another speculator who is of the contrary opinion, but he may just as well be buying in effect from a merchant or manufacturer who is conducting a hedging operation. The two functions of organised futures markets are both discharged more efficiently by an active market with a continuously large volume of transactions. The greater the volume of speculative transactions, the better are the facilities for hedging. The greater the volume of hedging transactions, the better will the function of price regulation be discharged.

This exposition of the evolution, operation and functions of organised futures markets has so far been related mainly to the situation before the outbreak of World War II. During the first forty years of the present century and indeed before that, the basis of the whole system of marketing primary commodities was private merchanting. Marketing was conducted by individual competitive merchant firms, and there was very little and only sporadic action by governments or by organisations of producers. In this system futures markets played a very important role, and were in their hey-day. Since 1939 the whole environment in which these markets functioned has been greatly changed. Their general importance has considerably declined, though they are still important in a narrower field, as the following sketch of developments since 1939 will show.

The outbreak of World War II at once brought into force severe regulations concerning foreign exchange, with the result that futures markets in the U.K. were all closed within a few days. Speculation could only be sheer gambling on the fortunes of war, and could serve no useful economic function. Government regulations and price controls rapidly resulted in the virtual disappearance of most spot markets also. In lieu of a private merchanting system there was soon created a governmental or centralised system. In the U.K., and later in the U.S.A., government bulk buying from producers' organisations or their governments was organised, and the supplies so obtained were distributed by government organisations and agencies. Thus in the U.K. the Ministry of Food bought all foodstuffs and animal feeding stuffs in bulk, and distributed supplies at controlled prices all the way down the line to the final consumers. The Ministry of Supply did the same for imports of raw materials. The executive committees handling the various commodities were usually run by the most outstanding men in the trades concerned. Merchant firms continued their functions of distributing the actual physical produce, but almost completely ceased to be concerned with the business of purchasing and therefore the making of prices. Much the same sort of controls were established in the U.S.A. In the later years of the war the two countries set up combined boards for the joint purchasing of many commodities and the allocation of these supplies between themselves and sometimes also between allied and neutral countries. These developments at the importing end naturally led to similar sort of developments at the exporting end. Exporters became faced with only one or very few large buyers. These monopolistic conditions gave rise to the establishment of governmental selling agencies as in Argentina and in the British Dominions, while in British colonies the price for exported produce was in effect fixed by the U.K. government departments concerned. The effect of the war on the marketing of commodities was thus to substitute a system of almost complete government control in place of private merchanting over all but a small part of the whole field.

When the war ended in 1945, a process of reversing the war-time system and of returning to private merchanting soon began. In the U.S.A. things moved faster than in the U.K., if only because of the more rapid removal of price controls. In the U.K. the restoration of free markets was a gradual and halting process, especially in the earlier years. There were two big obstacles, one political, the other economic. The political obstacle was, in short, the general aversion of the Labour government to private merchanting and particularly to futures markets. The economic obstacle was the difficult foreign exchange situation, and particularly the dollar shortage. A whole new technique had to be evolved for the conduct of markets within the framework of exchange control regulations. The government very naturally proceeded slowly and tentatively, beginning with commodities produced mainly within the sterling area, and gradually proceeding to those which involved purchases as well as sales in dollars and other 'hard' currencies. Thus the first steps were the resumption

53

THE ORGANISATION OF MARKETING

of the London wool auctions, and the reopening of the London Rubber Exchange, in the autumn of 1946. After this there was a pause for three years until November 1949 when the London Metal Exchange was opened for both spot and future delivery dealings in tin. In 1951 the London cocoa market and the London tea auctions were resurrected, and in 1952 the London coffee market. Dealings in lead and zinc were resumed on the London Metal Exchange, and in 1954 dealings in copper. That year also saw the reopening of the futures markets in Liverpool for wheat and cotton, and for barley and maize at the Baltic Exchange in London. Finally the sugar market was re-opened in 1957. Parallel, so to speak, with the restoration of commodity markets was the equally gradual restoration of freer dealings in the foreign exchange market, which are a necessary concomitant. As the foreign exchange position became easier, commodity markets got into their stride, and so the volume of business and the technical efficiency of the foreign exchange market increased: the effects were mutual.

By about 1956 the change-back to a system of private merchanting may be said to have been more or less completed. In 1946 about four-fifths of Britain's imports were being purchased by government departments. Ten years later virtually none of the chief primary products was so purchased. Yet the restored private merchanting system is very different from that of the inter-war period. Anticipating certain events and developments which will be described in the chapters which follow, it may be observed here that with the U.S. price support legislation for wheat, and with government selling of wheat in Canada, Argentina and Australia, together with the international wheat agreements of the last ten years concerning the control of supplies and prices, it is small wonder that the great markets for wheat function very differently from the pre-war system. The Liverpool futures market was reopened in 1954 but was very soon closed again. The Liverpool cotton market is a shadow of its former self, because the whole supply situation has been so dominated by the sales policy of the U.S. government and its enormous stocks. Similarly such factors as strategic stock piling, and subsequent liquidation by the U.S. and the U.K. governments, have made things difficult at times for the London and New York metal exchanges, as also have the International Tin Agreement and the concerted control of supplies by some of the large copper producers. Other markets have been affected by the existence of single sellers of significant quantities, such as Argentina and Brazil for most of their exports, or the cocoa boards of West Africa. On a smaller scale have been the producers' co-operative societies operating central selling organisations for the produce of their members. Many of these factors have of course affected New York's markets also, but the operations of the London markets were specially restricted by Britain's foreign exchange position right up to 1959, and are even restricted to some extent at present. The Bank of England still has powers to call for returns of all transactions, with a view to checking both dollar expenditure and excessive speculation. Nevertheless, with the notable exceptions of wheat and cotton, the spot and futures markets for the non-ferrous metals, rubber, wool, coffee, cocoa and sugar, as well as the Baltic Exchange for grains, are again all functioning effectively, even if in a rather different environment and in a rather different way as compared with pre-World War II.

Little has been said above concerning the accuracy with which private merchanting performs the task of determining world prices. The prima facie case that specialisation increases efficiency has been assumed to be correct in respect of the operation of organised futures markets and the activities of merchant speculators. As has been noted above, during World War II an alternative system of marketing was instituted, a system of centralised bulk buying, and in many cases also of selling, operated by governments. In Britain there was, and still is, a substantial body of public opinion which considers the post-war return to what is essentially a system of private merchanting to have been a retrograde step. In particular the restoration of organised futures markets is sometimes regarded as support for gambling devices performing no real economic function. Something has been said about this above, but no attempt has been made to weigh the merits of private merchanting versus centralised government bulk trading, or to determine the crucial question which system is likely to result in the most accurate determination of prices. This is an intricate and very difficult problem, and though its study, if inevitably somewhat inconclusive, does at least throw more light on the workings of the two rival systems of marketing, it has been relegated to an appendix to this chapter. To include it at this point would interrupt the presentation of the general study of primary commodities which is the main object of this book. It cannot be regarded as an integral part of this study.[1]

[1] It is nevertheless a subject on which the ordinary citizen, let alone the economist, ought to make up his mind—may indeed be virtually compelled to do so in the not too distant future—and it is therefore to be hoped that the reader will not be deterred from turning to this appendix, either immediately or later when he has finished the main text.

Appendix: The Economics of Private Merchanting versus Government Bulk Trading

Though there are other aspects of this whole general problem, such as the relative economies of the two systems in the physical processes of marketing, and their relative advantages in respect of general economic stability, yet the really crucial issue concerns the determination of prices. This will therefore be considered first. Which system results in the more accurate determination of prices—the system of private merchanting, with its markets and organised speculation for those commodities which satisfy the requisite conditions, or centralised government bulk trading, with its bargaining between politicans and civil servants representing each country? Now the private merchanting system claims in effect that the determination of prices reaches its highest pitch of efficiency in an organised speculative market. A comparative study of the efficiency with which organised speculation discharges its price-regulating functions, and of the corresponding efficiency with which prices are determined under government trading, should therefore reveal the relative merits and demerits of the two systems of marketing in respect of this crucial question. Such a study should also incidentally throw some light on the merits and demerits of bulk buying and selling by governments or by producers' co-operative societies, as compared with the competitive buying and selling of a private merchanting system, though these matters will not be directly considered here.

The two systems are, however, so different that it is more profitable to appraise each in turn than to compare them point by point. Organised speculation will therefore be considered first. Its price-regulating function covers both the maintenance of one price level in all the markets for the commodity in question throughout the world, and the determination of the level of that price. The former is comparatively easy, for it depends on actual ascertainable facts. If the price in one market gets out of line with the others, arbitrage operations, as explained in the preceding chapter,[1] offer the speculator a profit, and these operations will rapidly bring the price in that market into line with the rest. There is not much doubt that such regulation was achieved with a high degree of success during the inter-war period. Though this is in its essence a straightforward business which does not need further explanation, its importance should

[1] See page 45.

not for that reason be underestimated whether from the producer's or consumer's points of view; nor in particular from the manufacturer's point of view, for the maintenance of one world price level assures him that his competitors in other countries are not getting their supplies of raw materials on better terms. In the immediate post-war years, British manufacturers of cotton, metals, and other commodities which were still subject to government control of supplies, complained frequently and loudly that they were having to pay higher prices than some of their competitors. Though general trading conditions in those years were admittedly difficult and abnormal, so that it cannot be concluded that this is an inherent defect in government trading, yet the absence of such complaints in the last ten years or so is at least evidence that organised markets, even when functioning less freely than in the inter-war period, are still able to achieve this form of price regulation satisfactorily.

The other form of price regulation—the determination of what the world price level should be—is much more difficult, for this involves estimates not only of current, but also of future, demand and supply. The speculative market determines this price level by means of a very large and continuous flow of guesses, for that is what speculative transactions really are. Any important change in the conditions of demand or supply is usually detected as a likely development by some of the speculators well before the actual event. By their operations they start the price moving in the appropriate direction. As the change, and its exact magnitude, become more certain and clearer, the market gradually adjusts the price accordingly. Usually when the event actually takes place, for example, the harvesting of a larger or smaller crop, there is little change in the price because the effect has already been foreseen and gradually discounted in advance as the result of hundreds, or perhaps thousands, of speculative transactions. Thus a speculative market produces graduated price changes. This is an important economic gain, for a graduated price movement gives time for adjustments. An earlier rise gives time for all who are short of stocks to buy before they have to pay too dearly. It tends to hasten the flow of supplies to the markets, it may even encourage some expansion in the volume of future production if this is required, and it tends to curtail consumption smoothly. An earlier decline has similar but opposite effects. It is a common saying that 'it is easy to be wise after the event', meaning that if the speaker had realised the probability of an occurrence in advance, or even if he had had some inkling of it, he would have taken steps to minimise its effects. That is precisely what organised speculation helps the economic system to do. An examination of all the available evidence may well lead to the conclusion that in general it does it with fair success, considering how difficult it is to guess what even the immediate future has in store.

This method of price determination by a multiplicity of guesses, however, means a high frequency of small price changes, for it is usually through continual oscillations around a trend line that the price is gradually adjusted to a new level, and not along a smooth curve. This is an inherent feature of speculative markets. The speculators are always trying to turn to their personal advantage the news of the day, such as crop condition reports, weather reports, political events or rumours thereof, trade disputes, business failures, company reports and profits, changes in freight rates, and so on. On the precise significance of such news, the opinions of the speculators will almost certainly differ and so, therefore, will their operations. Consequently the price tends to see-saw, up a little, down a little, all the time, even when the news justifies little or no change in the price. When it does clearly indicate an appreciable adjustment of the price, opinions will differ as to the exact change required; and again it is by a series of oscillations that the correct adjustment is finally achieved. If the change required is large, the market tends to get excited, and very often the necessary adjustment will first be overdone, and then, so to speak, underdone. The oscillations start on a considerable scale, and gradually diminish until they die away as the new price level is established. Thus a speculative market tends to be oversensitive, and the more perfect a speculative market becomes the more sensitive it becomes. Critics of speculative markets often point to the frequency of price changes as unnecessary disturbances of the price. They may fail to realise that the reduction of the violence of price fluctuations is in a real sense achieved by the frequency of price changes. The benefits of the former cannot be had without the drawbacks of the latter.

There is little doubt that speculation does diminish the violence of price fluctuations, but there is also the question whether it diminishes their extent, that is, the range between the maximum and the minimum of any phase. The answer to this further question is that the extent of price fluctuations depends primarily on the elasticities of the demand for, and the supply of, the commodity in question. A speculative market cannot alter these elasticities. If the result of a graduated change in the price of a commodity has little effect on its demand or supply, then, though graduated, the price will in the end have to rise as high, or fall as low, as it would do in the absence of a speculative market. If the result has a large effect, the converse will be true. The extent of the fluctuation depends simply on the elasticities of demand and supply. The wide extent of the price fluctuations of certain commodities for which there are speculative markets is attributable to their low elasticities of demand and/or supply. Speculation cannot be blamed for failure to achieve something which in the nature of things it cannot do.

There are, however, better-founded criticisms of organised speculation, such as the possibility of a speculator, or a group of speculators, manipulating the price simply to their own advantage, and the extent to which they can do so. In accordance with the state of his transactions, every speculator at any particular moment wants to see the price move in one direction rather than the other; and if he buys or sells on a big enough scale, he can usually force the price up or down, assuming no opposite secular change in the price is taking place. But he will only do this if he thinks he can make a profit by so doing. Ultimately he must cover his liabilities; if he has been buying on a big scale at gradually increasing prices, he must eventually sell an equal amount; and his selling will cause the price to decline again, so that his sales will take place at gradually decreasing prices. The probability is, other things remaining unaltered, that the two series of transactions will just about balance (i.e. his average buying price and his average selling price will be much the same), and that he will make little profit, or even a small loss. If he can make other speculators think that the price will continue to rise so that they continue buying after he has stopped, he may then be able to make his sales at a higher average price than his average buying price. Such persuasion of others, however, is not easy to achieve. The rules of all organised markets forbid the spreading of false news or rumours and such-like practices, and the penalty is usually permanent expulsion from membership. This acts as a strong deterrent even if detection is often difficult. If his financial resources are very large, however, he may be able to achieve a speculative 'corner' by acquiring all, or nearly all, the available futures selling contracts for a particular month, so that he has a monopoly of these contracts, and will be able to dictate the prices at which the sellers (the 'bears') can cover their contracts. The price may then be pushed up quite artificially for a few days at the end of that particular delivery month, and the cornerer will make large profits. His victims will be in the main his fellow speculators, though merchants and manufacturers may lose on hedging contracts, and to that extent it may be argued that their costs are increased, and so the consumer ultimately suffers. At best a corner is likely to be a nuisance to merchants and manufacturers, because they will feel it wise to postpone their hedging contracts until the price disturbance has subsided, even if this means carrying additional risks themselves. The possibility of cornering is certainly a drawback to organised speculation, for there is no way of preventing it. Cornering is, however, a very difficult and risky operation, and so corners are very occasional events. It must be remembered that cornering of all the actual physical supplies of a commodity is by no means unknown, and a physical corner is likely to be immensely more damaging to merchants and manufacturers, and to the consumer, than a speculative corner. Apart from cornering, however, it must be reckoned that ordinary price manipulation—now one dealer, or group of dealers, and now another, trying to get a 'pull' on the market—is constantly exerting an influence on the price, though not of course chronically in one direction more than in the other, and not usually to any considerable extent, or more than very temporarily.

Finally, there is the criticism that the speculator is far more concerned with guessing what other speculators will do and the way in which they will move the price in the immediate future than with guessing at the true equilibrium price. This is the Keynesian thesis concerning speculation of the 2nd to nth degrees. It may first be observed that this thesis was developed by Keynes on the basis of the behaviour of stock exchanges, and with primary reference to dealings in stocks and shares. There are significant differences between stock exchanges and commodity markets. On a stock exchange, dealings take place in a fixed supply of assets, whereas on commodity markets the supply is a continual flow. Moreover, a much larger proportion of the transactions on a commodity market are normally made by specialists, who rely for their profits on their specialised knowledge of the commodity and their skill as operators, than on a stock exchange where the relatively ignorant general investing public still plays a significant role. On the other hand, there is no doubt that speculators on a commodity market are influenced, often to a considerable degree, even if half subconsciously, by what they think other speculators are thinking, and how they will therefore act. The dealers on a commodity market spend much of every day in a crowd together, and they naturally become responsive to what may loosely be termed 'crowd psychology' or, as it is often termed, 'market sentiment'. Profits can certainly often be made by intelligent anticipation of what others are going to do; but if all the operators are reckoned to be about equally intelligent at this game, which on a commodity market is usually a fair assumption, the game is not likely to be very profitable to any of them in the long run—not nearly so profitable as making better guesses at the true equilibrium price. The Keynesian thesis certainly applies to commodity markets, and such 2nd degree speculation, if only in its most general forms, plays a part and militates against the market's accurate determination of the price, but its effects should not be exaggerated.

There are, however, times when it is not true even of commodity markets that the bulk of the transactions are made by specialists, namely when the general public invade a commodity market and start speculating in large volume. This hardly ever happens in the U.K., for if the British public wants to speculate on a commodity, it does so in the shares of producing companies on the stock exchange; but it has happened periodically in the U.S.A., and occasionally in other countries. Such speculation by the general public is always for a rise in the price, since the public does not understand the technique of bear speculation. Prior to World War II the American public sometimes formed the idea—nearly always wrongly—that their wheat crop, or some other crop, was going to be a near failure, and so started buying futures on the Chicago or other markets. Relatively to the normal volume of transactions on the market this meant a tidal wave of purchases, and the price would shoot upwards. According to what may be termed the classical economic doctrine on this matter, the professional speculators on the market, if they see no cause for a rise, or think that the rise has gone far enough, should adopt a bear policy, and by their sales check and in due course reverse the rise. But this overlooks two very pertinent facts. The first is that the total financial resources of all the professionals may well be far smaller than the volume of buying which is being done by the public. Thus even if all the professionals sold short to the limit of their resources, the price rise might only be somewhat slowed down. The second, and more conclusive, point is that there is no reason to suppose that a bear policy would give the professionals more profits than they would get by following the rise as bulls until they judged that it had nearly spent itself; then selling out, and waiting until the price had definitely turned downwards as the result of liquidating sales by the public; and then following the decline in the price as bears until they judged this in turn had nearly come to an end. In other words, speculating on what the public is going to do should give the professionals more profits than speculating on what the price ought to be; and anyway much surer and safer profits, for the procedure outlined above is relatively easy provided that they are not too greedy and leave themselves an adequate margin of safety at the turning points. This is what happens on such occasions, and the result is that the price boom is stimulated by the professionals instead of being checked. So is the ensuing slump. When the public invade a commodity market in this fashion, organised speculation may legitimately be called mere gambling, and it is a real drawback to the system that the public can turn a market into a casino. It must, however, be emphasised that this sort of thing does not often happen. At most, less than half a dozen instances can be found in the whole inter-war period and, owing to the altered status of organised markets since World War II, it seems unlikely that earlier happenings of this sort will be repeated.

Organised speculation therefore has merits in respect of price determination and regulation, but it also has defects. Turning now to the consideration of government bulk trading—or, as it may be termed, centralised marketing in contrast to private merchanting—this is clearly free from the defects of organised speculation, such as price manipulation and 2nd to nth degree Keynesian speculation, for such matters simply do not come into the picture. But centralised marketing has its own drawbacks and difficulties of an essentially similar kind, in that those making the contracts are usually not solely concerned in trying to determine the true equilibrium price, but allow extraneous factors and motives to influence their decisions. In practice the negotiators on both sides will be politicians or their civil servants. Political considerations are consequently almost bound to intrude. For example, on the buyer's side the civil servants may be quite certain that the price ought to be lower, but a higher price may be accepted because the seller is a colony, or a very friendly country, or a country whose friendship it is desirable to win, or because the present political party in power is thought to be more friendly or more amenable than the opposing political party and therefore should be assisted to remain as the government. Similarly, a price which the buyer realises is below the equilibrium price may be fought for to the last extreme for the opposite of these sorts of reasons, or because the country is short of foreign exchange, and so on. The same sort of thing tends, of course, to happen on the seller's side. There were numerous contracts made during the period of centralised marketing during and immediately following World War II which seem to exhibit quite clearly the intrusion of such political considerations, and even in a sense personal considerations, as when the Prime Ministers of two countries made trade contracts during 'summit' political conferences. The possible, it might almost be said the certain, intrusion of political or semi-political considerations is the great drawback to price determination under centralised marketing. To measure their extent and effects in any sort of scientific way is, however, an impossibility, just as it is impossible to measure the extent of the defects in private merchanting. In both cases it is all a matter of personal opinion and personal valuations.

In order to try and push this analysis a stage further, however, let a bland assumption be made that these drawbacks of both systems in respect of price determination balance each other, and that so far there is therefore nothing to choose between them. Both systems, then, are up to a point guessing at the true equilibrium price. There is, however, the great difference that private merchanting, especially if organised speculation is possible, sets the price over any short period at the average or mean of a very large number of more or less independent guesses; whereas with centralised marketing over a corresponding period there are likely to be only two guesses, the buyer's and the seller's or, if more than one of each is concerned, still only very few, and the price as finally agreed upon is most likely to be somewhere between them. With private merchanting, individual merchants and speculators are continually guessing at the price all day and every day, and so there is a large and continuous flow of guesses. Under centralised marketing, the price of a large part, or even of the whole, of the world exportable production of a commodity for, say, six months ahead, or even a year, may be fixed by one contract, or at the most by very few contracts. Under private merchanting, over a period of, say, six months, thousands of guesses will be made, whereas under centralised marketing the number of guesses will probably be in single figures, and for longish periods not a single guess may be made. Now, if the guesses were sheer guesswork on no foundation of reasoning as in pure gambling, then, in accordance with the law of large numbers, the average of the very large number of guesses under private merchanting would be nearer the mark than the average of the very small number of guesses under centralised marketing. But in fact under both systems the guesswork is to some extent 'informed'. It rests on some foundation of facts and information. The foundation, however, is by no means the same for the two systems. Under centralised marketing, the negotiators on both sides will almost certainly take every possible step to collect every scrap of relevant information, and will study and weigh it all carefully and quietly before they form their guess at the correct price. The individual merchant, on the other hand, though he will take note of all the relevant information which comes his way privately, or through news agencies, newspapers and so on, is unlikely to get such complete information as the negotiators of centralised marketing contracts. He will certainly not have the time, even if he commands the sheer technical ability, to collate and arrange it, and study it and weigh it, as will those negotiators. The individual merchant must act quickly on most of the information which reaches him, or he will lose the race with his competitors at the start. There is no doubt therefore that the guesses under centralised marketing are far better informed guesses than those under private merchanting. It is, however, equally certain that even under centralised marketing the unknown and the uncertain remain a large, usually a very large, proportion of the whole problem, and so the proportion of sheer guesswork remains large.

The private merchanting system therefore has the advantage of a multiplicity of guesses, and centralised marketing that of superior information on which to found its few guesses. There is obviously no way of determining the relative importance of these totally different sorts of advantages. That is bound to vary with different commodities, and even at different times with the same commodity. There is therefore no way of deciding which system will result in the better determination of the price. It is, however, certain that centralised marketing, with its far fewer changes in the price at longish intervals, inevitably means that these changes will be large relatively to the much more frequent changes under private merchanting. Centralised marketing means intermittent adjustment of the price by fewer but larger changes. Private merchanting means continuous adjustment of the price towards the equilibrium level. As has been argued above, continuous adjustment of prices is very much preferable to all concerned and to the smooth working of the economic system as a whole;

and it may perhaps be concluded that until more evidence is available of the greater exactitude and singleness of purpose of centralised marketing in respect of price determination and regulation, the advantage of the continuous adjustment of prices under private merchanting outweighs the defects of that system.

This lengthy analysis of the relative merits of the two systems in respect of price determination has been inconclusive, but it has at least thrown some light on this part of the problem. Price determination is the crucial issue, but some few notes may be added here on some of the other aspects of the whole problem, such as the relative economies of the two systems in respect of the physical processes of marketing, and their relative contribution to the stability of the economic system. Under centralised marketing, buying takes one of two main forms—bulk purchases, i.e. buying by contract very large quantities for delivery within, say, a few months; or the making of long-term contracts for perhaps several years ahead for stated quantities, or sometimes the whole available supplies of a country as they come forward, at prices usually determined year by year, though sometimes for two years at a time. Both these forms of centralised buying should offer economies in the realms of transportation and handling as compared with private merchanting, simply because the contracts are usually for such much larger consignments. But on the question whether these economies are likely to be relatively large or inconsiderable, information is so far very scarce. It can safely be said that in peace-time they are nothing like so large as they were in war-time, if only because of the unusual organisation which the last war forced on the world's shipping industry. Beyond that it is largely at present guesswork. Probably for some commodities these economies might be considerable, though not for others. Centralised buying by long-term contracts, however, offers in addition a different kind of economy. It is the understood essence of such contracts that the buyer shall benefit somewhat when prices are rising, and the seller when prices are falling, i.e. that there should be some element of give-and-take in the prices. Consequently, buying by long-term contracts should give a greater security to the consumer of actual physical supplies of the commodity, and at more stable prices than those which he might have to pay to secure the same volume of supplies in an open world market under private merchanting. Similarly there should be greater security to the producer that he will be able to dispose of his output at more stable prices than he might get in an open world market. In this sense and to this extent, the long-term contract offers the real economy of greater stability and security. Whether this will be obtained by both parties at a worthwhile price, at an economical cost, depends upon a very exact determination of the average contract prices: in other words on the crucial issue of price determination.

All this applies equally to centralised selling. It may perhaps be concluded that centralised marketing as compared with private merchanting has certain economies to offer in the physical processes of marketing; and where the long-term contract is employed, in respect of security and stability, provided always that the average prices are accurately determined. On the other hand, against these possible economies must be set the automatic provision by organised speculative markets of a reasonably efficient risk-bearing service, whereas under centralised marketing there may have to be an ancillary scheme to take the place of hedging facilities, such, for example, as the British cotton insurance scheme during the last war. This involves an additional direct cost, and a risk of possible financial loss to the government. Again it must be remembered that centralised marketing does not necessarily result in the maintenance of one world price level. Processors or manufacturers in one country may sometimes find themselves paying less for a commodity than their competitors in other countries (which of course they will like), but sometimes more (to which they will take the strongest objection). Private merchanting, especially when organised speculation is possible, is almost certainly superior in this respect.

Thus, in considering the merits and demerits of these two systems of trading, many issues have to be balanced one against another. The truth is that, since most of these issues involve a large element of personal judgement, no agreed verdict or scientific solution is possible. This does not, however, prevent passionate expressions of opinion by those who are convinced of the superiority of one system over the other.

6. THE BEHAVIOUR OF PRICES

All, or nearly all, primary commodities are alike in one important respect. In the absence of any successful organised control scheme, their market prices fluctuate very widely, not only in the short term of a few weeks or months, or say within a year, but also in the longer term of several years. In either case, when demand shows a tendency to outrun supply, prices rise to levels which seem altogether out of proportion to the deficiency in supply. The position is reversed if supply exceeds demand. Examples of both short- and longer-term fluctuations in recent years could be quoted in large numbers, but a few will suffice here. Sugar has, of course, been specially affected by the Cuban crisis, but its recent record has even so been very remarkable. In May 1961 the New York price was 3·2 cents per lb; in January 1962 2·0 cents; in December 1962 4·5 cents; in May 1963 12 cents; in August 1963 6·0 cents; in November 1963 12 cents; in May 1964 7 cents; and in October 1964 3·6 cents. The price of cocoa was under 21 cents per lb in September 1961; over 26 cents in December 1961; and back to 20 cents in February 1962; and there was a similar and slightly larger if slower fluctuation between September 1962 and April 1964. The price of Brazilian coffee (Santos grade 4) was around 34 cents per lb in August 1963, and eight months later it was 47·5 cents. The price of Manilla hemp (abaca) fell from £201 per ton in March 1963 to £169 in July 1963, and was back again to £193 by February 1964; while sisal (East African no. 1) rose from £99 per ton in September 1962 to £148 in April 1963, only to fall to £110 in October 1964. Non-ferrous metal prices are even more volatile. In March 1956 the price of copper (cash wire bars) was at a peak of £437 per ton; in June 1956 it was £264 and by February 1958 £160; more recently the price doubled between January and October 1964. Similar examples are provided by lead and zinc. What may happen when there are doubts as to the adequacy of productive capacity may be illustrated, for a small deficiency, by wool prices, which for crossbred rose from 74 pence per lb in September 1962 to 110 pence in early 1964; and, for a feared large deficiency, by tin prices, which rose from £850 per ton in February 1963 to £1650 in October 1964. Similar examples can be drawn in quantity back to 1945, including the great fluctuations caused by the Korean War, of which some account is given in chapter 9 below; and from the inter-war and pre-1914 periods. Widely, one might almost say wildly, fluctuating prices have always characterised most primary commodities, and the contrast with the prices of manufactures is most noticeable. What then causes the prices of primary commodities to fluctuate so greatly, both in the short and the longer term?[1]

---

[1] The phrases short and longer term are deliberately used here as being more elastic and less rigidly defined than the standard short- and long-period conceptions of economic theory, which with primary commodities often seem to be unrealistic.

Short-term Fluctuations

It will make for clarity to investigate short-term fluctuations first, and then longer term, even though both are often found in active operation together. It is a commonplace that an equilibrium price may be disturbed by changes in the demand or in the supply, or by simultaneous changes in both. Now demand may change quite quickly in the case of some raw materials, owing to changes in the tempo of general economic activity in one or all of the main markets; but the demand for foodstuffs normally tends to be fairly steady over short periods, and changes from the prevailing trend are usually slow to take effect. With primary commodities, however, it is far more common for an equilibrium price to be upset by changes in supply. Everyone knows that agricultural crops can be greatly affected by the weather, and though below-average yields in some producing countries tend to be balanced by above-average yields in others, yet world production of very many agricultural products, tree crops as well as annual crops, does vary considerably from year to year. Mining industries are not much subject to the vagaries of weather, but their rate of output may be affected by geological and other natural factors outside the producers' control, as well as by strikes, and by stoppages due to mechanical failures. With almost all primary commodities, supply is continually altering and so, often, is demand. Surpluses and shortages are continually occurring, and equilibrium is a rarity and seldom lasts long.

The final consumers' demand for most foodstuffs tends without doubt to be inelastic over short periods. Consumers are slow to change their customary habits of eating and drinking, and if foodstuffs become dearer, they will economise on other things until this becomes relatively too burdensome. Manufacturers, as the consumers of raw materials, are unlikely to reduce their demand appreciably in the face of rising prices, unless a particular raw material forms such a large proportion of their costs that they must raise the price of their finished product. Still less are they likely to increase their demand if prices are falling, at least until the price of the particular raw material falls sufficiently to enable them to reduce the price of their finished product, so that they can anticipate larger sales. Thus, in the short term, demand for most primary products is markedly inelastic. Consequently their prices will fall very considerably if supply is even slightly larger than demand, and rise sharply if it is even slightly smaller. This result is all the more certain because of the short-term inelasticity of supply. With annual crops, producers cannot vary their acreages until sowings are made for the next crop. Unless they are convinced that the higher or lower price level will continue at least until that crop is marketed, they are unlikely to make much change simply on account of the price. With some tree crops, a small change in current supply can be evoked quickly by a change in price. Rubber trees can be tapped harder or less hard, and the collection of the produce of palm trees can be intensified or slackened. There are, however, limits to such variations of the normal production programme. Mining is much more under the control of the producers. By working overtime or short time, by concentrating on the richer or the poorer veins of ores, an appreciable response to price changes can usually be secured even with a few months. In general, however, the supply of most primary commodities is inelastic over short periods. Thus a first approach to answering the question 'Why do the prices of primary products fluctuate so widely in the short term?' is that the main causes are continual variations in current supplies, coupled with the inelasticity of demand and the general inelasticity of supply, though to these factors may often be added, especially in respect of raw materials, variations in the demand itself.

This first approach to the answer should and can be refined by a little further analysis. So far demand has been taken as the demand of the final consumers of foodstuffs and of the manufacturers of raw materials, but with primary commodities merchants usually play an important role in the marketing process, as the previous chapter has shown, and it is mostly merchants who actually make prices at the big markets. Importing merchants certainly base their operations on current physical consumption, but with variations arising from their judgement as to how the price will change, and from the consequent intensity of their desire to increase or decrease their stocks. Thus market demand is, so to speak, superimposed on final demand for physical consumption, and it is market demand which directly affects the price. If importing merchants have adjusted their stocks to what they consider a level of convenience, and confidently expect no change in supply or demand or therefore price, market demand and final demand will coincide. But if importing merchants think that the price will rise, they may decide to increase their stocks, and then market demand will be greater than final demand; and vice versa if they think that the price will fall and decide to reduce their stocks. Importing merchants, moreover, are not the only holders of stocks. Manufacturers and processors, especially large firms, often 'take a view' on price changes, and vary their stocks of raw foodstuffs or raw materials, and thus help to determine market demand.

Market demand may not only differ from final demand, but the elasticity of market demand may differ from the elasticity of final demand. If prices are falling and are expected to fall further, market demand may for a time contract much below final demand, and the price may have to fall a great deal before it evokes an appreciable increase in the quantity demanded. If, on the other hand, prices are rising and expected to rise further, the price may have to rise a great deal before it causes any appreciable contraction in the quantity demanded. Thus in both situations market demand becomes extremely inelastic. In the former situation—falling prices expected to continue—buyers may for a time almost disappear, while in the latter situation all want to buy as much as they can. In many cases of the latter, demand will for a time actually increase with each rise in the price, as buyers become more and more anxious to cover their requirements before the price rises even higher: in other words, for a brief period the whole demand curve is shifted to the right. This may well happen when what is commonly called a 'market scramble' occurs. Thus market demand, instead of, as is usual, varying inversely with price, may vary directly with price—i.e. a falling price will lead to a fall in market demand, so long as price is expected to continue to fall; while a rising price will lead to a rise in demand, until the point is reached when no further rise in price is anticipated. The extensive buying which takes place during the upward price movement is an additional reason why the subsequent reaction, when the price falls back from the peak, is apt to be so violent. Buyers will have covered their requirements, often for months ahead, during the period of rising prices. Even relatively low prices will not tempt them to buy until the time comes when they have to start restocking again; and even then they will only buy 'from hand to mouth' until they are sure that prices are not going to fall any further. Thus the vagaries of market demand are likely to accentuate the fluctuations of price arising from variations in the final demand for physical consumption, or variations in the current supply.

Much the same sort of considerations affect supplies to the market as contrasted with current production. If exporting merchants are confident that the price will rise, they may decide to reduce their offers for sale and to hold larger stocks, and thus market supply will be reduced below the rate appropriate to current production. If they think that the price will fall, they may press some of their stocks on to the market before the price falls too far, thus accentuating the price fall just as their reaction to a rising price accentuates the rise. Market supply may therefore fluctuate more than current production as the result of the exporting merchants' speculative operations. Basically of course current production determines supply, just as the final demand for consumption basically determines demand, but as market demand can modify final demand, so market supply can modify current production. Market demand and market supply tend to increase the fluctuation of prices, and often do so to a very high degree.

It may be objected that this account of the merchant's role in price-making runs counter to the common doctrine that stocks cushion changes in demand and supply, and so reduce fluctuations in prices. It is commonly argued that if the price rises, the merchant will sell any stocks which he is holding over and above the barest minimum for the smooth working of his business, because such sales will now yield him a profit; and, if the price falls, he will buy for stock, because he is buying cheap, and reckons he will in due course be able to make a profit even if the price only returns to the normal equilibrium level. This is logical enough if the merchant reckons that the price change is small and temporary. Importing merchants certainly draw on their stocks to meet slightly larger orders, especially if the market price has risen somewhat and they can get a higher price from their customers. In the case of a price fall, they may well decide to increase their stocks if they think the price fall is only temporary. Similarly, exporting merchants may decide to increase their stocks if they think a price fall is only temporary, or to run down their stocks if they think a price rise is only temporary. It is reasonable, therefore, to say that stocks cushion small temporary changes in demand and supply, and so reduce price fluctuations. But what merchant is going to sell stocks if he is confident that the price is going to rise further and so give him higher profits? Or what merchant is going to increase his stocks if he is confident that the price is going to fall further? He will obviously wait to sell until he thinks that the price rise has reached, or nearly reached, its peak. He will obviously wait to buy until he thinks the price fall has gone as far, or nearly as far, as it will go. By acting in these ways, he will maximise his profits, assuming that his forecasts are correct. When he sells stocks at or near the peak of a price rise, he admittedly checks any further rise, and in that sense his stocks have a cushioning effect. His action has a similar effect when he starts to buy at or near the bottom of a price fall. During the waiting period, however, his stocks are unchanged and have no effect at all, and the common doctrine that stocks reduce price fluctuations has to be modified almost out of recognition. But even this is on the assumption that stocks are unchanged, and it has been argued above that if stockholders are confident that the price will continue to rise appreciably further, they may well increase their stocks, either in order to safeguard their supplies before the price goes very high, or in order to make larger profits on an increased turnover; and vice versa in the case of a price fall if they are confident as to their supplies and content with the profit already secured on their stocks.

Even if the common doctrine is true of small temporary changes in demand and supply, it is not true of larger and more lasting changes which give scope for speculative activity by stockholders. Such speculation tends to increase the swing of price fluctuations, even if it stops them earlier than would otherwise be so. Thus a price rise, due to a short crop, is likely to be steeper as the result of speculative activity by stockholders, though the peak may be lower because the speculators will sell when they think it is within sight. Similarly with a price fall, because speculators will buy when they think the price has fallen far enough. In this sense the common doctrine still has some element of truth, but it does not alter the fact that market demand and market supply often increase the fluctuations of price arising from changing final demand and current production. This analysis is undoubtedly supported by the behaviour of the prices of many primary commodities over short periods as illustrated in the pages which follow.

To round off this account, however, attention must be drawn to the cost of holding physical stocks of a commodity when speculation cannot be performed by making contracts for future delivery, i.e. with commodities for which organised futures markets have not developed, or where such contracts do not meet the merchant speculator's requirements. The cost of holding physical stocks is composed of the costs of physical storage, which vary with different commodities but are unlikely to be less than 5 %, and the costs of financing the operation, for which the merchant will require 10 % at least, and more if he considers that there is any considerable risk involved. Thus, the total costs may well be in the order of 20 % or even more, and therefore the merchant must be confident that he will be able to sell within the year at a price higher than his purchase price. Suppose that there is a bumper crop; demand being highly inelastic the price will fall heavily, and there will be no check to its fall until merchant speculators are induced to buy up the surplus with the prospect of holding it until a short-crop occurs. This may be the next season but may not be for two or even more seasons. Under such circumstances it is obvious that the price of the bumper crop will fall a very long way, since in the short-crop year the price will not rise much above normal because the merchants will make up the deficiency of the crop by selling the surplus of the bumper crop which they have been carrying. This is a rather extreme example of stockholding, but it does emphasise its limitations as a check on large price fluctuations under certain circumstances. Under other circumstances stockholding may, as we have seen, actually increase price fluctuations instead of checking them.

Longer-term Fluctuations

Longer-term fluctuations arise mainly from changes in final demand for consumption and in current production. Market demand and supply are relevant only in the short term, and without this complication longer-term fluctuations can be dealt with briefly, even though they are no less important. In the longer term, final demand usually continues to be inelastic for small changes in price, as in the short term, but if there is a really large and sustained change in price, demand may also change substantially, and often rather suddenly. The new demand curve may well be more elastic than the old. Moreover, the new demand may not respond to a restoration of the original price for a longish period. For example, when coffee prices rose very high in 1954, consumption in the U.S.A., the largest market, dropped by nearly one-fifth as housewives stretched a pound of coffee to make 60 instead of 40 cups. Consumers soon got used to this weaker brew, and there has so far been little return to the old standard. This sort of occurrence is most likely to affect commodities which have competitive substitutes. If the price of natural rubber were to rise above a certain level, manufacturers would soon substitute synthetic rubber. When tin was scarce during World War II, the use of substitute metals was much increased, and the post-war demand for tin did not recover its pre-war level even when the price became moderate or cheap for several years. Producers of other metals are now well aware that sustained high prices may result in reduced consumption.

Similarly, a period of sustained low prices may surely bring about a more or less lasting increase in demand. Of this sisal is a good example, for its low price during most of the inter-war period, and in the latter part of the 1950's, was undoubtedly of great benefit in its competition with manilla and other fibres as the raw material for agricultural twines, ropes and string. Moreover, in general, a low price is obviously of great service in warding off the development of synthetic or other substitutes. If the cause of a sustained rise in the price is a temporarily reduced supply, and a fall in demand results, then when the supply returns to normal there will be a surplus, and the price will fall heavily. Similarly, if the cause is an increase in demand, a large sustained rise in the price may choke the demand, which may then fall to an even lower level than before the increase. The results will be the same. This course of events may happen in reverse in the case of a sustained fall in the price. Thus changes in demand may occur in the longer term as the result of large sustained changes in price. The elasticity of the demand may also change, and if this happens, the results will often be to set up large oscillations of the price.

The effects of changes of price on supply, however, are usually more important than the effects on demand. The supply of annual crops, like demand, tends to be inelastic for small changes of price, but a large sustained price change may bring about large changes in capacity for production. Supply may become more elastic for large sustained price changes. Often the change in capacity is overdone, especially if the producers are small and numerous and each acts without thought, or perhaps knowledge, of what others are doing. The result may be too large an increase in supply or perhaps, more rarely, too large a reduction. Thus again considerable oscillations of the price may be set going. On the other hand, with some tree crops, such as coffee and tea, rubber and sisal, coconut and other palm tree products, any change in capacity for production is only likely to take place in response to very large and very prolonged price changes. The gestation period and the productive life of the trees are both long, and the effect on current supplies will be very slow because of the gestation period of several years. Again, when a very high price does at last evoke an increase in capacity, the increase is apt to be too large. When the obvious natural reluctance of producers to destroy trees is at last overcome by sheer despair, the result may be excessive destruction. With minerals, the exploitation of even proved reserves

74

is likely to be a relatively slow business. If the discovery of new sources and their proving is necessary, this will only be stimulated by very high prices, for the costs and the risks are usually great. Any increase in capacity will take even longer to materialise. This latter situation appears to be true of the tin industry during the last few years, but in general the large concerns which are typical of other non-ferrous metals and of petroleum usually have ample proved reserves. Even so, they will not exploit them unless they are confident that the high price will be sustained for a sufficiently long period to make the new investment worth while. Conversely, they will be very reluctant to close down mines or oil wells until there is no prospect whatever of the price leaving a margin over prime costs, and these are commonly only a small proportion of total costs.

The supply of many primary commodities is usually therefore very inelastic in the longer term, for appreciable changes in capacity for production are only brought about by large sustained price changes. Small changes in price have little or no effect in increasing or decreasing productive capacity. This is broadly true even of annual crops, for though increasing or decreasing the acreage of such crops is not difficult from a physical point of view, the farmer must change his crop programme, and in the case of a decrease must find an alternative use for the land. Farmers in most countries appear to be conservative in such matters. It is also true that rotations may be adversely affected by such changes. When changes of capacity are brought about they often tend to be excessive, and this may well initiate from the supply side an oscillation of the price, just as oscillation may be initiated from the demand side. The general combined result is that in the longer term the prices of many, if not most, primary commodities are continually swinging over a wide range, sometimes relatively gently, but more often perhaps with relative violence.

Summary

With most primary commodities, the equilibrium of demand and supply is being constantly disturbed for one reason or another, and there are several different factors, both on the demand and the supply side, which tend to cause violent reactions and large fluctuations in the price, both in the short and longer terms. Hence it is that a small temporary surplus or shortage results in price changes on a scale far greater than seems reasonable on a superficial view. Similarly, if a change in productive capacity is required, this will be brought about only by a very large sustained change in the price. Moreover, short-term fluctuations are continually being superimposed on such longer-term trends, and these often mask the true longer-term situation. When the situation is at last fully realised, the price changes far more than it would otherwise have done, with the result that productive capacity is increased or diminished too much. Large oscillations of the price follow. Large and frequent price changes create serious economic difficulties for the producers of primary products, and for the national economies of countries dependent on exports of primary products, and sometimes also for consuming countries. The problem of stabilising the prices of primary products is indeed in the forefront of international economic policy, and forms the central theme of part IV, Commodity Control Schemes.

PART III

GENERAL TRENDS AND FLUCTUATIONS OF INTERNATIONAL TRADE SINCE WORLD WAR I

---

7. THE INTER-WAR PERIOD

Part III will endeavour to provide a historical sketch of the changing fortunes of the primary industries as a group since World War I and of any outstanding developments in particular industries. In order to appreciate correctly the significance of what has been happening since World War II, it is certainly necessary to have some general ideas of what happened in the inter-war period, but it seems unnecessary to go back further than that for this purpose. This sketch therefore starts at the end of World War I. Since this is now nearly half a century ago, some brief reminders of the state of the world at that time may be a suitable prelude.

The economic situation at the end of 1918 was very different from that of 1945. National economies were not disrupted to the same extent by World War I, except in Russia and in those areas which were affected by the break up of the Austro-Hungarian Empire or by the political and resulting agrarian revolutions in the Balkans. These are important exceptions, and in particular the world's wheat production and trade had been greatly changed thereby. But France, Italy, the many countries which had remained neutral, and even Germany in essentials, were still effective economic concerns in 1918, though certainly much distorted and strained. So also was the economy of the United Kingdom. By contrast the economy of the United States had been greatly developed and strengthened. Even during the eighteen months of actual participation as a belligerent, the economy of the United States had been relatively little distorted.

Outside the U.S.A. and Canada, however, most of the world's primary producing countries were in some difficulty with their exports. This was mainly owing to the shortage of shipping, and of imported manufactures of which Europe and the U.K. had little to

77

spare to send them. Stocks of some primary products had piled up in many of the producing countries, but stocks in consuming areas, both of foodstuffs and raw materials, were very low. Viewing the world as a whole, the ordinary pre-war price mechanism was still functioning. In general it was suspended to a limited extent only, whether in respect of particular commodities or particular countries, though many futures markets were closed. In comparison with 1945, however, the extent of 'controls' was small, though in several cases by no means negligible. The economic situation of the world at the end of 1918 appeared at the time extremely difficult and depressing, but by comparison with 1945 it now seems a relatively simple and manageable sort of problem.

The economic policy of 1919 may be summarised as 'back to business as usual as quickly as possible'. There was a general world scramble for supplies of primary products, both for immediate use and for rebuilding normal working stocks. In a number of cases, such as wheat and sugar, there was a genuine world shortage of supplies, but in many others the difficulty was only overseas transport from the producing countries. The result of this scramble was the post-war boom of 1920—a boom of high prices and profits rather than of expanding actual production or consumption. At the end of 1918 the U.K. wholesale prices index, which was a fair indication of the world price level of primary products at this period, stood at around 230 as compared with a 1913 base of 100. By the middle of 1920 it was around 300.

As soon as the demand at high price levels began to be satisfied and shipping difficulties diminished, the boom broke, and there was a tremendous readjustment of all prices, and especially those of primary products. The average level of U.K. wholesale prices in 1921 was well under 200, and in 1922 about 150–160. Such approximations are best because the standard index numbers varied a good deal under the stress of so much movement. This post-war slump was however comparatively short. Towards the end of 1922 recovery was rapidly beginning, and went ahead fast so that by the end of 1923 the world's economy as a whole was back on an even keel, the big exceptions being Russia, and Germany where there was the great inflation and final collapse of the mark. The years 1923–5 were really the final stages of post-war readjustment in Europe (Britain returned to the gold standard in 1925), but on the whole, and certainly for the rest of the world, production and trade in primary products on the one hand, and in manufactures on the other, was again proceeding relatively smoothly and in a normal manner.

From the end of 1925 until the end of 1929 was a period of rapid expansion of production and trade throughout most of the world. In particular there was a great general boom in the U.S.A. which culminated in the Wall Street crash in the autumn of 1929, which in turn ushered in the world depression of 1930–3. These years 1926–9 are the key years of the whole inter-war period, in that they must contain the seeds of that depression, with its lingering effects during the rest of the 1930's, even if it is not easy to sort them out so far as the primary industries are concerned. Further, these years of expansion saw the first widespread development of the commodity control schemes which were to become an important feature of the organisation of primary production and trade. This period of four years therefore merits special attention, and for that reason will be considered here at rather disproportionate length.

The primary industries shared in the general expansion, but the picture of these industries in this period is complicated, and in many respects puzzling. The world's production of foodstuffs certainly increased, though probably not much faster than population. The production of raw materials increased much more than that of foodstuffs, continuing the tendency that had been in operation since 1913. Though this was a period of expanding production and trade for the primary industries, it certainly lacked balance in the sense that conditions in individual industries varied greatly. Not all the signs which are normally associated with a general healthy economic expansion were in evidence. If the conditions in individual industries are examined in detail, there seems to have been an apparently satisfactory situation of steady expansion in meat and dairy products, cereals other than wheat, tea and cocoa and, among raw materials, wool, cotton and zinc, though with some qualifications for the last two. Then there were certain industries in which by 1929 production was definitely threatening to become excessive in the near future, for example wheat, rubber and tin. A third group consisted of industries in which supply was by 1929 running right away from demand, even though that was expanding quite reasonably well: coffee, sugar, petroleum and lead. With a classification on these lines, it might be expected that in a period of rapid general expansion there would be a group of industries in which supply was falling short of demand. There appears, however, to have been only one, namely flax, and that was simply because the chief source of the pre-World War I supply, Russia, had almost ceased to export, and new sources had not yet been developed. The absence of such a category of industries seems curious, because it would surely be natural in such a period of expansion for the supplies of quite a number of commodities to run short at any rate temporarily. On the contrary, it seems that in this period of expansion there was, if anything, a rather general tendency for supplies of primary products to outrun demand. In some industries this actually happened, in a few cases to a marked degree. In other industries the tendency was manifestly in operation, and while in still others it was not apparent by 1929, in no ordinary case was the reverse tendency evident.

Further light on the situation can be obtained by a brief study of the movements of prices and of stocks. *The Economist*'s index of wholesale prices as recalculated on a 1927 base includes crude iron and steel products, leather and a few other semi-manufactures, but it suffices as a general guide to the world price level of primary products. On the 1927 base, this index registered the following results:

Index of wholesale prices (1927 = 100)

1925	112	1928	98
1926	104	1929	92
1927	100		

Thus over the period there was an appreciable fall in the prices of primary products, though in no sense a serious one as the rate of decline was so steady; but it is certainly unusual for prices to fall throughout a period of expanding production and trade. The significance of this is not easy to determine. An examination of the individual prices which compose the index shows that foodstuff prices as a group remained nearly stationary, and that it was mainly a fall in raw material prices which brought about the decline in the general index. But in the foodstuffs group, the prices of wheat, sugar and some other commodities declined considerably, while the prices of cereals other than wheat rose substantially, and the prices of meat, dairy products and some other commodities remained more or less unchanged. Thus the result for the group is an average of some rather widely different movements. Similarly, some raw materials rose in price, though the majority tended to fall. Over-all there was a general steady decline, but there was also very considerable variation in price movements.

The prices of primary products in this period, however, were not all what may be termed competitive free market prices, i.e. free from any appreciable monopolistic control. Commodity control schemes, or as economists in the 1920's termed them 'artificial control schemes', were already in operation in a number of primary industries. A fuller account of these schemes is given in chapter 10 below, but brief mention of them must be made here. The British rubber restriction scheme, covering the output of Malaya and Ceylon, had raised the world price to a wholly artificial level in 1925 and 1926, but in 1927 it lost control, and was terminated at the end of 1928. A Brazilian coffee valorisation scheme was started in 1923, and until 1929 successfully maintained the world price of coffee at a level much above what it would otherwise have been, though at the cost of an enormous accumulation of stocks. From 1926 Cuba, by far the largest exporter of sugar, was restricting the size of her crops with an appreciable effect on the price. From 1926 also, an international cartel of the principal exporters of copper greatly raised the price by restriction of output, and maintained it at a high level until 1929. In 1928 the Canadian wheat pools held back part of their bumper crop in order to prevent the price falling unduly low. During 1927 and 1928 attempts were made to establish partial restriction of output schemes for petroleum, lead and zinc, though the effect on prices was not really significant. Thus the prices of several commodities were subject in this period to monopolistic influences, and were higher than they would otherwise have been. Even more important than their effect on prices is the rapid spread of such schemes during a period of expanding production and trade. Most of them were established to meet producers' difficulties and dissatisfactions, and their desirability was being actively discussed in 1929 with reference to other primary industries, notably cotton and tin.

Turning to stocks, the available statistics at this period can only be relied upon to a limited extent. They do not cover all the important primary products, and they relate, of course, only to visible supplies as then composed. Nevertheless, the index numbers produced by the League of Nations are probably at least a rough guide to relative movements over a few consecutive years. These show quite definitely that stocks of primary products increased considerably and at an accelerating rate from 1925 to 1929, and that stocks of foodstuffs rose considerably more than stocks of raw materials. This information by itself does not imply that supplies were tending to exceed demand. With expanding consumption, the stocks of convenience—that is the stocks which merchants, processors, and manufacturers hold in order that their work may proceed smoothly—will automatically tend to increase, because the factors which make for a reduced ratio mostly operate only slowly, and produce appreciable effects only over longish periods of years.[1] No accurate measurement of final consumption is possible; but imports modified for changes in stocks held by importing merchants give a reasonably close approximation to current absorption by producers and manufacturers; and the ratio of the visible supply to current absorption is a definite indicator of the relationship between supply and demand. If these ratios are examined over the period 1925-9 there seems to be only one case where the ratio declined heavily, namely copper, and that was entirely due to the international cartel and its restriction of output. The ratio appears to have declined slightly for tin and petroleum, and probably for meat and dairy products, wool, flax and jute, rye, oats and maize, though the available statistics are limited and rather unreliable. On the other hand, the ratio increased slightly for cotton, lead, zinc and tea. Finally there are three spectacular increases: sugar and wheat, for which the ratio about doubled, and coffee, for which it nearly trebled. Yet each of these three commodities was affected by special factors: sugar stocks would probably have been much greater still but for the restriction of the Cuban crop: *per contra*, coffee stocks would almost certainly have been much smaller if the Brazilian control had adopted restriction of output instead of control of exports: and the doubling of the ratio for wheat was caused by unpredictable bumper harvests in many parts of the world in 1928. In a period of expanding trade it might be expected that the ratio of stocks to current absorption would tend to decline as increasing demand pressed on the available supplies, which, in the case of most primary products, cannot be immediately or rapidly increased. Such a tendency was not much in evidence during this period. While the ratio for certain commodities greatly increased so that stocks increased far above the level of convenience, there appears to have been no general tendency towards the piling up of surplus stocks, any more than there was a general tendency towards shortage. All that can be said with certainty on the subject of changes in stocks during this period is that there were great variations in what happened.

Summing up these investigations, the following broad conclusions have to be set side by side and considered together. First, that there

---

[1] See chapter 4, page 40.

appears to have been a rather general tendency for supplies of primary products to outrun demand. Secondly, that taking all primary products together there was a general steady price decline, though this was the result of widely divergent movements in the prices of individual commodities, and was mainly brought about by a decline in the prices of raw materials as a group rather than foodstuffs. Thirdly, that changes in stocks, while showing no general tendency towards shortage, indicated no general tendency towards surplus, but only great variation. To these conclusions may be added another facet of the whole situation. Relatively to pre-World War I the absolute price level of primary products in the period 1926–9 was much lower than the price level of manufactured goods. There are, even for this period, indexes of the prices of products purchased by agriculturists in the U.S.A. and in Sweden, but the simplest and most general evidence can be obtained by a study of the changes in the barter terms of trade between countries which are mainly exporters of primary products in return for manufactures, and countries which are mainly exporters of manufactures in return for food and raw materials. Thus, as compared with pre-World War I, the United Kingdom in 1926–9 was having to give only 80–85 units of exports for 100 units of imports, while the Netherlands East Indies and Argentina were having to give 120–30 units of exports, mainly of primary products, for 100 units of imports, mainly of manufactures. Linked with this absolutely lower level of the prices of primary products relatively to manufactures is the probability that while the real wages and incomes of manufacturing producers during the period 1925–9 rose appreciably, those of primary producers remained more or less stationary. The available statistical evidence is, however, neither sufficiently adequate nor reliable to warrant any definite pronouncement on this matter.

To what do all these conclusions add up? The answer is far from clear or certain, but it is at least a likely hypothesis that behind all these signs and symptoms there was taking place in the primary industries in this period, and probably throughout the 1920's, a rise in productivity and a fall in costs of production at rates much increased as compared with the immediate pre-World War I period, and still more as compared with the war and immediate post-war years: and that this was taking place fairly generally, though varying very considerably, as would be natural, between different industries. This would be consonant with the conclusion reached above that there seemed to be an underlying tendency for supply to outrun demand even in this period of expanding production and trade; consonant too with the overall decline of prices and yet great variations for different products; consonant with the great variations in respect of stocks; and consonant with the lower absolute price level of primary products relatively to that of manufactures. It could be, in short, an important contributory factor to the general malaise, or lack of balance, which the primary industries appear to exhibit in this period of expansion. The reader may wonder why this rise in productivity and fall in costs of production should thus be deduced as a hypothesis instead of stated as a historical fact. The answer is that the available information and statistics on this matter are far too limited, and lacking in measurability, to establish the true extent of its influence. General evidence is available for quite a number of industries. Mechanisation was certainly being rapidly introduced in the 1920's for the cultivation and harvesting of wheat, and of cereals other than rice, especially in Canada and the U.S.A. Sugar costs in Cuba were being reduced by larger-scale mills, and in Java by improved varieties of cane. New very fertile lands in the north-west of São Paulo state were being rapidly planted up with coffee, and this was undoubtedly the root cause of Brazil's overproduction as well as resulting in reduced costs. The rapid development of the Katanga and Rhodesian copper mines was disturbing that industry, and in all the non-ferrous industries there was considerable technical progress both in mining operations and in initial processing. But without detailed studies of productivity and cost changes it is impossible to assess in quantitative terms the influence of these factors in particular industries, still less in the primary industries as a group. Such studies are lacking. Even if the fact of an unusually rapid general advance in productivity were to be established and its results quantitatively assessed, it is not suggested that this would provide an adequate explanation of the troubles of those primary industries which were in trouble or threatened to become so. The rapid restoration of Europe's beet-sugar industry was certainly a more powerful factor in bringing about excessive sugar supplies than rapid technical progress in Cuba, while the overproduction of coffee in Brazil was at least as much due to faulty management of the valorisation or control scheme as to the inherent superiority of the new coffee lands. Nevertheless, rapid technical progress, in at least many of its varied forms, necessitates rapid adjustment of the structure and organisation of the industry affected. This rapid adjustment is often painful to some producers when, for example, it involves the closing down of high-cost producers or producing areas. This they naturally resist, and so prolong the process of adjustment, which is anyway usually very difficult to achieve quickly in the primary industries. If there are a large number of primary industries so affected, they give to the primary industries as a group a general malaise and the appearance of lack of balance, even in a period of expanding production and trade.

So much then for the period of expansion from 1926 to 1929. If this rather lengthy study of it has not yielded very clear-cut results in respect of the causation of the ensuing severe depression, at least it has shown that the primary industries as a group were not enjoying, even in this period of expansion, the sort of robust health which would enable them to offer solid resistance to the onset of a world depression; and that in several cases supply was, or was threatening shortly to become, excessive even while demand was still increasing. The Wall Street crash in the autumn of 1929 upset business confidence throughout the world. Market demand for primary products virtually ceased because merchants and manufacturers were reducing their stocks to the absolute minimum, no one wishing to hold stocks at any price, or for that matter able to obtain the finance to do so. The result was a catastrophic fall in the prices of many primary products, much more rapid and much larger than the fall which took place in the prices of manufactures. Between December 1929 and December 1930 the export price of wheat fell by over 50%, the price of rubber by nearly 50%, the prices of cotton and jute by about 40%, and those of wool, copper, tin and lead by well over 30%. Though the prices of sugar, meat, timber, hides and petroleum and several other products fell much less, the average fall over the twelve months was about 23%. By the late spring of 1930 market demand was reappearing because merchants, processors and manufacturers had to buy to meet the requirements of current absorption, but since that was beginning to decline considerably, the rate of fall of prices did not slacken very much throughout 1930, though it did in 1931. In September of that year Britain abandoned the gold standard. Sterling prices naturally rose, though not by much, and soon resumed their fall. In June 1932 sterling prices reached their lowest point at 59 as compared with 100 in 1927, though it was not until the devaluation of the U.S. dollar in March 1933 that any genuine rise began. Even then it was small, and prices continued to 'bump along the bottom' for nearly three years. Throughout these years of depression it cannot be said that foodstuffs as a group fell in price more heavily than raw materials, or minerals than other raw materials. Nor can any other such groupings be made. The best generalisation is that those commodities of which supplies were already excessive in 1928–9, or were tending to be excessive, fell most in price, and those which were more or less in equilibrium in 1928–9 fell least. Even to this there were some exceptions, for much depended on other conditions peculiar to each industry and particularly on the response of production and consumption to falling prices.

Under these conditions stocks in the hands of producers and of some of their governments, notably the U.S. government in respect of wheat and cotton, increased sharply as the combined result of current supplies not being fully absorbed and of the practical difficulties of contracting production. Stocks of both foodstuffs and raw materials as groups probably reached a peak at the end of 1931. During the next two years the former continued to increase, but the latter declined slowly, and had returned to something near normality by 1935, whereas foodstuffs did not do so until at least a year later.

Further light on these changes in stocks is shed by the changes in production. World production of raw materials declined during 1930, and more rapidly in 1931 and 1932, when the index was only about 80 as compared with 110 in 1929 and 100 for the average of 1925–9. Thereafter it began to rise again, and by 1936 had recovered to the 1929 level. But the production of foodstuffs remained appreciably unchanged from 1928 until 1936. A reader's first reaction might be to question the reliability of these League of Nations statistics in view of the tremendous fall in prices, and of the probability of declining consumption which might be expected during this severe and prolonged world depression. It must, however, be realised that world population was increasing by at least 1 % a year, and that even the unemployed man must eat quite a large proportion of his normal consumption. Moreover, as standards of living fall, it is not the staple or basic foodstuffs which are reduced but the semi-luxuries, and the former are recorded statistically much more completely at this period than the latter. Account must also be taken of the increase in stocks though this is a relatively small matter over the period as a whole. Thus, with an increasing population, this stationary production of mainly staple foodstuffs is consonant with an appreciable fall in total consumption per head. What this stationary production, despite the heavy fall in prices, does show is the inelasticity of the production of basic foodstuffs, especially in a period when all agricultural products were suffering depression and there was no other product to which the farmer could profitably shift his activities. The demand for foodstuffs was very much better maintained than the demand for raw materials. If it had not been, prices would have fallen still lower, and the pressure to reduce production would have been greater. As it was, the holding of large stocks, the natural growth of population, and after 1932 the revival of the income of the world's manufacturing population kept the pressure on producers sufficiently great to prevent any expansion of production for eight years, but prevented the pressure of low prices being so severe and prolonged as to reduce production. Gradually demand and supply drew nearer together and stocks were reduced to a more normal level. Though prices remained relatively low, technical progress had continued, and primary producers had, to put it shortly, got used to lower wages and incomes.

Stability in the production of foodstuffs did not, however, mean a maintenance of the volume of world trade in foodstuffs. For this period the simplest overall measurement of this volume is provided by the League of Nations index numbers of world exports plus imports revalued at the prices of the base year. This is commonly called the quantum of world trade. For foodstuffs this shows a fall from 100 in 1929 to a little over 80 in 1933–5, rising to around 90 for the next three years. The increase in stocks accounts for a large part of the difference between unchanged production and the declining quantum in the earlier years. By the later years many food-importing countries had increased their home supplies by means of tariffs and subsidies, in their efforts to preserve their own agricultural industries and to economise in foreign exchange, and there was some decline of production in the exporting countries. In other words, for foodstuffs the world depression caused a lasting movement towards autarky and the contraction of world trade. For raw materials the quantum also fell to about 80 (1929 = 100) in 1932, but it then began to rise again, reached nearly 100 in 1936, and appreciably exceeded that in 1937. In other words, world trade in raw materials fluctuated similarly to production, and stocks were back to normal by 1935. Importing countries found it less politically necessary, and anyway usually more technically difficult, to increase home supplies of raw materials than of basic foodstuffs.

The fall in the prices of primary products was, as has been said above, much more rapid and much larger than for manufactures.

Hence the swing in the barter terms of trade against the primary producing countries, which had taken place between 1913 and 1925-9, was much intensified by the world depression. Comparing 1932-3 with 1925-9, the ratio shows much the same change as in the previous comparison, i.e. 80-85 units of U.K. exports obtained 100 units of imports. The reverse was true for primary producing countries like Argentina, while as an exceptional case the Netherlands East Indies was having to give nearly double the amount of its export produce for a given volume of imports, the prices of its particular exports being specially low.[1] From 1929 to 1932, therefore, the terms of trade moved violently and greatly in favour of the industrialised countries. From 1933 a reversed relative movement began, and the terms of trade swung slowly back in favour of the primary producing countries, until in early 1937—to anticipate the next paragraph—the price relationship had almost returned to the 1929 position, though in 1938 it fell back again.

The story of the years 1936-8 can be told briefly, for it has no lasting significance. Recovery was proceeding smoothly and more rapidly during the first half of 1936; indeed expansion would be the more correct term, for production was now ahead of the average of 1925-9. Then, in the late autumn of 1936 and the spring of 1937, there was something of a general trade boom in the U.S.A. Foodstuffs were little affected, but with manufacturing production expanding fast, the demand for raw materials, especially those imported largely by the U.S.A., reached a level at which real shortages seemed possible. A speculative demand was superimposed on the already high trade demand, and prices increased rapidly. The non-ferrous metals were perhaps the leaders, but rubber, wool and cotton followed them closely. By March–April 1937 supplies of the non-ferrous metals were responding freely to their very high prices, and supplies of other materials would clearly do so before long. Various political developments hastened and intensified the collapse of this short-lived price boom. Prices of raw materials broke heavily, and then continued to fall as a result of the decline in manufacturing activity in the U.S.A. during 1938, and of the gradual spread of this recession to other

---

[1] So far as producers' real incomes and the foreign exchange earnings of their exports are concerned, adverse changes in the barter terms of trade, i.e. in the real value of exports, may be wholly or partly offset by simultaneous increases in the volume of their exports. This was happening to some extent in the case of a good many primary products between 1925 and 1929, and as compared with 1913, but not during the depression of the 1930's. The converse may of course be equally true.

countries. Most raw materials, though some much more than others, experienced this upward and downward fluctuation in prices during 1936–8. There were similar movements in production. Foodstuffs, however, as has already been said, were little affected, though there happened to be large bumper crops of wheat in 1937. There was also in that year a bumper crop of American cotton, so that both these important industries were unsettled. Substantial quantities were carried over, and stocks were swollen much above the level of convenience.

Recession continued until the autumn of 1938, when after the Munich agreement the world generally may be said to have begun really active preparation for the coming war. Economically, 1939 and to some extent the end of 1938 belong to the period of World War II, and will therefore start the next chapter. This picture of the period 1929–38 has been sketched in general terms, and little reference has been made to the experiences of individual primary industries. But there is one feature of the period which lies between the general and the particular, and which must at least be mentioned if the picture is to be reasonably complete, namely the role played by commodity control schemes. The violent falls in prices during the winter of 1929–30 virtually broke the effective control of nearly all the current schemes, though most of them continued to exist on paper. The earliest attempts at restoring some degree of effective control were in fact the work of governments rather than of the industries themselves. The governments came in to try and relieve situations which were becoming politically or socially dangerous. Thus the Canadian federal government came to the rescue of the wheat pools in November 1930 and the Brazilian federal government took over the valorisation scheme from the coffee-producing states, because the whole economic stability of these countries was in peril. The U.S. government took essentially similar steps to organise and finance stock-holding schemes for wheat and cotton. Otherwise, large and important sections of the country would have been ruined to an extent which the government dared not contemplate. The continuation of Brazil's control of coffee exports, reinforced by the policy of large-scale destruction of stocks, undoubtedly held up the price above what it would otherwise have been, as is clear from the fall in the price from roughly around 10 cents a lb to 7 cents when control was abandoned in 1937. Similarly the intervention of the Canadian and U.S. governments in wheat and cotton certainly had some effect in preventing prices falling too much. Cuba went on restricting her sugar crop, though with little effect on the world price, but the copper control, and the attempts at control in petroleum, lead and zinc, had all been swept away by the events of 1929–30.

These government interventions were made with the ultimate objective of ending control as soon as this could be safely accomplished. The year 1931 saw, however, the establishment of the first of several new control schemes. Fuller accounts and further study of these schemes will be found in chapter 12. Here little more than a catalogue will suffice, together with the briefest appraisals of their influence. The first was the International Tin Restriction scheme of 1931, which was renewed in 1936 for another five years. By very severe restriction of production, the price of tin was rapidly raised from a little over £100 a ton at the end of 1930 to over £200 by mid-1933, and held there, though not without considerable fluctuations, until the outbreak of World War II. From this point of view it was a very strong and efficient control scheme, which preserved all the tin-producing capacity of the world through the stress and strain of the Great Depression. Indeed it made the latter half of the 1930's a definitely profitable period for most producers, even if it was creating less satisfactory long-period results. Also in 1931 came the International Sugar Agreement for the control of exports of beet as well as cane sugar. This achieved some reduction of the large surplus stocks, but did not prevent a continuing fall in the price. It expired in 1936, and there was no new agreement until 1938. In 1933 an agreement was made between the chief wheat-exporting countries and the chief importing countries, whereby the former undertook to limit their exports and reduce acreage, and the latter not to raise their tariffs any higher, and to reduce them if and when a certain price level was established. Its only effect was to ease the pressure of exports somewhat during the 1933–4 season, for after that it ceased to be observed. In 1933 also came the International Tea Agreement. By a moderate restriction of exports this succeeded in reducing stocks and raising prices by 50% as compared with their level in 1932, though not without creating some undesirable tendencies from the long-period point of view. It was renewed in 1938. The International Rubber Agreement was not signed until mid-1934, when the world was beginning to recover from the depression, and this made its task easier. It was moderately successful in disposing of large stocks at steadily rising prices. Finally in 1935 a control scheme for copper was established by the producers in Chile, Rhodesia and the Belgian Congo. This had considerable monopolistic control outside the U.S.A., where a high tariff on copper imports had been imposed in 1932, virtually isolating the American industry from the rest of the world. This scheme, like the sugar agreement but unlike all the others, was a purely private agreement between producers. Governments took no official part. It had some effect in steadying the price, but no attempt was made to raise it unduly by severe output restriction.

It cannot therefore be said that international control schemes played any important general part in the history of the primary industries as a group during the 1930's. Only for tin, tea and rubber did they play a decisive part, though they exerted some influence in sugar and copper, and to a very small degree for a short time in wheat; while national controls affected coffee, wheat and cotton. The mere fact, however, that control schemes were established for so many industries, and that so many industries were sufficiently well organised to enable these schemes to operate with reasonable mechanical efficiency, is important. Moreover, though the British and Dutch governments were leaders in the tin, tea and rubber schemes, many countries were concerned in the sugar and wheat agreements. In particular the U.S.A. was a party to the latter, and in 1938 may be said to have taken the lead in initiating discussions about the possibility of an international cotton agreement. Thus commodity control schemes were an actual and potential feature of the 1930's, which must certainly not be overlooked, even if their achievements were confined to a somewhat limited field.

8. THE PERIOD 1939–50

Rearmament and the stockpiling of strategic materials began after the Munich agreement in the autumn of 1938. As noted in the previous chapter, the end of that year marks the beginning from the economic point of view of the war period. The demand for a few raw materials, mostly metals, increased, and their prices rose rather steeply during 1939. In general the previous downward trend of prices, which had followed the sharp break at the end of the short-lived boom in early 1937, only flattened out somewhat, and there was no radical change in the situation of primary products as a group until the outbreak of war. The threat of war, however, was clearly exerting an influence on the markets.

The history of the primary industries during the actual war years exhibits three clearly defined periods, each with its own outstanding characteristics. The first was from September 1939 until the German invasion of Europe in May 1940 and was characterised by a general stocking up of supplies by both the Allies and the neutral countries, especially those in Europe. The second period was from May 1940 until December 1941 when the Pearl Harbour attack by Japan brought the U.S.A. into the war, and may be termed the period of surplus supplies, or impending surpluses. The third period was from December 1941 until the end of the war in mid-1945, and may be termed the period of increasing shortages and deficiencies. These three periods will now be considered in turn.

The first period, September 1939 to May 1940, was from the primary producers' point of view a time of rapidly rising prices and excellent profits. The Allied blockade of Germany meant of course the loss of a considerable market, but this loss was more than made good by a general stocking up of non-perishable foodstuffs and raw materials on the part of the Allies at war, and of every neutral country in Europe which still had access to the world at large. The only troubles of primary producers were due to a shortage of shipping, which in this period resulted, not from German submarine activities, nor very much from the diversion of tonnage by the Allies to military ends, but mainly as the result of the delays consequent upon the inspection system at specified anchorages by which the blockade of supplies to Germany was being enforced.

This short period of wartime prosperity in the primary industries came to an abrupt end with the German invasion of Europe. The result was that virtually the whole of the European continental market, and not merely Germany, disappeared from the view of overseas primary producers throughout the rest of the world. A glance back to chapter 3 will remind the reader what this meant. In addition, the Germans captured an appreciable amount of the world's ocean shipping tonnage. Though a great deal of previously neutral tonnage got away, or stayed away, from European ports, and so became available to Britain, the increasing demands for shipping for military purposes, coupled with the effects of the German submarine campaign, rapidly resulted in a cumulatively stringent shortage. Thus the world's primary producers lost not only a large and important market, but also an increasing part of the means of getting their exports to the remaining markets. Stocks of primary products therefore began to pile up rapidly in many exporting countries, even though the remaining consuming markets, particularly the U.K., would have liked to import much more than could be transported to them. On the other hand, despite the piling up of stocks and the restriction of production, prices were at least maintained. For what could be shipped, consuming countries were willing to pay whatever in reason exporters asked. Surpluses of cotton began to pile up in India, Brazil and Peru, and in Egypt, French Africa, and the Belgian Congo, in addition to the very large stocks which the U.S.A. was still holding from the record crop of 1938. British Commonwealth wool producers were safeguarded by Britain's agreement to buy the whole of their clips for the duration of the war, but Argentina and Uruguay had lost almost all their markets. Jute and sisal producers were seriously affected by the complete loss of the European market, and it even seemed certain that there would be a surplus of copper unless production in South America and Africa was drastically curtailed. Prospective surpluses of food were still more numerous, and likely to be more serious from the producers' point of view. In the summer of 1940 it was estimated that the already considerable surplus of wheat in the four principal exporting countries would double to 20 million tons in 1940–1. This is approximately what happened. Large surpluses of sugar seemed inevitable in the Netherlands East Indies, Dominica and Peru, and a smaller surplus in Cuba, due to shortage of shipping and rationing in the U.K. as well as the blockade of Europe. The 200,000 tons of sugar exports of the French African colonies had no market at all, since all had previously gone to France under a tariff preference. Argentina used to export around three million tons of maize to continental Europe, while British imports had now been reduced by about one million tons. In 1940–1 Argentina had a bumper crop. Half the world's exportable supplies of coffee were reckoned to be surplus, irrespective of any previous surplus stocks. A largish surplus of cocoa was impending. Last, but far from least, surpluses of some oilseeds seemed certain to become almost astronomical unless production was drastically reduced. The economic situation in some primary producing countries appeared likely to become extremely serious, for example, in Argentina, Brazil, Peru, the Netherlands East Indies and the French African colonies.

There were, however, a few shortages even in this world of actual or impending surpluses, and these were the few primary products of which continental Europe had been a large exporter. Thus Denmark used to provide before the war about half the U.K. supply of butter, and a great deal of bacon. The closing of the Baltic meant almost a complete stoppage of timber and wood pulp from the Scandinavian countries, and supplies of petroleum from Rumania and Russia ceased just as the war demand became almost insatiable. But apart from these commodities, and some metals of minor importance, such as molybdenum for hardening steel, the world outside Europe was faced not merely with more supplies than could be shipped, but more supplies of some products than were wanted even if they could have been shipped. For many primary producers the war at this stage meant, or looked like meaning, problems of surplus stocks and surplus capacity of a magnitude which made the similar problems of the Great Depression look in retrospect as nothing.

These problems were, however, in most cases only just becoming actual, as distinct from prospective, when in December 1941 Japan and the U.S.A. became belligerents. From the point of view of Britain and the U.S.A., the Japanese invasion of South-east Asia changed many of the impending surpluses into deficiencies almost overnight. Thus supplies of vegetable oilseeds from the Philippines, the Netherlands East Indies and Malaya ceased, and only those from Africa, Ceylon and India remained available, and the export surplus from India, mainly groundnuts, was not only difficult to ship, but was rapidly diminishing in volume owing to rising home consumption. The supply of sugar from the Philippines to the U.S.A. ceased, as did tea supplies to the U.K. from the N.E.I. and from China, but these were not vital. Rice virtually disappeared from international trade with the Japanese occupation of most of Burma, Indo-China and Thailand. This was of course serious for India and Ceylon, though not directly of any great moment for the rest of the world. From the military point of view, however, the disappearance of these supplies of food-stuffs was unimportant compared to that of certain raw materials. All the main sources of natural rubber disappeared with the exception of Ceylon, and the result was an acute shortage, and a desperate struggle to make the available stocks, which fortunately were considerable, last out until the U.S.A. could develop a large-scale supply of synthetic rubber. The other great shortage was tin, of which only about one-quarter of the pre-war world supply remained available, from Bolivia, Nigeria and the Belgian Congo. But the disappearance of manilla hemp from the Philippines, and of the large supply of sisal from the N.E.I., created a desperate shortage of hard fibres for ropes, twines and string. Also the loss of petroleum supplies from the N.E.I. was, to say the least, most inconvenient.

The Japanese invasions thus changed certain surpluses into deficiencies within a few months. As the war proceeded, some new long-period factors became increasingly powerful. The most important was the cumulatively increasing demand by the U.S.A. for almost all primary products, especially raw materials but also many foodstuffs. The next was the cumulatively increasing shortage of shipping, consequent on the one hand from the growing U.S. demand, and on the other from the German submarine campaign, not only in terms of shipping losses, but also of the longer time taken on voyages owing to the need for convoying. The effect was uneven as between different primary products and between the countries producing them. High-war-priority products received preferential shipping treatment, and supplies were drawn from the nearest sources. Thirdly, there was the still-longer-period tendency for primary production to decline owing to the non-renewal of worn-out plant and equipment, and to the diversion of labour to meet the need for increasing domestic supplies of food and where possible manufactures, as international trade had become so restricted. Again the effect was uneven, for the production of high-priority war supplies was naturally kept up as far as possible to requirements. By 1945, however, there were few primary industries in which the tendency to declining production was not in operation, and in some it was marked. Where there were local surpluses owing to the shortage of shipping, this tendency was of course all to the good. Where production was barely enough, it led to increasing stringency of supplies. In nearly all cases it was laying up trouble for the post-war period.

Thus after the immediate effects of the Japanese invasions these long-period factors gradually took effect, so that the combined result brought about the very opposite general conditions to those which characterised 1940-1. This made the third period of the war, from 1941 onwards, a period of increasing shortages and deficiencies. But just as in the second period there were some shortages, such as dairy products and timber, which simply grew worse as the years went on, so in the third period there were some commodities which remained in surplus supply. Some of these were very important commodities. Thus wheat remained in heavy surplus supply, even though acreage in the chief exporting countries was appreciably reduced in 1942 and 1943. In 1943 stocks reached their peak.

Argentina found maize almost unsaleable, and used large quantities as fuel in place of coal which was no longer obtainable. Cotton and wool stocks continued to pile up despite declining production. Coffee was always in ample supply, though production declined everywhere, and especially in Brazil owing to a run of bad weather conditions. So too there were ample supplies of cocoa, even though production in West Africa was falling owing to the onset of a disease. There were also a few commodities of which supplies remained adequate, especially as production increased, for example, copper, aluminium and zinc, while the production of lead was restricted to the amount needed. Thus, though its dominant characteristics were certainly increasing shortage and, in general, declining production, the picture during the later years of the war was considerably mixed.

The situation, therefore, when the war ended in mid-1945 did not appear to be generally desperate. Some commodities were clearly going to be in short supply for some considerable time, for example, meat and animal fats, tin, timber, jute and hard fibres, but the shortage of some others could reasonably be expected to ease fairly quickly, for example, sugar, vegetable oilseeds and oils, and natural rubber. Production of other commodities was being maintained at a level which seemed reasonably adequate to meet peace-time demand, for example, copper, aluminium and zinc. Surplus stocks of wheat, over and above the normal level of convenience, amounted to six months' pre-war world imports; cotton stocks to about the same, though mostly consisting of the middle and lower grades; wool stocks to as much as two years supply; and coffee and cocoa stocks seemed to provide a comfortable margin. Given an extension of the war-time international regulation of the available supplies to meet what would clearly be for a time an abnormal restocking demand, the immediate post-war outlook as regards primary commodities seemed to be a manageable situation, and reasonably satisfactory after six years of world war.

This forecast was to be proved quite wrong. Instead, for the next three years there was a general excess of demand over available supplies, and a tremendous rise in the prices of almost all primary commodities. This turned the terms of trade greatly in favour of primary producing countries and greatly against their industrialised customers. Why this happened could only be fully explained by a detailed study. All that will be attempted here is to note the four

96

main reasons which together provide the skeleton on which such an explanation would be built up. The first, and by far the most generally important, was the very great increase in the consumption of primary commodities, and particularly raw materials, by the U.S.A. during the immediate post-war years as compared with pre-war together, in the case of some raw materials, with the additional demand for the building up of strategic stockpiles: and all this took place despite the great rise in prices. In other words, and as a very broad generalisation, the U.S.A. was taking a much larger slice out of a reduced general supply of primary products. Though the increase in the U.S. consumption of many foodstuffs was only in line with the 12 % increase in population since pre-war, yet the consumption of vegetable oils was about 30 % greater, and of coffee 40 % greater. The U.S. consumption of raw materials was in many cases much greater still, for example, copper and rubber about double pre-war, and wool 60–70 % greater. In mid-1945 no one really expected American industrial activity to accomplish the change-over from war-time to peace-time production as quickly as it did or to reach such a high tempo so soon. The rest of the world thus had to compete for such supplies as they deemed essential with an enormous and insistent American demand, and so prices were forced up far higher than they would have been with a less active and prosperous United States. The second reason is a more limited one, though of great importance within its field, namely the disastrous harvests of cereals and sugar in all western Europe and the U.K. in 1947, as the result of the weather. This turned an insufficiency of wheat into a desperate shortage, and greatly intensified the shortage of sugar. The third reason, of still more limited importance, was the political disturbances in the Netherlands East Indies, which led to the creation of independent Indonesia. These prevented any appreciable resumption of exports from this previously very important source, with the exceptions of rubber and tin which, coming from other Indonesian islands than Java, were less affected by the disturbances. Even small supplies of vegetable oilseeds and oils, tea, sugar, and sisal, with the promise of an accelerating rate of exports, would probably have greatly helped the world situation in these products. Finally there was Argentina's export policy. Exports were handled entirely by a government central marketing organisation to which the producers were legally bound to sell, and its buying prices were fixed much lower than the prices at which it was able to sell. Consequently the high prices paid by consumers for wheat, maize,

4   97   RPC

wool, and linseed did not bring about the usual corrective of increased supplies. In fairness, it should be added that some British colonies in Africa followed the same policy with certain of their export commodities, even if with different motives.

These are the main reasons for the great rise in the prices of primary commodities between 1945 and 1948—a rise on the average of about 60%—though there are many other factors which ought to be taken into account in a full study. The year 1948, however, saw the end of this general upsurge of commodity prices, and the end, therefore, of the first of the periods which may be distinguished in the post-war history of primary commodities. This period, 1945-8, may be termed the period of restocking and of the recovery of production and consumption after the war; or, from the other end, so to speak, the period of the seller's market. The next period, from mid-1948 to mid-1950, is characterised by the easing of the generally tight supply position of the first period, and by the end of the immediate post-war seller's market: this might have continued until some sort of general equilibrium had been regained, had it not been brought to an abrupt end in mid-1950 by the oubreak of the Korean War. It started in February 1948 when the prices of most cereals led by wheat, and also that of cotton, fell sharply. In the second half of that year good harvests brought a further considerable decline, while the prices of merino wool, fats and vegetable oils, tea, sugar, cocoa, rubber and sisal all began to fall. But most metals, cross-bred wool, jute and coffee continued to rise in price throughout 1948, so that price movements during that year were very varied. During 1949, however, the downward trend became more general and more marked. Metal prices broke heavily, and those of wool and jute declined, leaving only coffee to continue its rise for which there were special reasons. Wheat and other cereals, and cotton, ended the year at much the same price level as at the beginning, having had their revision downwards during the previous year. In the last quarter of 1949 sterling prices rose with the devaluation of sterling, but in most cases not by the full extent of the devaluation. They really continued to decline as dollar prices did.

In the early months of 1950 a case could be made out for anticipating some stability in prices. It seemed as if the pressure of restocking, and of rising consumption on supplies which were mostly increasing only slowly, had eased; that the consequent sharp revision of prices downwards had been more or less completed; and that the outlook was for a steady but slowly declining price level as supplies steadily but slowly expanded. Yet this is far too simplified a picture, for in the general background there were a number of different complications. There was the complication of the dollar shortage, which was leading towards two price levels in the world—a dollar price level in certain countries and a sterling price level in the rest—and this reflected a big difference in the supply and demand situations in the two areas, surpluses or threatening surpluses in the dollar area and still shortages in the sterling area. There was the complication of the current uncertainty as to whether the slight slackening in the tempo of American industry since 1948 was just a temporary recession or betokened the long-expected post-war world depression on the pattern of 1920. There were the complications of the stockpiling of strategic raw materials by the United States, and of the U.S. policy of price support for their domestic agricultural products; of Britain's policy of bulk buying, and particularly of long-term buying contracts, with all the political issues which may influence such contracts; of the possibility of other commodity control schemes as well as the International Wheat Agreement signed in August 1949; and so on. The situation in the first half of 1950 was in fact confused and involved. It lacked any real stability, even though the one complication which was to change the picture completely, namely the Korean War, was not of course visible or foreseen.

The Korean War starts a third historical period. But a further aspect of prices, and some account of the recovery of production between 1945 and 1950, will help to complete the above account of this second period. The trends in the general level of the prices of primary commodities have been sketched, but nothing has been said about the great differences in the price levels of individual commodities relative to their pre-war relationship. In this respect four fairly distinct groups of staple commodities with standardised, and therefore comparable, world prices may be distinguished at the beginning of 1950, taking the average prices of the immediate pre-war years as a base of 100.

Expensive commodities with price ratios over 600—coffee, cocoa, sisal, jute.
Moderately expensive commodities with price ratios between 400 and 500—cotton, merino wool, lead.
Moderately cheap commodities with price ratios between 300 and 400—wheat, sugar, fats and vegetable oils, zinc.
Cheap commodities with price ratios under 300—tea, copper, tin, rubber.

4-2

There was thus an enormous range of price levels as compared with pre-war, and this obviously invites comparisons with the volume of production of these commodities in 1950 relatively to pre-war. Were the commodities which had risen most in price those whose production had failed to expand as fast as the others, and vice versa? Very broadly the answer is in the affirmative, though such a generalisation demands qualification and explanation in several cases. Thus, in the expensive group, world production of coffee and jute in the 1949–50 season was only about 80 % of the pre-war average, and cocoa about the same as pre-war. Sisal production was definitely greater but, despite this, its price was high because the production of manilla fibre from the Philippines was still far below pre-war, and sisal was required as a substitute. In the moderately expensive group, the production of cotton and of lead was still below pre-war, and that of wool only just larger. The demand for both cotton and lead had been relatively reduced by the growing use of substitutes, while the demand for wool was much greater, and the price would certainly have been much higher if large stocks had not been available. Production of all the commodities in the moderately cheap group was above pre-war, though not by much except for zinc where production had increased by 130 %. In the cheap group, tea production was only about the same as pre-war. Its price in 1950 was being held down by the bulk-buying policy of the U.K. as the largest single buyer, while copper production was well above pre-war, and total rubber supplies, i.e. natural plus synthetic, were nearly doubled. The tin situation was peculiar, for though production was running at only 90 % of pre-war, the acute war-time shortage had led to the development of substitutes, and demand was much reduced. Thus there are various exceptions to the general proposition that prices were highest where the recovery or expansion of production was least. This should not mask the fact that the production of nearly all primary commodities, with the exceptions of coffee and wool, had increased considerably since the end of the war. Nor should this in turn suggest that the sources of exports had remained the same. On the contrary, many commodities had experienced large changes in this respect as compared with pre-war. Further study of the subject will be more conveniently made in the next chapter.

9. THE PERIOD 1950–64

The outbreak of the Korean War in July 1950 was a surprise to the whole world. It caught the commodity markets completely unawares just when they were in a rather confused and unstable condition. The upward surge in prices which then took place was not due to any appreciable increase in actual physical consumption, but essentially to a terrific scramble for stocks of raw materials of all kinds, and of certain materials in particular. Most foodstuffs also rose substantially in price, but they were, so to speak, followers and not leaders. The scramble was considerably intensified by the efforts of the U.S. government to build up strategic stockpiles to larger sizes just when merchants and manufacturers were bent on building up their stocks. There were thus very wide variations in the extent of the price rises of different commodities, and a single index is largely useless and by itself very misleading. Table IV overleaf therefore shows price quotations for a selection of staple commodities in March 1950, which was well before the outbreak of the Korean War and provides a comparison over twelve months with the peak of the price rise in March 1951. The third column shows the percentage increase in prices during the boom, and the fourth column the extent of the fall in actual prices during the following six months, while the last column shows the position a year later, i.e. in September 1952, by which time the effects of the war may be said to have largely passed away.

Cross-bred wool showed the biggest rise in price, and merino, though a long way behind, obtained third place in the race. The enormous stocks of wool accumulated during the war had clouded the inadequacy of the current rate of production, and with their exhaustion the supply of wool had become too small to meet the demand even at the fairly high prices of 1949 and early 1950. When, therefore, the Korean War brought about a scramble for stocks, a big rise in price naturally ensued, though certainly no one would have expected it to be so fantastic. The next largest rises were in rubber and tin, despite the fact that the production of both was well ahead of current physical consumption, i.e. leaving strategic stockpiling out of account. An international restriction scheme was indeed being actively discussed to deal with the overproduction of tin. There was, of course, the fear that the Korean War or communist

TABLE IV. *Commodity prices and the Korean War*

	March 1950	March 1951	% rise (1950–1)	September 1951	September 1952
	pence per lb			pence per lb	
Wool, crossbred (48's)	55	214	290	61	71
Rubber no. 1, R.S.S.	19	60	216	48	22
Wool, merino (64's)	127	314	147	112	132
	£'s per ton			£'s per ton	
Tin, standard	590	1260	114	1030	963
Jute, firsts	116	230	100	160	73
Sisal, B.E.A. no. 1	130	250	93	224	110
	U.S. cents per lb			U.S. cents per lb	
Copper[1]	19·5	24·5	26	27·5	36
Lead[1]	11·0	17·0	55	19·0	13·5
Zinc[1]	11·0	17·5	58	19·5	12·5
Cotton, middling	33	46	40	38	36
Cocoa, Accra	24	38	58	32	32
Sugar, Cuban	4·5	5·5	24	5·4	4·0
Coffee, Santos 4	50	56	12	55	54
Wheat, Chicago	2·25	2·48	10	2·52	2·38

[1] U.S. Official Prices: free market prices much higher, but inadequately recorded.

aggression would spread southwards to the main producing areas of Malaya and Indonesia, just as the Japanese invasions had done in the recent world war. This fear was apparently shared by the U.S. government, judging by its avidity to increase its stockpiles of these two commodities in particular. The combined result was to treble the price of rubber, and double that of tin. Jute and sisal prices also doubled, but these commodities were in barely adequate supply before the Korean War began. Copper and zinc were in adequate but not excessive supply, though lead production was ahead of commercial consumption. The early imposition by the U.S. government of official prices undoubtedly prevented their free market prices from rising more than they in fact did. Cotton showed a relatively moderate rise, but even this was surprising considering that production was well ahead of consumption despite a heavily restricted U.S. crop. Foodstuffs, as the lower part of the table shows, rose only moderately compared with materials and metals, and a longer list would confirm this, though cocoa with its customary price volatility was an exception. Nevertheless, the prices of nearly all primary commodities rose appreciably between July 1950 and March 1951, while some far surpassed all records of short-period price rises. It was a period such as commodity markets in general had never previously known, and it may be hoped will never know again.

By March 1951 the scramble had largely spent itself. All such market scrambles will come to an end in due course from internal causes, but on this occasion some powerful external factors came into operation at much the same time. Thus towards the end of January 1951 the U.S. government imposed maximum prices for a large range of commodities, and introduced restrictions on the quantities which might be used in civilian manufacture as distinct from rearmament orders. At the same time invitations were sent out to the International Materials Conference to be held at Washington. The objective was to establish allocation schemes for materials in short supply, and so to restrict any further rise in their prices. Early in February it is probable that strategic stockpiling purchases were reduced, and a little later an announcement that such purchases of tin would cease forthwith broke that price immediately. These external factors came into operation just at the right time, when the scramble was beginning to subside from internal causes. They certainly hastened the turn downwards. Wool, though not the earliest commodity to fall in price, crashed in April even more spectacularly than it had boomed. American manufacturers just ceased to buy, and the price may be said to have collapsed overnight. The fundamental cause was fear that consumers would cease to buy finished goods at the high prices which the cost of their raw materials would involve, a fear which events proved to be fully justified. How such a factor suddenly takes general effect overnight is one of those psychological problems of economics which are hard to explain convincingly even though it repeatedly presents itself in commodity markets. Rubber, tin and cotton prices all fell substantially, and the price of jute very heavily. Sisal was less affected. As a comparison of the columns in the table for March and September 1951 shows, the collapse was by no means general. Prices of foodstuffs showed little general change, though there were in fact some considerable fluctuations during this period, while the prices of copper, lead and zinc continued to rise. These metals were now definitely in short supply for rearmament requirements, and copper and zinc were two of the seven materials for which allocation schemes were established by the Washington Materials Conference. The other materials were four other metals of minor importance quantitatively, though essential for rearmament, and sulphur. It cannot be said, then, that there was a general and simultaneous collapse of this unprecedented boom in commodity prices, even though there is no doubt that March 1951 marked its end. Some prices collapsed very quickly thereafter, and many more declined considerably, but in a few special cases prices continued to rise.

Between September 1951 and September 1952 the downward readjustment of prices continued. Those commodities which had so far maintained relatively high prices, such as jute, sisal, rubber, lead and zinc, now fell heavily. Those which had risen least, such as wheat, sugar, coffee and cotton, naturally fell least. As always there were some exceptions. Cocoa and tea, though still high above their pre-Korean price levels, fell little, and the same was true of tin. Wool prices turned slightly upwards, and copper continued to rise considerably. By the end of 1952, however, the effects of the Korean boom were passing away, and the more fundamental readjustment of supplies to what may loosely be termed the normal trend of peace-time demands, which had begun in 1948, was now resumed.

During the next four years to 1956 there was no considerable general movement of commodity prices, but rather a slow drift downwards punctuated by some very large fluctuations in the prices of particular commodities. Sugar, wool, jute, lead and zinc prices were very steady. Wheat prices fell in 1953 and then held steady. Sisal continued to fall during 1953, and then steadied. Cotton was steady in 1953 and 1954, and then fell. But for some commodities the tale was very different. Thus there was the so-called 'beverages boom' of 1954, when coffee, tea and cocoa prices all boomed, though for very different and unconnected reasons. They then fell sharply, especially cocoa. The price of rubber rose to a peak of 44 pence in September 1955, and then fell to around 25 pence by the end of 1956. The greatest boom was in copper, which, after rising steadily from 1950 and escaping any post-Korean decline, continued to rise until a peak was reached in March 1956 at £437 a ton. This was the highest price ever recorded and about ten times the 1938 price. From this there was a tremendous fall to about £180 in October 1957. These heavy fluctuations were all due primarily to circumstances peculiar to each industry, which need not be explained here. As has already been said, there was no considerable general movement of commodity prices, though index numbers were of course temporarily influenced by these special cases.

Two matters, however, deserve mention in this summary account of the course of events from 1950 to 1956. The first is the reappearance of commodity control schemes, starting with the International Wheat Agreement of August 1949, and its renewal (though without membership by the U.K.) in 1953. This was followed by a sugar agreement in January 1954. The draft of a tin agreement had been approved in December 1953 but, owing to Indonesia's delay in ratification, it did not become operative until July 1956. A coffee agreement was to follow in 1957. Up to the end of 1956, however, only the wheat and sugar agreements were exercising any direct influence, and that was not considerable. These control schemes will be considered in some detail in chapter 13 below, and no more need be said at this point.

The other matter is the effects on commodities of the Suez Canal crisis at the end of 1956, especially in comparison with the effects of the Korean War. That war caused far less dislocation to the physical flow of commodities from producing areas to the big consuming areas than the closing of the canal. Whereas the Korean War produced an unprecedented boom in commodity prices, the Suez crisis, though raising some prices somewhat for a short time, really caused a major disturbance only in the freight market. The Korean War boom was admittedly much intensified by U.S. stockpiling, and this virtually stopped during the Suez crisis. Even allowing for that considerable difference and the general differences between the two situations, the contrast in what happened does seem to underline the fact that in 1956 the supply position of most primary commodities was a good deal easier than it was in 1950, especially as stocks in the hands of merchants and manufacturers were certainly not excessive in 1956, and many were in fact probably near the minimum level of convenience.

This comment leads on to a more important and fundamental observation on the whole period from 1945 to 1956. Up to 1948-9 commodities were in short supply relative to the current post-war demand, and prices rose steeply. A process of readjusting prices and costs to a new 'normal' or peace-time supply and demand situation then began, but was quickly interrupted by the Korean War price boom. The effects of that boom largely passed away by 1952-3, and so the general readjustment process was resumed. In other words, the course of commodity prices since the end of the sellers' market in 1948-9 should be viewed as a single period of transition to the essentially buyers' market of 1956, interrupted generally by the Korean War, and interrupted for certain commodities by the development of special temporary situations in those industries individually. In a sense all periods are periods of readjustment, for nothing in the economic world ever ceases to change. It is not suggested that readjustment was completed by 1956, but rather that by then the unusual readjustments required by six years of world war were in the main accomplished. The process was becoming one of normal adaptation to the more usual sort of changing world.

During the year 1956, however, a new phase of the downward movement of prices began. Until then world consumption of most primary commodities had been increasing, but in 1956 and 1957 many showed no increase, and some a reduction, while market absorption tended to contract still further, because in some cases stocks at the consuming end were reduced to the bare minimum of convenience. In the summer of 1957 the general trade recession in the U.S.A. became more marked, and many commodity prices, which had already been showing signs of weakness, began an accelerating decline. For some, notably wheat and cotton, the decline was reinforced by the more liberal disposal policies for surplus farm products which were adopted by the U.S. government. For others it was reinforced by the ending of U.S. and U.K. strategic stockpiling and by some sales. As usual there were exceptions to this considerable downward movement. The price of sugar rose very sharply and then fell almost as sharply in 1957. Cocoa prices did much the same in 1958. After the tremendous boom of 1955, copper prices reached a low point in February 1958 and then staged a rapid recovery. But in general the marked downward trend continued until the autumn of 1959, when for a short time the prices of several commodities began to rise. With improving trade in the U.S.A., and in industrialised countries generally, it seemed that the consumption of many primary commodities might be resuming its upward trend, and that in view of the low level of stocks at the consuming end prices might start rising appreciably.

By May 1960 the *Economist* price index had risen by 5 % as compared with July 1959. Then the brighter outlook faded away, and by the end of 1960 the index was slightly lower than in mid-1959. The rise was mainly due to the non-ferrous metals, which reached a peak in early 1960, and then fell heavily. It was also partly due to rubber, which soared from around 24 pence per lb in early 1958 to 42 pence in May 1960, only to drop to 26 pence by the end of that year. The trend of foodstuffs prices was a continuous gentle fall, increasing its pace a little in the latter part of 1960. Early in 1961 the prices of many commodities rose, and again the *Economist* index rose 5% by May. Then it started to fall again, and ended the year at about the same level as it had been at the beginning. Up to August 1962 prices declined only slightly, and then at last a genuine upsurge began. World industrial activity, notably in the U.S.A., had been increasing especially since early 1961. Manufacturers' stocks of raw materials were extremely low, for there seemed no possibility of any shortage. Low, too, were stocks of many foodstuffs at the consuming end, while population and incomes in the main consuming countries had increased. On the supply side the long decline of prices had tended to diminish any surplus obsolescent capacity, as well as stimulating efficiency. In short, the stage had been gradually set for a new phase in the fortunes of the primary industries.

By the end of 1962 the *Economist* index registered a rise of some 4%. By March 1963 it had regained the level of the base year 1958. By June it was up to 108. After a relapse in June and July, the rise was resumed even more sharply, and by mid-November the index reached 115·5. The prices of foodstuffs, boosted by sugar and to a lesser extent coffee and cocoa, led the way (the food index rose 40% between August 1962 and May 1963, and after a setback in the summer rose appreciably higher still by November); fibres also rose, especially sisal; while metals joined in more definitely in the second and fourth quarters. During the first half of 1964 foodstuffs prices turned downwards. This was started by a drastic fall in the price of sugar, but with the increasingly definite prospect of good harvests cereal prices declined, and also coffee and cocoa. Though sisal fell heavily, other fibres remained fairly steady. The prices of the non-ferrous metals rose still faster up to June 1964, and shot upwards from June to October, in which month the *Economist* metals index reached 236 (1958 = 100). By comparison the foodstuffs index in October 1964 stood at a mere 107, and the fibres index at 104, though the former had been nearly 130 and the latter 109 a year before. The combined index stood at about 110. In October 1964[1] there were signs that the boom in non-ferrous metals was giving way though, in view of the depleted stocks situation and the difficulties of expanding production quickly, especially in the case of tin, no dramatic collapse seemed likely. Any further fall in the prices of foodstuffs or fibres seemed equally unlikely. So did any renewed substantial rise.

[1] I.e. at the time of writing.

A brief note may be added concerning the boom in metal prices, with special reference to copper. The fundamental cause has been the increasing demand due to rising manufacturing activity, swollen by the attempts of merchants and manufacturers to rebuild stocks which they had allowed to fall to the lowest level in 1962, coupled with the inelasticity of supply once full production had been reached in 1963–4. In addition the copper situation has been complicated by the policy of the big producers, both in Africa and Chile, of selling direct to large consumers instead of on the London Metal Exchange. This was thus reduced to the status of a residual market, with all the susceptibility to small changes in its demand or supply inevitably characteristic of such a market. During 1962 and 1963 the big producers had been trying to hold up the price, by restriction of output or sales, to around £234 per ton. Early in 1964 there was very little difference between the producers' price of £236 and the price on the London Metal Exchange. The restrictions were then withdrawn. But the L.M.E. price then started a rapid large rise. Consumers wanted larger quantities than the big producers could supply, and there was a scramble for the residual supplies available on the Exchange. The producers raised their price to £244 and then to £260, and later Chile raised her selling price to £280. Meantime the L.M.E. price soared upwards, and at the end of October reached £522, stimulated by the Rhodesian producers having to declare *force majeure* on their contracts because of strikes. How these three prices for copper will finally come together should be an interesting story. Zinc and lead prices also rose greatly, as the result of the unexpectedly large increase in demand. The price of tin soared from a little over £1000 per ton at the beginning of 1964 to £1655 in mid-October, substantially above even its spectacular Korean War peak. For some time tin consumption has been well ahead of production, which can now only be increased by the exploitation of new sources of supply.

Altogether the 1964 simultaneous boom in all four of these metals has been on an unprecedented scale. There has been no general boom in the prices of other primary commodities, but there has been a definite upsurge of their general price level after ten years or so of virtually continuous decline. As always there were individual commodities which at times broke away from this general trend. This upsurge has been sufficient to make a great difference to the export earnings and national incomes of primary producing countries. No longer is the aid given by the richer countries to the poorer primary producing countries being largely neutralised by the fall in the prices of the latter's exports. Though the richer countries have still been getting richer, the poorer countries in 1963 and 1964 were no longer getting poorer.

The summary history of primary commodities in this and the preceding chapter has been largely in terms of price movements, and requires supplementing in respect of changes in the volume of trade, and relative changes in the main sources of supply. For the volume of a commodity's exports may alter as well as its price, and it is of course the two together which determine the total return to the producers, and the total export earnings of the particular producing countries. Table II (p. 7) listed the principal exporters of primary products outside Europe in 1959–61, but this only shows the recent situation, and does not give any information as to the growth in the volume of exports, or the changes which have taken place since, say, before World War II in the relative importance of different sources of supply. Table v (p. 113) therefore attempts to fill this gap by showing for 1934–8 and 1948–52 as well as 1959–61, the average exports of the same twenty primary commodities from the principal exporting countries. The 1934–8 figures represent the pre-World War II position; and those for 1948–52 the position when production and trade had in general recovered from the effects of the war, and were settling down to a new pattern. The 1959–61 figures are the latest which were generally available in tabulated form in October 1964 (these of course being the same figures as in table II). As will be seen, there are a few variations of dates, and in the information given, for different commodities, but the general form of the table is as nearly homogeneous as possible.

This table should be studied from two points of view: the growth in the volume of exports, and the relative changes in the main sources of supply. The former is indicated for each commodity in the totals of the exports of the principal exporters. The figures speak clearly for themselves, but the following rough classification in note form may be of assistance in obtaining an overall view (the number in parentheses after each commodity mentioned refers to its number in the table):

(a) The only commodities showing a continuous decline in the volume of their exports are rice (13) and tin (17)—rice owing to reduced demand from the consuming countries of the Far East, and tin owing to production declining even more than consumption.

(b) Manilla fibre (18) exports were much reduced in 1948–52 as compared with pre-war owing to the Japanese invasion, and have not recovered since.

(c) Exports of lead (20) have changed little.

(d) Beef (2) and maize (14) exports were still much reduced in 1948–52 as the result of the war (particularly Argentina's exports), but the former has since recovered to the pre-war volume, and the latter to much above it (though the sources have changed greatly—see below).

(e) Cotton (5), tea (15), cocoa (16) and sisal (18) exports were about the same in 1948/52 as pre-war, but since then sisal exports have increased about 60%, tea nearly 40%, and cotton and cocoa about 25%.

(f) Coffee (6), copper (7), wool (8), sugar (9) and tobacco (12) exports were all considerably larger in 1948/52 than pre-war, and had increased even faster by 1959/61. Comparing 1959/61 with pre-war, coffee exports increased over 60%, copper more than 100%, wool 270%, sugar 40%, and tobacco 60%. Oils and fats (4) increased over this period nearly 40%.

(g) Zinc (19) exports were double pre-war in 1948–52, but have increased relatively little since.

(h) Wheat (3) exports were nearly double pre-war in 1948–52, and have largely increased since, so that the 1959–61 exports were much more than double pre-war.

(i) The crude petroleum (1) exports shown in the table have increased ten times since pre-war.

Turning to the relative changes in the main sources of supply, two developments have affected a number of commodities, and in that sense constitute outstanding general changes. One is the large fall in exports from Indonesia of vegetable oilseeds and oils (4), sugar (9), tea (15), tin (17) and sisal (18). Indonesia has ceased to be a principal exporter of sugar, tea and sisal, which were the great Dutch plantation industries; only exports of rubber (10), mainly a smallholders' industry, have increased since pre-war. The other general change—and of much greater importance—is the emergence of the U.S.A. as the largest exporter of wheat, oils and fats, and maize, and as a principal exporter of rice. This is all the more remarkable when it is remembered that the U.S.A. was a net importer of wheat in 1934–6, and up to the war an exporter of maize only after specially good harvests, while exports of oils and fats were virtually confined to lard, and rice exports were very small. Attention has been drawn to these two changes, the general nature of which might not be realised when studying the individual commodities in the table. The relative changes in the sources of supply of individual commodities are obvious, but the following observations comparing 1959–61 with pre-war may highlight the more important.

Meat (2). Argentina's beef exports have not nearly recovered to the pre-war level, while those from Australia and New Zealand have nearly doubled. New Zealand has increased her absolute pre-eminence as an exporter of mutton and lamb.

Wheat (3). Apart from the emergence of the U.S.A. as by far the largest exporter, Canada shows a large increase, and Australia some increase, but Argentina's exports have fallen.

Fats and oils (4). Large reductions in exports from Indonesia, China, Argentina and, especially, India have been far more than balanced by the huge increase of U.S. exports, assisted by increases from the Philippines, former B.W.A., Congo and 'Other Africa'.

Cotton (5). U.S. exports are little changed. Brazil's exports have declined considerably, but this has been more than balanced by increases from Mexico and 'Other Africa', with some assistance from Sudan.

Coffee (6). Africa's exports (mainly robusta) have increased five times, to more than half Brazil's exports.

Copper (7). Rhodesia (Zambia) and the Congo (Katanga) have gained on Chile, but Peru shows the biggest proportionate increase of all.

Wool (8). Australia, New Zealand and South Africa have gained on Argentina and Uruguay.

Sugar (9). Indonesia has ceased to export since the war, and Formosa (Taiwan) exports rather less. Quantitatively, the doubling of Cuba's exports is the most important increase, but other countries have also doubled, or nearly doubled, their exports.

Rubber (10). Indonesia's exports have increased to parity with Malaya. Thailand and Africa have become principal exporters.

Tobacco (12). Turkey, Bulgaria and Greece have doubled their exports. U.S.A. shows only a small increase, but Rhodesia's exports have increased six times, though still small relatively to the others.

Rice (13). Greatly reduced exports from Burma and Indo-China are only partly balanced by the large increase in U.S. exports, which were insignificant pre-war.

Maize (14). U.S.A. has taken Argentina's place as the largest exporter: Argentina's exports are much less than half pre-war. South Africa's exports have considerably increased.

Tea (15). Indonesia's exports are only half pre-war, but India and Ceylon have considerably increased their exports, and exports from Africa are becoming appreciable.

Cocoa (16). Ghana has increased her pre-eminence, but Nigeria and 'Other Africa' show increases. Brazil's and Ecuador's exports are unchanged since pre-war.

Sisal (18). Brazil has emerged as a principal exporter, more than taking the place of Indonesia, which has virtually ceased to export. Tanganyika, however, retains her pre-eminence. Exports from Mexico have fallen heavily, but partly because exports of manufactured fibre products have taken the place of fibre exports.

Zinc (19). Canada and Peru show the largest increases. Algeria and Morocco have become substantial exporters.

Lead (20). Australia has nearly maintained her exports of metal, but exports from Canada and Mexico are smaller. Peru shows a substantial increase.

With these notes, table v may be left to speak for itself.

TABLE V. *The principal exports of primary products outside Europe in 1934-8, 1948-52 and 1959-61*

(All figures are annual averages for these periods in thousand tons, unless otherwise stated.)

(1) PETROLEUM (MILLION TONS)

	1934–8	1948–52	1959–61
Crude production[1]	(1936)	(1950)	(1962)
Total Middle East	13	85	240
Venezuela	23	93	114
Total of above	36	178	354

[1] Production of crude is shown as a general indication of growth since almost all is exported either as crude or refined products, and the details of the latter do not justify the space required. Figures are for 1936, 1950 and 1962 only. In 1936 U.S.A. produced 149 million tons, and was a large exporter: in 1962 U.S.A. produced 357 million tons, and was a very large net importer.

(2) MEAT

	1934–8	1948–52	1959–61
Beef			
Argentina	409	195	321
Uruguay	54	53	39
Brazil	43	12	15
Australia	107	69	190
New Zealand	48	58	101
Total of above	661	387	666
Mutton and lamb			
New Zealand	182	257	342
Australia	90	46	67
Argentina	49	51	33
Total of above	321	354	442

(3) WHEAT AND WHEAT FLOUR (MILLION TONS)

	1934–8	1948–52	1959–61
U.S.A.	1·3	11·2	15·4
Canada	4·8	7·3	8·9
Argentina	3·3	1·9	2·2
Australia	2·8	3·1	3·4
Total of above	12·2	23·5	29·9

TABLE V (*cont.*)

(4) FATS AND OILS

Exports of all kinds in terms of oil or fats	1934–8	1948–52 Not available	1959–61
U.S.A.	100	—	2395
Philippines	348	—	620
Former British W. Africa	455	—	688
Former French W. Africa	298	—	261
Congo Republic	97	—	241
Other Africa	212	—	310
Indonesia	529	—	284
Australia and Oceania	363	—	311
India and Ceylon	589	—	190
China	742	—	325
Argentina and Uruguay	577	—	344
Total of above	4310	—	5969

(5) COTTON

	1934–8	1948–52	1959–61
U.S.A.	1294	1047	1330
Mexico	23	148	342
United Arab Republic	375	350	330
Sudan	50	67	137
Uganda	70[1]	70	63
Other Africa	63	124	201
Brazil	194	140	64
Peru	75	65	109
Turkey	17	50	52
Total of above	2161	2061	2628

[1] All B.E.A.

(6) COFFEE

	1934–8	1948–52	1959–61
Brazil	875	1006	1030
Colombia	230	304	360
Other Latin America	292	304	503
Africa	130	282	633
Indonesia	85	13	48
Total of above	1612	1909	2574

TABLE V *(cont.)*

(7) COPPER
(Unrefined and refined unwrought)

	1934-8	1948-52	1959-61
	1	2	
Rhodesia (Zambia)	186	372	536
Chile	320	340	486
Peru	33	21	186
Congo Republic	150	204	286
Canada	150	118	228
Total of above	839	1055	1722

[1] Column 1: averages 1936-8.
[2] Column 2: 1953 only, with a representative figure for Chile as 1953 exports much reduced.

(8) WOOL

Australia	206	300	610
New Zealand	87	132	246
Argentina	77	78	140
Uruguay	28	36	47
Union of S. Africa	45	50	120
Total of above	443	596	1163

(9) SUGAR (MILLION TONS)

Cuba[1]	2·6	5·3	5·4
Dominican Republic	0·4	0·5	0·8
Peru	0·3	0·3	0·5
Philippine Republic[2]	0·9	0·5	1·1
British Commonwealth[3]	1·6	1·6	2·7
Formosa (Taiwan)	0·9	0·4	0·7
Indonesia	1·1	—	—
Total of above	7·8	8·6	11·2

[1] Cuba received limited tariff preference from U.S.A. until 1961.
[2] Philippine Republic exports all to U.S.A. preferential rate after independence.
[3] Preferential rate in U.K. tariff.

TABLE V (*cont.*)

(10) RUBBER, NATURAL

	1934–8	1948–52	1959–61
Malaya[1]	421	648	693
Indonesia[2]	347	628	664
Ceylon	64	100	96
Thailand	32	103	175
Africa	9	59	130
Total of above	873	1538	1758

[1] Exports minus imports.
[2] Including estimates of unrecorded shipments.

(11) DAIRY PRODUCTS[1]

[1] Little change in relative position of exporters: simply steady growth. Requisite space for details not justified.

(12) TOBACCO UNMANUFACTURED

U.S.A.	198	210	221
Turkey, Bulgaria and Greece	97	133	198
Rhodesia	15	48	87
India	21	42	42
Brazil	31	30	37
Total of above	362	463	585

(13) RICE (MILLION TONS)

Burma	3·1	1·2	1·7
Thailand	1·4	1·3	1·3
Indo-China	1·3	0·4	0·5[1]
U.S.A.	0·1	0·5	0·8
Total of above	5·9	3·4	4·3

[1] Exports from Cambodia and Vietnam Republic.

(14) MAIZE (MILLION TONS)

Argentina	6·5	1·1	2·5
U.S.A.	0·8	2·3	6·2
S. Africa	0·3	0·1	0·8
Total of above	7·6	3·5	9·5

TABLE V (*cont.*)

(15) TEA

	1934–8	1948–52	1959–61
India	157	193	205
Ceylon	100	137	184
Indonesia	68	27	32
Africa	Very small	Very small	41
Total of above	325	357	462

(16) COCOA BEANS

Ghana	266	241	325
Nigeria	91	109	163
Other Africa	105	130	181
Brazil	114	98	103
Ecuador	36	37	32
Total of above	612	615	804

(17) TIN (PRODUCTION OF ORE IN TERMS OF METAL CONTENT)

	1	2	3
Malaya	77	56	56
Indonesia	38	32	19
Thailand	16	10	13
China (est.)	11	6	18
Bolivia	25	34	20
Nigeria	11	8	8
Congo	9	15	7
Total of above	187	161	141

[1] Column 1: 1937 only, as international restriction scheme in operation in all other years.

[2] Column 2: 1953 only.

[3] Column 3: 1960–2, as restriction in operation in 1959.

TABLE V (*cont.*)

(18) JUTE AND HARD FIBRES

	1934–8	1948–52	1959–61
Jute			
Pakistan	N/A	760	724
Sisal, etc.			
Tanganyika	90	136	209
Kenya	33	37	56
Portuguese East Africa	28	39	86
Brazil	—	35	117
Mexico	85	56	35
Indonesia	85	7	15
Total sisal	321	310	518
Manilla fibre			
Philippine Republic	165	93	94

(19) ZINC

	[2]	[3]	
Canada			
Ore[1]	22	172	164
Metal	121	141	177
Australia			
Ore[1]	97	122	155
Metal	42	45	36
Congo			
Ore[1]	3	80	47 (est.)
Metal	0	6	50 (est.)
Mexico			
Ore[1]	116	150	188
Metal	31	51	32
Peru			
Ore[1]	19	87	144
Metal	0	9	26
Algeria and Morocco			
Ore[1]	Small	70 (est.)	87
Total of above	451	933	1106

[1] Estimated zinc content of ores and concentrates.
[2] Column 1: average 1936–8.
[3] Column 2: 1953 only.

TABLE V *(cont.)*

(20) LEAD—METAL

	1934–8	1948–52	1959–61
	1	2	
Australia	195	142	185
Canada	146	92	91
Mexico	206	202	153
Peru	18	60	63
Morocco	22	50	26
Total of above	587	546	518

[1] Column 1: average 1936–8.
[2] Column 2: 1953 only.

PART IV

COMMODITY CONTROL SCHEMES

---

10. EVOLUTION AND DEVELOPMENT OF COMMODITY CONTROL SCHEMES TO 1929

In the course of the historical survey of the last three chapters reference has been made from time to time to commodity control schemes in various primary industries. A fuller study of the whole subject was promised in this section. Such a study is justified because control schemes have become a very important and distinctive feature of the organisation of certain primary industries, and because their merits and demerits in different circumstances are being actively discussed by study groups representative of other industries. As a general proposition, they look like playing, if indeed they are not already playing, an important role in international political economy, that is, in the arrangements which governments, or groups of governments, make for their economic relations with other countries or groups of countries. Commodity control schemes are no longer mainly the concern of individual industries, the governments of their countries taking only a mild interest. They are now becoming the key with which primary producing countries hope to open the door to prosperity, and with which industrially developed countries hope to open new markets and so at least maintain their national incomes. It is therefore very important to study and analyse the economics of this relatively modern development in order to understand its fundamental characteristics, its limitations and practical difficulties, and its potentialities for good and evil both in the short and the longer run, and both from the economic and the political points of view. These are matters on which personal assessments as yet differ sharply. The present investigation seeks to reach balanced conclusions, but the reader must be warned that these are unlikely to command general assent in view of the varying importance which is attributed by individual economists and politicians to the different factors involved.

A study of commodity control schemes in the primary industries must start with the proposition that these schemes are fundamentally part of the general movement towards industrial combination, which has long been proceeding in all industrialised countries. The customary limitation of a study of that movement to manufacturing industries, or at the widest to manufacturing and certain mining industries, should not be allowed to obscure the fact that commodity control schemes are fundamentally forms of monopolistic combination of the cartel type adapted to the rather different problems and conditions of primary industries. It is true that the government of a country producing a primary product is usually more intimately concerned in a control scheme for that product than the governments of industrialised countries are in cartels covering manufactures, but this is a characteristic, not a distinguishing or definitive, feature. Governments played no part in the international copper control schemes of 1926 and 1935, nor directly in the sugar scheme of 1931. Mining industries seem indeed to be common ground in the treatment which economists have usually given to these developments. Coal cartels and potash cartels have, at least in the past, usually been discussed under the heading of industrial combination, while copper cartels and tin cartels come under the heading of commodity control schemes along with rubber or sugar or tea cartels. The only reason for this differential treatment appears to be that the evolution of cartels in manufacturing industries, and in some mining industries, took place earlier than it did in agricultural and other mining industries. Put very summarily, the former dates a long way back before World War I, while the latter is a post-World War I development. Nevertheless, as long as it is realised that both developments come from the same root and are parts of the same tree, namely the general movement towards combination in industry—using that word industry to cover as it should, both primary production and manufacturing and marketing and transportation—it is convenient to study them separately. As groups they do have certain important differences.

The statement that control schemes in the primary industries did not develop until after World War I needs some small qualification. Before that war, there were some attempts to form international cartels in zinc and certain other metals and minerals of minor importance. There was also a technically very interesting scheme for

regulating the export of currants, in which Greece then held a monopolistic position in the European market. But there was only one
larger-scale attempt to control the world price of an important
primary product, namely the Brazilian coffee valorisation scheme of
1907. Brazil at that time supplied approximately 80 % of the world
exports of coffee and was faced with large surplus supplies. No other
country was concerned in the scheme, which was in fact operated by
the government of the state of São Paulo, then the chief coffee-
producing state, and not by the federal government of Brazil. The
scheme may thus be described as an incomplete national cartel of a
compulsory character seeking to influence the world market by
regulating exports. It was in no sense an international cartel, even
though it was largely financed by bankers in a number of European
countries. All that need be said here is that the coffee planters and
politicians of São Paulo state were convinced of the benefits of the
scheme—even if a more impartial judgement is that it was not a
success, though not a complete failure. It certainly taught them
some lessons in the technique of operating such a scheme, and paved
the way for the one established in the early 1920's.[1]

During and immediately after World War I, the Allied governments operated a number of control schemes affecting primary
products, most of them from the consumers' and not the producers'
end. Arising out of the war and the post-war boom and slump, there
were some interesting cartel agreements for the regulation of output
in copper, tin and rubber; and also the British government's war-
time scheme for the marketing of Australian wool (B.A.W.R.A.).
Though these control schemes arose directly out of the circumstances
created by the war, they were nevertheless direct forerunners of later
schemes. The war thus exercised a considerable influence on the movement towards combination in the primary industries, as it did,
though in rather different ways, in manufacturing industries. What
was created to meet the special and often desperate situations in
which primary producers found themselves as the result of the war
could be adapted to meet the equally desperate situations with which
they often found themselves faced in peace-time, as the result of the
vagaries of nature and the weather, or of the trade cycle. By the
early 1920's primary producers in general were beginning to grasp

---

[1] For a fuller account of the 1907 valorisation scheme, reference may be made to
the Royal Economic Society's *Memorandum*, no. 34, dated February 1932, pp. 8–9,
by the present author.

the idea and the possibilities of control schemes; especially as the short duration of the post-war depression, and the relatively rapid recovery, particularly in the U.S.A., helped these pioneer attempts at control to achieve a considerable apparent measure of success.

The rubber industry may be taken as an example of the continuity of development. In 1917 there was a great shortage of shipping owing to the war, and at the same time the very large area which had been planted in Malaya as the result of the great rubber boom of 1909–10 began to come into production.[1] Consequently, output in Malaya increased largely and rapidly, but could not all be shipped to the U.S.A. and Europe, even though demand was urgent and the price in London and New York high. Stocks therefore began to pile up in Malaya, on such a scale that in 1917 a voluntary scheme was established by the plantation companies to restrict output to 75 % of capacity. At the same time the F.M.S. government appointed a committee to consider a compulsory restriction scheme. After the voluntary restriction scheme had run for twelve months, the war ended, and the scheme was not renewed, since there was every prospect that the shipping shortage would speedily end. The government committee made its report and this was pigeon-holed. But when in the late autumn of 1920 the post-war boom collapsed, and the price of rubber dropped from nearly 2s. a lb to about 10d. in four months, it was natural that voluntary restriction of output should be reintroduced. For reasons which need not be detailed here, there was insufficient support for its continuation after one year's operation. This immediately led to the appointment by the British government of a committee to consider compulsory restriction. Naturally this committee got the report of the F.M.S. government committee of 1917 out of its pigeon-hole, and took note of its recommendations. Eventually a compulsory restriction scheme was established in 1922, not only for Malaya but also for Ceylon. The circumstances of the two crises were, however, quite different. The crisis of 1917 was due to the war-time shipping shortage, while the 1921 crisis was fundamentally due more to excessive production than to a fall in demand, despite the world depression. Moreover, the excessive production was in no way due to the war, but to the rubber boom of 1909–10. The voluntary restriction scheme of 1917, however, was clearly the

---

[1] A rubber tree takes about seven years to reach what plantation technique considers to be tappable size.

forerunner of the compulsory scheme of 1922. The ideas, and to some extent the mechanism, of the war-time scheme were adapted in 1922 as a remedy for the same problems of excess supplies, even though the setting was so different.

Other examples of this continuity of development are supplied by the copper and tin industries. These were greatly expanded during the war, and so found themselves with rapidly mounting stocks when even the smaller normal peace-time demand was much reduced by the post-war slump. Both industries experimented with stockholding pools, which as such turned out to be financially profitable. The copper industry experimented also with organised restriction of output. Both industries learned positive and negative lessons which were later applied to more ambitious schemes of control.

By 1925 further experience and knowledge of the potentialities of control schemes was becoming available. By November of that year the British rubber restriction scheme had succeeded in three years in raising the price from 8d. a lb to 4s. As a result, the so-called pivotal price, which the scheme was intended to establish and stabilise, was raised from 15d. to 21d. By the end of 1926 things did not look quite so cheerful from the producers' point of view, but the disastrous end of the scheme was still more or less hidden in the distance. There had been a striking demonstration of what such a scheme could achieve, and producers in other primary industries had witnessed it. Another kind of control scheme was also showing by 1925 at least its practicability in operation, namely the Brazilian coffee valorisation scheme. This had really got under way in 1923 after some further unsatisfactory trials of market intervention as a remedy for surplus supplies. This was a scheme for regulating the flow of coffee on to the market at an even rate estimated to stabilise the price at a desired level; any temporary surplus due to a specially good crop being held as stocks which were to be released when there was a short crop; and the farmers receiving substantial cash advances on delivery of their crops to the official warehouses. The scheme was at first operated by the federal government, but in 1925, owing to political differences, it was handed over to the government of the state of São Paulo. By then the price had risen substantially. For this the Brazilians gave the valorisation scheme most of the credit, though in fact it was mainly due to a genuine tendency for supplies to fall short of an increasing demand. Certainly, however, the mechanism of control was functioning smoothly. Though there had been no severe test of the scheme by

1925, its practicability seemed well established, and its potentialities most promising, at least in the eyes of the producers.

It is not, therefore, very surprising that control schemes began to increase in number from 1925 onwards. In that year the European beet-sugar crops staged an unexpectedly rapid recovery after their near extinction during World War I. Consequently Cuba, then the largest exporter of sugar in the western hemisphere, found it impossible to sell at any reasonable price the very large crop which was the result of a big expansion of acreage during the preceding two to three years. Moreover, there was little prospect of the world absorbing the still bigger Cuban crop which was growing for the 1926 harvest. Restriction of output seemed the obvious and necessary remedy, for the whole economic life of Cuba at that time depended on sugar exports, just as Brazil's did on coffee, and to a large extent Malaya's on rubber. In Cuba, as in the other two control schemes, the government was drawn in to help in creating a sufficiently solid centralised control over the very numerous individual producers, large and small. The Cuban sugar restriction scheme began, therefore, in 1926. It lasted, with one short interval, until it was merged in the international sugar control scheme established by all the leading exporting countries in 1931. Up to 1929 it was having an appreciable effect in maintaining the world price above what it would have been without restriction of the Cuban crops. After the Wall Street crash, its effects on the price were negligible.

The year 1926 also saw the establishment of the international copper cartel known as Copper Exporters Inc. This was a control scheme of a rather different kind from those already in operation, inasmuch as governments played no part in it; moreover, it did not originate as a remedy for surplus supplies, for though the current price in 1926 was a little on the low side, the statistical position was very promising from the producers' point of view. The cartel was simply a deliberate attempt to secure monopolistic profits for the American capital then controlling around 75 % of world mine production. In this attempt the Union Minière du Haut-Katanga in the Belgian Congo, then supplying about 15 % of world exports and the only other important exporter, was persuaded to join. By a system of rationing the European markets and so reducing merchants' stocks to a very low level, supplemented later by restriction of output, the cartel succeeded in raising the price by 1928 to the same sort of outrageous level as the British rubber restriction scheme had previously raised the price of rubber. From about 13 U.S. cents, a peak of 24 cents a lb was reached in March 1929 when a buyers' strike began. The cartel then pegged the price at 18 cents. Despite the virtual cessation of buying after the Wall Street crash, the cartel held the price at that level until April 1930, after which control was lost and the cartel broke up. There is no doubt that while the high prices lasted, the members of the cartel made very large profits. There is also no doubt that these high prices greatly stimulated the development of the new copper field in Northern Rhodesia. Though the actual output of Rhodesia by 1929 was not the cause of the cartel's debacle, the cartel's price policy undoubtedly hastened the day when low-cost African production was to put the relatively high-cost industry in the U.S.A. out of the world export market.

While Copper Exporters was thus giving another demonstration of what could be achieved by combination, the British rubber restriction scheme was demonstrating its dangers in the longer run. Just as the high-price policy of the copper cartel was hastening the development of a large, new low-cost source of supply, so the earlier high price for rubber had stimulated production by the peoples of the Netherlands East Indies, and from all sources outside the scheme. Just as Copper Exporters encountered a buyers' strike in 1929, so in 1926 the British rubber cartel was faced with considerable consumer resistance, and in particular the formation of a centralised buying pool by the large American consumers. Despite successive reductions of exports from Malaya and Ceylon, the world price of rubber continued to decline. It became obvious that the higher pivotal price of 1s. 9d. established in 1926 could not be held. Eventually the British government gave six months' notice that the scheme would be terminated on 1 November 1928, whereupon the price promptly dropped to 8–9d., only a little higher than it was in 1922 before the scheme started. The plantation industries of Malaya and Ceylon were then faced with the problem of very large and rapidly increasing supplies from the Netherlands East Indies.

This dismal story, however, did not check the general spread of control schemes. In 1927 and 1928 there were attempts to run restriction schemes of a limited character in petroleum, and in lead and zinc. In 1928 there was also the first big attempt by the Canadian wheat pools to control the price of wheat. Until then, these cooperative marketing organisations had as their main objective the equalisation of the flow of wheat on to the market over each crop year, so avoiding the alleged depression of the price when individual farmers all sold their wheat as soon as it was harvested. In 1928, however, faced with a very large crop, the central selling agency of the pools decided to hold back part of it so as to prevent prices falling unduly low, and to carry this as stocks until there was a short crop. It was the same valorisation idea as the Brazilian coffee scheme, and essentially the same technique was used.

By 1929, therefore, control schemes were becoming quite numerous. Their desirability was being actively discussed in respect of other primary industries, especially cotton and tin. The Wall Street crash and the world depression, however, began a new phase in the history of commodity control. This chapter will therefore be rounded off by a brief inquiry as to whether there was any general cause of the outburst of control schemes in the 1920's, such as some widespread new feature in the general economic conditions of the primary industries during this period of expansion. After the relatively intensive study which was made of this period in chapter 7, the answer seems quite definitely to be in the negative. It certainly was not the case that a large number of the primary industries were suffering from some common difficulty, and that some of them experimented with control schemes as a remedy, while the rest were frightened to do so because they were not convinced of their efficacy. Rather, the situation seems to have been that in certain primary industries, for reasons peculiar to each, supply got ahead of demand, the prices of their products fell greatly, and the producers found themselves in difficulties. Then, instead of waiting as in time past for the storm to blow itself out, the producers rapidly reflected on what manufacturing industries commonly did when in such difficulties; and on what governments had successfully done in the way of centralised control in World War I; and on the success of certain immediate post-war control schemes for primary products, reinforced by further experience as the decade went on. As a result of these reflections, successive industries decided to try and solve their difficulties on the same sort of lines, despite the often quite different causes of those difficulties, calling upon their governments to render any legislative assistance within their powers, where that seemed necessary or desirable. This the governments were usually willing to do, if indeed they were not already taking some initiative themselves, because with primary industries, so much more often than is usual with manufacturing industries, the whole economic welfare of the producing countries, as well as the state revenues, depends on the foreign earnings of one or two exporting industries. Moreover the governments had also learned during and since World War I how much more could be done, and done with at least temporary success, by government collaboration than by producers' own unaided efforts.

This analysis does not need to be stretched too far to include the copper cartel of 1926, even though that did not originate in conditions which could reasonably be described as oversupply. Copper producers could argue that if a control scheme could raise the price from a very low level to a very high level, as the British rubber restriction scheme had done, then surely the price could be raised even more easily from a much better starting point. This argument does not, however, take into account the one widespread factor which emerged from the study of this period in chapter 7, namely the rapid rise in productivity and decline in costs of production in many primary industries, which may well have been an important contributory factor to the general malaise, or lack of balance, exhibited by these primary industries as a group. This is a very different thing, however, from saying that rapid technical progress was the cause of the tendency to excess supplies which gave rise to control schemes. As was noted in chapter 7, there were more specific and powerful factors bringing about excess supplies in the different industries where this condition developed. Certainly technical progress was no direct major cause of the crop of control schemes in the 1920's. On the other hand, rapid technical progress, using that term in the widest possible sense, is likely to be a serious complicating factor in the successful conduct and administration of a control scheme, and one which often jeopardises its chances of ultimate success. Technical progress necessitates rapid adjustment of industrial structure and organisation, and the speedy elimination of obsolete high-cost capacity, whereas the object of most control schemes has usually been to freeze the existing position. Raising prices tends to speed up technical progress outside the control's sphere of influence, and often surreptitiously inside it. This may have the result that the production of outsiders increases, so necessitating more and more restrictive action by the control, or that its position is undermined from within. The rubber, copper and coffee control schemes of the 1920's all illustrate these effects. It will, however, be best to delay further study of these matters until the story of control schemes has been completed.

This analysis of the evolution and development of control schemes bears out the point that their origins are not to be found in the circumstances of the 1920's but lie further back. While World War I and its aftermath undoubtedly had a powerful influence on their development, their real origins lie in the general movement towards industrial combination which had started long before in manufacturing and certain mining industries. In the 1920's combination in the primary industries was merely added to that main movement.

11. THE CRISIS OF 1930 AND GOVERNMENT INTERVENTIONS

Towards the end of chapter 7 above, a very summary account was given of the history of control schemes after the Wall Street crash and during the 1930's. This will now be somewhat expanded, particularly in respect of one or two schemes, so as to form a more adequate basis for an appraisal of the changing character of control schemes up to the outbreak of World War II. As was explained in chapter 7, the Wall Street crash completely upset the confidence of the business world. In the closing months of 1929 and early 1930, even though actual physical absorption was still proceeding at much the same rate as before, current market demand virtually ceased, because merchants and manufacturers were bent on reducing their stocks to the absolute minimum. This naturally sent the prices of commodities tumbling downwards in company with the prices of securities on Wall Street. The result was to break the effective control of nearly all the existing commodity schemes. Obviously no restriction of output could recreate a demand which had ceased to exist, and no scheme for the holding of stocks could be floated when no one would lend money for that or indeed any other purpose. Thus, during the winter and early spring of 1929–30 conditions of *laissez-faire*, or free competition, ruled in fact for almost all primary commodities, even though several control schemes still existed on paper. For a brief period it looked as if the era of commodity control had come to an abrupt end. By the late spring of 1930 two developments began. On the one hand, market demand reappeared as merchants and manufacturers, having more or less exhausted their stocks, had to buy to meet the requirements of current physical absorption. On the other hand current physical absorption was itself contracting sharply. The result on balance was that the fall in prices became steadier, and the rate of fall slackened somewhat. At the same time it was becoming obvious that prices would, so to speak, never stop falling, still less start rising again, until production had been contracted to meet the current demand, and in many cases even below that demand by such an amount as would absorb the surplus stocks which producers had perforce accumulated. Obviously under such circumstances there was a good deal to be said for restriction of output schemes. However, the practical difficulties of organisation were rendered almost insuperable by the rapidity with which prices and general conditions were changing. In some industries, too, the lower-cost producers still felt that they could weather the storm, provided it did not last too long. They were prepared to carry on independently in the hope that the higher-cost producers would sink, and so be out of the way when demand revived. Thus, as outlined in chapter 7, the earliest measures to resurrect controls were taken by governments because the situation of the producers of certain commodities, notably wheat in Canada, wheat and cotton in the U.S.A., and coffee in Brazil, was becoming so desperate as to threaten the political and economic stability of their countries. Where there was not this pressure on governments to intervene, they naturally did not take any initiative in promoting control schemes which the industries concerned were not yet sufficiently unanimous to demand. This did not begin until about 1931.

The objective of these government interventions was simply to relieve existing critical conditions, and then to terminate their responsibilities, and any form of government control, as soon as this could be safely accomplished. These interventions by governments in 1930 are not therefore of any considerable lasting interest in themselves, but they have some importance as the forerunners of things to come, and so merit brief accounts. The Canadian wheat pools had withheld from the market a substantial proportion of the bumper crop of 1928 in order to maintain the price at what was considered a reasonable level, the argument being that sooner or later there would be a short crop. These stocks were successfully financed. Though the 1929 crop was somewhat small, there was no appreciable reduction in the carry-over in August 1930. On the 1929 crop the pools made initial payments of $1 a bushel, the price in September being around $1.50. Two months later, the price was down to $1.25, and the pools then sought assurances from the banks that they would not force them to sell in order to safeguard their loans. The banks refused. However, the provincial governments were persuaded to guarantee the accounts of the pools with the banks. The idea that wheat could fall below $1, the amount of the initial advance, was considered ridiculous. Yet in 1930 this happened. The Canadian federal government had to take over the selling side of the pools' business, leaving them to function only as the owners of elevators. A wheat merchant was appointed to control the sale of the surplus stocks, which was gradually accomplished, and the farmers marketed the 1931 and subsequent crops through private merchants in the old way. A reaction, however, set in after a time. In 1935 the principles of co-operative marketing were resurrected by the establishment of the Canadian Wheat Board as a *voluntary* government marketing agency, making initial advances and selling as the pools had done. When the need for complete centralised control of marketing arose as the result of World War II, the Wheat Board naturally became the government organ for such control, receiving monopoly powers as the only legal seller of wheat for export. Its position and powers remain about the same today. Thus what was intended in 1930 to be a temporary government intervention has, in effect, had lasting, almost permanent, results.

In the U.S.A. the fall in wheat prices in 1930 led to heavy government purchases by the Federal Farm Board through the Grain Stabilisation Corporation. By the early summer of 1932 this government holding was nearly 7 million tons. As a result, Chicago wheat prices were maintained well above world prices, with the inevitable result that exports virtually ceased. The 1932 U.S. crop was small, and so further purchasing by the government was unnecessary. Then in 1933 the Roosevelt administration came in, and introduced a scheme of direct acreage control, combined with a subsidy to the farmers financed by a tax on flour. Direct acreage restriction was the right way to control wheat production, for low prices had very little effect in discouraging production in the prevailing conditions either in the U.S.A. or other exporting countries. But this policy was almost too successful. Owing to drought, the 1934 crop was so small that the remaining government stocks which had not already been given to the Red Cross for the unemployed, or sold cheap in Asia, were all required for home consumption. For the first time in history the U.S.A. became a net importer of wheat, though the amount was inconsiderable. The 1935 and 1936 crops were well below average, and in these years also there was a small net import. Thus the acreage reduction scheme was almost still-born, and so the subsidy fund was devoted to furthering mixed farming and soil fertility conservation.

However, the Agricultural Adjustment Act of 1933, and the Commodity Credit Corporation established to make loans to producers on stocks, were direct forerunners of the Act of 1938, and of the permanent U.S. support policy for agricultural prices, which has played such an important role since World War II. Thus again temporary market intervention by a government in 1930 had lasting results.

The story of American cotton is in essence very similar, though the problem was to prove much more difficult, and the attempted remedies much more complicated. No detailed account will be attempted here. The story starts with the Federal Farm Board coming in 1930 to the rescue of the cotton-growers' co-operative societies. These had carried over large stocks in an attempt to prevent the price falling too low, and had also assumed large liabilities in respect of sales contracts for future delivery, in the expectation that the fall in the price would be only temporary. To safeguard its own position, and to relieve distress in the cotton belt, the Board accumulated still bigger stocks from the large crop of 1931. This did not prevent a further considerable fall in the price, and a small crop in 1932 did nothing to improve the situation even if it prevented its worsening. Then in 1933 the Roosevelt administration introduced successive schemes of voluntary subsidised acreage control, which, with the help of bad weather in 1934 and 1935, eventually enabled the government to reduce its stocks and liabilities to a relatively manageable amount by the end of the 1936–7 season. During this season, however, these schemes of control were declared unconstitutional by the U.S. Supreme Court. The farmers were therefore free to produce as much as they liked in the 1937–8 season, and with very favourable weather they produced the biggest crop on record. The government had to resume purchasing on a very large scale, and in 1939 was holding the equivalent of more than 18 months' requirements. Purchase taxes had reduced domestic consumption, and other exporting countries, notably Brazil, had stolen much of the U.S. share of the expanding foreign demand. Government intervention in cotton in 1930, like that in wheat, led on to later developments in internal agricultural policy; but cotton was also responsible for a further development in U.S. trade policy, namely direct participation in international commodity control agreements. For in the summer of 1939 the U.S. government took the lead in convening an international cotton congress; and this was actually in session when the outbreak of war terminated it before any decisions had been reached.

An account of the liquidation of the Brazilian coffee valorisation scheme has been deferred until last, because it was a radically different sort of affair, and because it is so important and interesting as to merit somewhat fuller treatment here, especially in view of what has been happening since the mid-1950's. The summary account at the beginning of this chapter may well have given the impression that the scheme's control of the market was swept away by the Wall Street crash. Although the two events closely coincided in time, and are up to a point linked together, such a generalisation would be misleading, for the coffee crash would have taken place in due course even if there had been no Wall Street crash. From 1923 up to the end of 1928, all went according to plan. Total supplies up to 1927 were barely equal to the world's requirements, and the price had been relatively high, not on account of the control scheme which in those years meant only regularised marketing, but because demand was being barely met. A large part of the bumper crop of 1927 was successfully held off the market, and in 1928 these stocks were somewhat reduced as the result of the usual succeeding short crop. By the end of 1928 it, however, was becoming clear, to the horror of the coffee farmers and the São Paulo government, that, contrary to all the rules of the coffee cycle,[1] 1929 would bring another bumper crop. The São Paulo Coffee Defence Institute went on bluffing—and very successfully—that all would be well, while the state government tried to obtain further loans to finance stockholding. This, however, proved impossible in New York or London or anywhere else in the financial conditions of early 1929. Eventually the federal government refused to authorise the necessary issue of paper money for a loan from the Bank of Brazil. The end was dramatic. On 11 October 1929 the Institute's broker sat silent in his place at the Santos futures market throughout the morning session, and when he still made no offers to buy in the afternoon, the market suddenly realised that the Institute had spent its last penny, and that the end had come. Prices fell headlong until the close of the year, and then continued to decline.

The breakdown of the valorisation scheme is still usually attributed, except in Brazil, to new planting brought about by the control's

---

[1] A bumper crop like that of 1927 exhausts the trees, and it was reckoned to take three to four years before they could bear another bumper crop, which would then take place whenever a really good weather season ensued. In the 1930's, however, bumper crops took place almost biennially owing to the large proportion of young vigorous trees.

high-price policy. This is an untenable argument, for no tree planted after 1925 would be in bearing by 1929. As has been said above, the relatively high price level of 1923–5 was due to barely adequate supplies and not to the machinations of the Institute. It is true that the new planting of 1923–5 contributed to the bumper crop of 1929, as it is also true that the prosperity of the farmers over the whole period 1923–9 had led to more careful cultivation, which had probably increased the recuperative powers of the older trees. But when full weight has been given to such factors, the weather must be adjudged to have played the most important part. The 1929 bumper crop was mainly just bad luck from the control's point of view, just as it was pure chance that it should have occurred when the impending Wall Street crash made further borrowing impossible. Nevertheless, from Brazil's longer-period point of view, these were fortunate events, for at least they forced the control to draw in its horns, and face the problem as one of liquidation, not continued valorisation. The volume of new planting in the years from 1925 to 1929, and especially in 1927 and 1928, had raised the average size of the crop to well over 20 million bags during the first half of the 1930's. Exports were then running at less than 15 million bags, despite low prices, but after 1928 there was not a single crop below that figure. This situation could not be righted by any feasible stockholding scheme. The explanation of the vast amount of new planting is not that the control contrived a boom in the price of coffee, for the price from 1926 to 1929 was no higher than it had been from 1923 to 1925, though that was on the high side. The true explanation is that with confidence in the Institute established, coffee was regarded in São Paulo as a sure money-maker. Also the Institute was providing lavish supplies of cash for new planting by making quite unnecessarily large advances to the farmers on deliveries of their crops to the official regulating warehouses.[1] This rather complicated matter need not be explained in detail here. What matters is that the valorisation scheme, not through its price policy but through its unwise and mistaken internal mechanism, was the main cause of the great increase in production in the early 1930's. This would inevitably have brought about the breakdown of the scheme, even if that had not happened for other reasons in 1929. It was this which rendered the liquidation process such a prolonged and, it might well be said, such a terrible and shocking affair.

[1] For an explanation, see the Royal Economic Society's *Memorandum*, no. 34 (1932), pp. 40–4.

This liquidation process must now be briefly described. During the winter of 1929–30 chaotic conditions prevailed in coffee markets. In April 1930, however, the São Paulo state government succeeded in arranging a £20 million loan in London, whereby most of the estimated existing stocks were to be liquidated over ten years. As money was again available to pay advances to the farmers, the general regulation of market supplies could be resumed. The crisis thus appeared to have been surmounted. The existing stocks had however been grossly underestimated, the 1931 crop looked like being another very large one and, most serious of all, the fall in the price of coffee had greatly diminished the value of Brazil's total exports. The foreign exchanges were also falling to an extent which was threatening the value of Brazil's currency, and indeed the stability of the country's economy. From 1924 to 1929 the average annual price of Santos 4, a typical grade, was a little over 20 cents in New York. In 1931 it was 9 cents. So, in the late autumn of 1930, the federal government took over the whole control scheme from São Paulo, and in April 1931 decided that destruction was the only remedy. It imposed a large export tax to pay the costs and to provide some compensation to the farmers for what was to be burned, though later no compensation was given. For the excess of supplies proved to be vast. The 1931 crop was very large, the 1932 crop, though much smaller, exceeded exports, and the 1933 crop was a record at 29 million bags. By the end of 1936 about 40 million bags had been burned, and another 17 were added to the holocaust during 1937. As a result the price was raised a little, and held between 10 and 11 cents (Santos 4, New York). Throughout these years Brazil made repeated efforts to induce the other Latin-American coffee-exporting countries to establish an international export restriction scheme. When the last of these conferences broke down in November 1937, it was decided to abandon the policy of price maintenance and try competitive price warfare. The export tax was therefore virtually abolished. The price fell as low as 7 cents, and though Brazil's exports increased substantially, the crops of all the other Latin-American exporters found a market. It must therefore be concluded that Brazil's additional sales went to rebuild stocks at the consuming end, rather than to replace other coffees. What would have happened if World War II had not started, it is difficult to say, but Brazil's chances in a price war were not very promising. Meantime destruction continued, though at a diminishing rate after 1938, for in the second half of the 1930's the average size of the crops was no longer rising. But the German invasion of Europe in 1940 virtually reduced Brazil's markets, and of course those of other exporters, to the U.S.A. only. Though the situation was greatly alleviated by an agreement, engineered by the U.S. government, for the sharing of the American market by the fourteen exporting countries in the western hemisphere, destruction did not finally cease until 1943. By this time well over 70 million bags had been burned, or say nearly five years' average Brazilian exports, or say two years' world consumption of all coffees. And yet, as the result of the same policy of retaining supplies to maintain the price, Brazil in 1962 had well over 50 million bags in stock! But how that came about belongs to a later chapter.

12. THE NEW CONTROL SCHEMES OF THE 1930's

After this summary of the liquidation of the control schemes of the 1920's and interventions by governments during the crisis year of 1930, the way is clear for a study of the new international control schemes established from 1931 onwards. In chronological order, these new schemes were as follows:

February	1931	Tin
May	1931	Sugar
April	1933	Tea
August	1933	Wheat
June	1934	Rubber
January	1936	Copper

Although various accounts[1] of these schemes are available, some in considerable detail, it seems desirable and convenient to include summaries of their histories here, in order to provide a continuous narrative of the evolution and development of commodity control schemes. Most readers of this book will probably not need the detailed knowledge which would justify the time required to consult other sources, and in any case some are out of print. Before embarking on the stories of the individual schemes, however, some of their common characteristics, particularly as compared with earlier schemes,

---

[1] Short summaries are to be found in *Commodity Control* by Lamartine Yates (1943). Some detailed studies are: Knorr, *Tin under Control* (1945); Wickizer, *Tea under International Regulation* (1944); Bauer, *The Rubber Industry* (1948).

will be considered first. Though this may seem like putting the cart before the horses, it will provide a general background, and will save a certain amount of repetition in the accounts of the individual schemes. The following notes and comments are therefore to be taken simply as a general introduction to these new schemes of the 1930's. The economics of these schemes will be considered later.

(1) The experiences of some of the control schemes of the 1920's had emphasised the dangers of an insufficient degree of monopoly, i.e. the undermining of a restriction scheme by increased production from outsiders. Hence the new schemes of the 1930's covered 80–90%[1], or even more, of exportable production. No scheme was now launched with the inadequate monopolistic position of the British rubber restriction scheme of 1922, or the Cuban restriction scheme of 1926, or even the São Paulo Coffee valorisation. The only qualification to this proposition is an exception which, so to speak, proves the rule: the sugar agreement of 1931 included almost all the countries exporting under free market conditions, but it did not include the tariff-protected 'sugar empires' of the U.S.A. and Britain, which by greatly increasing their production so reduced their demand for outside imports that the agreement failed to achieve its objectives.

(2) This sugar agreement of 1931 was made between trade associations of exporters, and the copper agreement of 1936 was also between the large producing groups; so that in these schemes governments played no direct part, though the governments of some of the sugar-exporting countries were very active behind the scenes. The tea agreement was also signed only by associations of exporters, but the governments of the three countries concerned—India, Ceylon and the Netherlands East Indies—undertook to prohibit exports in excess of the scheme's quotas, and were represented on the controlling committee; and so it may be regarded as a governmental scheme in substance though not strictly in form. The tin, wheat and rubber agreements were signed by the governments concerned, though on the controlling committees civil servants and politicians were in a minority. The majority were men engaged in the industries. It was gradually becoming realised during the 1930's, though not yet fully accepted, that except possibly in industries with highly centralised ownership, such as copper, really strong control schemes of a stable character, and their effective administration, could only be secured in practice by governments; and that where the prevention of new

[1] Except the rather special case of the copper scheme which covered only 70–75%.

additional capacity is part of the control, legislation is in most cases absolutely necessary.

(3) Consuming countries were full members of the short-lived wheat agreement of 1933; and the rubber scheme provided for the representation of rubber manufacturers on the controlling committee, but in an advisory capacity only. The other schemes made no provision for consumer representation as such, and even the rubber scheme must be reckoned as almost exclusively administered in the interests of producers, for not much real attention appears to have been given to the manufacturers' views. With the exception of wheat, these control schemes of the 1930's were conceived solely in the interests of producers, and conducted for their supposed benefit only. But it must be added that the controllers had learned from the earlier schemes how dangerous extreme exploitation of the consumer can be, and how effectively the consumer can retaliate when once roused. Some of the controls of the 1930's almost certainly raised prices considerably above what may be termed an equilibrium level, but there was no attempt to repeat the outrageous exploitation of the British rubber restriction scheme of 1922, or of Copper Exporters Inc. It was realised more and more clearly that the interests of producers and of consumers are not so wide apart even over periods of only a few years, and that consumer exploitation is usually a boomerang.

(4) The price policy of these controls of the 1930's was one of opportunism or expediency. There was no repetition of the automatic price regulation of the British rubber restriction scheme, and no public declaration of price objectives. Experience had shown that such were apt to lead to unwise policies and practices simply in order to try and reach the promised specific objectives. Instead, the objectives of these later schemes were laid down only in the most general terms, and the controllers pursued a policy of making the most they dared of a favourable situation. When economic conditions were against them, they tried to soften the results in so far as that could be done without making matters worse. Admittedly the controllers had certain ideas as to where they would like prices to be, but these ideas were not definite objectives to be secured at any cost, and were continually being revised in the light of existing and prospective situations.

(5) It may be observed in this connection that such opportunist policies have their own drawbacks. The holding of ample stocks of convenience or speculative stocks by merchants and manufacturers tends to become too risky when views on market trends depend to a

large extent on exactly what a commodity control chooses to do, for example, the exact degree of restriction which will be imposed in the next quarter. If merchants and manufacturers are holding only the minimum stocks of convenience, and there is an unexpected increase in consumption, no stocks are available to ease the temporary shortage while production is being speeded up. Thus a market scramble is apt to ensue, and the price to rise out of all proportion. The result is likely to be that too much production is released and the price slumps correspondingly. An unnecessary and most undesirable oscillation of the price is thus set going. Automatic regulation of output or exports by a price scale, as in the British rubber restriction scheme of 1922, does not get over the difficulty, as events showed. If the changes in the degree of restriction are announced for, say, six months ahead, that is not much help, because merchants and manufacturers know well enough that the control will alter its programme if the situation changes appreciably. The international rubber control of the late 1930's tried this remedy, but with conspicuous lack of success. The only effective remedy is for the control itself to establish a buffer stock. This usually means that merchants and manufacturers will hold only still smaller stocks, and therefore the buffer stock must be of considerable size and correspondingly expensive. In the 1930's only the tin control experimented with buffer stocks, and then only in a limited fashion, while the size of the stocks was quite inadequate. Some further comments on these so-called buffer stocks is given below in the account of the tin control scheme.

(6) With the partial exception of the tin scheme, all the other schemes of the 1930's relied on quantitative control of production or exports. The total capacity of the exporting countries was assessed at a standard figure, and no provision was made for altering these standards during the lifetime—mostly five years—of the agreements. The capacity of individual producers in each country was similarly assessed. Quantitative control thus froze the structure and organisation of the industries, and no attempt was made to shut down any excess high-cost capacity, or to encourage the expansion of new low-cost capacity. Some of the smaller producing countries exacted very good terms in respect of their standard production for joining the control schemes, but these were not necessarily low-cost producers. These aspects will be further considered in chapter 14 below, for they really belong to the economics of commodity control schemes in general. Suffice it to point out here that the control schemes of the

1930's were in their very essence restrictionist. They sought to raise prices to what the producers considered a satisfactory level, that is, one as high as would not arouse too much resistance by consuming interests, and to maintain them at such a level: and to do so by reducing supplies to the necessary extent, which even after the passing of the world depression was sometimes extremely severe. This involved the freezing of the structure and organisation of the industries concerned, and it is a matter for interesting speculation what would have happened in the long run if there had been no World War II.

The history of the individual schemes established in the 1930's will now be sketched against the background provided by the above notes and comments. Of the six schemes, that for tin is by far the most interesting to the student of commodity control, and justifies fuller treatment. The rest will be summarised more briefly.

Tin

In the mid-1920's tin enjoyed, or suffered, a price boom. Consumption greatly increased, and though production was stimulated by the rapidly rising price, consumption exceeded production for nearly two years in 1925–6. By 1927 supplies were gaining the upper hand, and the price fell from nearly £300 per ton in 1926 to below £200 in mid-1929. Between 1922 and 1929, world production increased from 125,000 tons to 193,000 tons: in Malaya production nearly doubled and contributed nearly half of the increase in world output, and in Bolivia it increased by nearly 50%. But there was not much increase from the third important source, the Netherlands East Indies, because the Dutch government, which really controlled the industry, was pursuing a policy of producing at a predetermined and only slowly increasing rate irrespective of the price, treating its tin ore as a wasting national asset which must not be used up too quickly. Among the smaller producers, Nigeria and Thailand both doubled their production, but there was little increase from the others. It was in short the common story of a rapid expansion of consumption leading to a boom in the price and a tardy, but excessive, provision of new capacity. Overproduction was indeed staring the industry in the face well before the Wall Street crash, and the Tin Producers' Association was formed in July 1929 to advocate and promote a restriction of output scheme.

After the Wall Street crash, the price began to fall more heavily. Under the leadership of the Tin Producers' Association two attempts at voluntary restriction of output were made in Malaya during 1930, but this did not have much effect because of the opposition of the lower-cost producers. There was also some curtailment in Bolivia. The Netherlands East Indies government and their tin companies, however, argued that as they had not expanded their output during the boom, it was unreasonable to expect them to curtail it in a slump for the benefit of those who had. The Netherlands East Indies was at this time almost certainly the lowest-cost producing country in the world. By the end of 1930 the price of tin was down to about £112, visible stocks had doubled, and even the Dutch saw the advisability of a restriction scheme. Hence in February 1931 an international agreement for the control of exports was signed by the governments of Malaya, the N.E.I., Bolivia, and Nigeria, with the declared objective of securing 'a fair and reasonable equilibrium between production and consumption with the view of preventing rapid and severe oscillations of the price'. Thailand joined the agreement in July 1931, which then covered 90 % of the current world exports. The agreement was renewed from 1 January 1934, and was soon joined by French Indo-China, the Belgian Congo, Portugal and the U.K. When it was renewed again in 1937 the two last-named countries dropped out.

Restriction of exports started at 78 % of the agreed standard amounts for each country, and was rapidly tightened to only $33\frac{1}{3}$ % by July 1932. This level was maintained throughout 1933, by which time the price had risen to over £200, and it may be said broadly that the industry was back on an even keel. In 1934 and 1935 consumption began to recover, and restriction was eased so as to maintain the price around £230. This seems to have been reckoned the desirable level. To assist its stability a buffer stock scheme was established, though this was soon liquidated and wound up. In 1936 the price fell considerably, but this was only due to the long protracted negotiations for the renewal of the agreement, and the expectations by merchants of their ultimate failure. As soon as renewal was certain, the price jumped back to a £230 level. Then, under the influence of the general raw materials boom of 1936–7, and the fact that permissible exports were now at 100 % of standard, the price rose to £280 in March 1937 and restriction was virtually removed. Nevertheless, in common with nearly all raw materials, the price of tin began to decline rapidly during the second half of 1937. Though restriction was reimposed and tightened to 35 % by mid-1938, even this was not sufficiently rapid in its effects, and the price went down to £160–£170. In the last quarter of 1938, however, as the result of this drastic restriction, the price was got back above £200, while producers' difficulties were at the same time eased by a special additional quota to provide supplies for another buffer stock. In the second quarter of 1939, exports were still restricted to 40 %. With the outbreak of war, restriction was rapidly removed, and the buffer stock was liquidated in the endeavour to meet the world-wide scramble for supplies.

It is to be hoped that this brief sketch of the scheme's history will provide a reasonable basis or background for the following broad conclusions and comments.

(1) The agreements provided a very strong and technically efficient control of exports, and so of output.

(2) Judged by such criteria as the rapid raising of the price from the extremely low level of 1931, the reduction of stocks, and the preservation of practically all the tin-producing capacity of the world through the stress and strain of the prolonged general depression, this was a highly successful control scheme.

(3) Around 1931 the tin industry was composed of all kinds of producing units. The range of costs was certainly very wide, with widely varying proportions as between capital and labour. It is indeed quite impossible to form any idea of the supply curve for tin at this period. All that can be said as regards the price policy of the control scheme is that for the great majority of producers in Malaya and for the N.E.I., the years 1933–9 were fairly comfortably profitable despite the very great increase in costs of an often heavily restricted output, while in 1937 when the price did not average much above £230, which appears to have been the price objective of the scheme, and when there was little restriction of output, Malayan producers and the N.E.I. may be said to have had their most successful year of all time. The profits then made went far to recoup the losses or lack of profits in 1931 and 1932. Bolivia and Nigeria probably did not find this price level so profitable as Malaya and the N.E.I., though it was a good enough year. It may thus be concluded that the price policy of the control was on the high side of 'fair and reasonable', but by how much it is impossible to assess with any accuracy.

(4) The Big Three—Malaya, the N.E.I. and Bolivia—produced approximately 80 % of the world's output in 1929, and in 1937 (the

year of full production) only 70%. The smaller producers who joined the scheme exacted good bargains for doing so, and those who did not join roughly doubled their production.

(5) To merchants of tin the scheme was of course anathema, but the control's policy of keeping supplies, and so stocks, on the short side rendered them powerless. Manufacturers, especially in the U.S.A., loudly condemned the maintenance by restriction of a price which they considered outrageously high; but they had to pay, for there was no quick escape though the search for substitutes and substitute techniques in manufacture was much stimulated.

(6) Finally a little more must be said about the buffer stocks of 1934 and 1938. There had been a private stockholding scheme in 1931 which was operated in close conjunction with the international agreement. The objective of this scheme was not to stabilise the price at a predetermined level, but simply to dispose of surplus stocks. This it successfully accomplished in 1933–4. The official buffer stock scheme of July 1934, however, was announced as a price stabilisation scheme. Stocks of a little over 8000 tons were provided by a special additional 5% on export quotas, which were then at only 40% of standard. When supplies were short in June and July 1935, this stock was rapidly released in order to avoid prices rising too far before increased export quotas could give relief. The scheme was then terminated. As a buffer stock it was far too small, and must be regarded as not much more than an experimental toy. However, when the control scheme was faced in mid-1938 with a rapidly falling price despite increasing restriction of exports, there was a repetition of the previous experiment. A stock of 10,000 tons was obtained as before by a special addition to export quotas and not, as might have been expected in these circumstances, by purchases in the market. This stock was held until the war scramble began in July 1939. It was then freely sold, though of course the amount was quite insufficient to have any effect on prices under those conditions.

These tin buffer stocks are the only examples in the inter-war period of that form of price control, and their history does not provide much guidance or experience for its operation. They were used to check rises in the price, but never falls. As things turned out, they would seem to have had two objectives: the prevention of the price rising too far above the level which was the control's objective and, secondly, the easing of producers' difficulties when the control ordered large reductions in output. These are worthy objectives, but they are not the objectives of a true buffer stock scheme for the stabilisation of short-period price fluctuations. This the control of exports equally failed to achieve.

The soundness of the policy of price control by means of export restriction may well be questioned in the circumstances of the tin industry in the 1930's. The creation of a very large amount of new capacity in the previous decade had resulted in an excess of capacity, and the industry ought to have shed something like 20,000 tons, or even more, of the highest-cost capacity, which had become obsolescent. It may be argued that if the price had remained around £100 for a year or two longer, this would have happened. It did not do so because the international control scheme froze the structure and organisation of by far the greater part of the whole industry. But a competitive struggle would almost certainly have revealed that a large part of the obsolescent highest-cost capacity was in Bolivia. If a substantial part of the Bolivian tin industry had been closed down, Bolivia's whole national economy, being so dependent on tin mining and tin exports, would have been imperilled. Some form of temporary control might well have been justifiable on social grounds in order to ease the difficulties of such a readjustment, but that would have been a totally different thing to the control scheme which was in fact established. Certainly, if a large part of the Bolivian industry had been closed down, it would have been little short of disastrous for the U.S.A. and the U.K. during World War II. The international scheme can, however, hardly claim credit for avoiding this.

After this relatively lengthy account of the tin control scheme, the other schemes may be treated briefly. None really approached the thorough-going character of the scheme for tin, and none really achieved the same technical success in reaching its main objective.

Sugar

Any understanding of the international sugar agreements requires a knowledge of the general organisation of the world trade in sugar. At the beginning of the 1930's the eastern and western hemispheres were broadly self-contained. Little of the sugar produced east of Suez was normally shipped west of Suez, except the exports of Mauritius and Australia which came to Britain under the imperial tariff preference, and the exports of the Philippines which was still then a U.S.

possession and so within the U.S. tariff wall. In the eastern hemisphere Java was the only big exporter. Java supplied India's requirements over and above her domestic production, Japan's over and
above her supplies from Formosa, and those of China, Hongkong
and Malaya. In the western hemisphere by far the biggest importers
were the U.S. and Britain, and each had what may be termed its
'sugar empire'. This comprised in the case of the U.S.A. the domestic
production, the exports from its possessions (Puerto Rico, Hawaii and
the Philippines), and a tariff preference to Cuba for the balance of
requirements (about 2·5 million tons). In the case of Britain it
comprised the domestic production of beet sugar, and the exports of
her colonies and of South Africa and Australia, which, all told,
still fell short of requirements by about 1 million tons. Continental
Europe, with its beet-sugar crop of some 8 million tons, was broadly
self-sufficient, Czechoslovakia and Poland exporting to deficiency
countries, and sometimes even to Britain. North Africa was an importer. Thus the 'free market' covered only a small proportion of
the world's production of sugar. Taking both hemispheres together,
its supplies at the beginning of the 1930's consisted of Java's crop
(about 3 million tons), the surplus of Cuba's crop over and above
the requirements of the U.S.A. (say 2·5 million tons), the crop of the
Dominican Republic (say 350,000 tons), and the small balance of
Peru's exports which was not absorbed by other South American
countries—a total of, say, 6 million tons out of a world production
of 27–28 million tons. Yet this small residual market set the general
level of world sugar prices.

As related in chapter 10 above,[1] Cuba had begun restricting her
production in 1926, and had made repeated efforts to persuade the
other exporting countries to join with her in an international scheme.
Though the European exporters were on the whole sympathetic, Java
refused to consider participation; and the European countries feared
that if Java stood out she would send sugar to Europe. But in 1930
Java found it impossible to sell even at the low level to which the
price had fallen as the result of the Wall Street crash and the world
depression. Opinion in Holland, from which the Java sugar industry
was closely controlled, rapidly swung round in favour of restriction.
In the autumn of 1930 Mr Chadbourne, an American, came to Europe
as spokesman for the Cuban industry, with proposals for an international restriction scheme. In May 1931 this was adopted by Cuba,

[1] See page 125.

145

Java, and the main European exporters. The agreement[1] was between the producers' associations in each country, and not between their governments, which were, however, in full sympathy and undertook to pass any legislation required to implement the scheme. Its main objective was to liquidate the large surplus stocks of about 4 million tons. These were to be segregated, and released by not less than 25% each year of the four years' agreement. National export quotas were fixed, and each country undertook to limit its total production to domestic consumption plus its export quota, the latter inclusive of the annual disposal of its surplus stocks. There was thus no direct control of markets or of the price, but provision was made for percentage increases in the export quotas if the price rose above 2 cents gold per lb, or say 9s. per cwt in depreciated sterling, which was about its average level in 1929 as compared with a little under 6s. in 1931.

The scheme was in general soundly conceived but, so far from raising prices, it failed to stop them falling to the very low level of 4s. 8d. per cwt in 1934 and 1935. On the whole the export quotas were observed. The European countries were able to reduce their sowings of beet to the requisite drastic extent, and to dispose of their surplus stocks. Cuba also reduced production, but not sufficiently, and still held at least half a million tons when the agreement came to an end in 1935. Java found her biggest market, India, almost disappearing owing to reduced consumption, coupled later with increased domestic production as the result of the raising of the Indian tariff in 1932. Java's Japanese market was failing owing to increased production in Formosa. By 1933 Java was holding 2·4 million tons of unsold sugar, and despite extreme reductions of the crops of 1934 and 1935, the surplus was still over 1 million tons at the end of the latter season. Thus, at the end of the four years of the agreement, surplus stocks still amounted to at least 1·5 million tons instead of the designed zero.

The stock position explains in part the scheme's failure to raise prices, but this was only a reflection of the real trouble, namely the increase in production outside the agreement, which more than matched the reduced production of the countries within it. The so-called Chadbourne countries roughly halved their production from 1932–3 onwards as compared with 1929–30. The rest of the world,

[1] For a fuller account by the present author of this agreement and its history, reference may be made to a section on Sugar in the *London and Cambridge Economic Service Special Memorandum*, no. 45 (November 1937), p. 23. (This memorandum was also published as *Royal Economic Society Memorandum*, no. 69.)

however, increased its production by more than two-thirds of the 6 million tons' reduction by the Chadbourne countries. The British 'sugar empire' contributed the largest increase, most of it being India's domestic production. The U.S. beet crop and the cane crop of the Philippines both increased substantially, though in 1935 the former was brought under restrictive government control. Russia and Formosa added to the total increase. Consequently the restriction of production by the Chadbourne countries was quite inadequate in face of the resulting large shrinkage of sales in the free market. This explains why the price failed to rise, despite what was after all a very considerable reduction of the surplus stocks, and despite the resumed increase in world consumption in 1934–5.

It is therefore small wonder that after all their sacrifices the Chadbourne countries felt that the agreement had achieved little, though the historian's verdict must surely be that without the scheme the situation would have been very much worse. Renewal at the time seemed pointless, and the scheme came to an end on 30 September 1935. During the rest of that year, and throughout most of 1936, the price fluctuated somewhat. Then began a definite rise reaching 6s. 9d. in March 1937, for though a large increase in production was in prospect, so was a continuing large increase in consumption. The U.S. had limited its domestic production, as had Britain, and the preferential duty to the British 'sugar empire' producers was most unlikely to be raised. With the prospects for the free-market producers thus brightening, an international sugar conference was called in London in February 1937 with government delegations from almost all the sugar-producing countries of the world. In May a new agreement, operative as from 1 September, was signed. This provided for the control of exports by quotas, and the restriction of stocks to about 25% of basic export quotas. The U.S.A. undertook to reduce the existing ratio of imports to total requirements, and Britain undertook to share any increase in consumption between imperial and foreign producers.

The export quotas of this new agreement may be said to have been based on a generous view of probable consumption. This certainly became true when, in the autumn of 1937 and during the first half of 1938, consumption, instead of continuing to increase, declined as the result of the general trade recession of that period, especially in the U.S.A. By April 1938 the price had fallen from 6s. 6d. to around 5s. per cwt, and the Sugar Council reduced export quotas by 5%. This was quite insufficient to meet the situation, but during the second half of 1938 the world began to stock up for fear of war, prices rose as stocks in producers' hands declined, and by June 1939 the London price was over 8s. Then the Council raised the original basic quotas quite considerably. With the outbreak of war, the international agreement naturally became void. How the scheme might have fared, if there had been no war, is idle speculation, but at least it can be said that both the 1931 and the 1937 agreements were on the right lines as remedies for most difficult situations. Both made things better rather than worse.

Tea

Britain is of course overwhelmingly the largest market, taking in the 1930's half the world's exports of 'black tea' (i.e. Indian as contrasted with China teas): the U.S.A. was the next largest market, but took only one-fifth as much as Britain. The only large exporters of black tea were India 38 % of total exports, Ceylon 25 %, and the Netherlands East Indies 17%: China, Japan and Formosa exported 'green' teas, but in the 1930's black tea accounted for over 87 % of the total world exports of all kinds of tea, and the two were only competitive to a limited extent. Since the international agreements have only covered black tea, no specific attention will be paid here to green tea, and in this account tea means black tea only.

Final demand for consumption is very inelastic to price changes, and responds only slowly and moderately to changes in consumers' incomes or taste. Production is fairly steady, at least relatively to many agricultural crops and, though weather plays a part, it often tends to affect quality rather than quantity. Variations in yield can to some extent be neutralised by finer or coarser plucking. Tea production has always been a plantation industry[1]—production for export from smallholdings was quite unimportant in the 1930's—and the capital investment required was relatively heavy. This and the long gestation period—about 3–4 years, and more for maximum yield—result in only gradual increases in capacity, and equally an even more gradual elimination of obsolescent capacity. Thus production tends to be fairly elastic in the short term, mainly because of the possibility of varying the severity of plucking, but very inelastic in the longer term.

Fundamentally tea is therefore a relatively stable primary industry.

[1] For the reasons see chapter 2, page 20.

Short-term fluctuations in demand or supply are not a great problem; but if capacity becomes excessive and surplus supplies emerge, the inelasticity of demand and of supply in the longer term makes it very difficult to remedy the situation, except by organised collective action: and similarly in the event of a prolonged shortage, though this has not occurred for a very long time. Once equilibrium is upset, its restoration is difficult, but collective action is easier to achieve with tea than with most commodities. As a plantation industry tea is relatively well organised, and only three countries were concerned in the export trade, India, Ceylon and the Netherlands East Indies. In the 1930's this meant the governments of Britain and Holland only. Control of output is facilitated by the possibility of resort to finer or coarser plucking and by the fact that it is administered through a relatively small number of producing units. Demand is still difficult to estimate exactly, but relatively easy compared with most primary commodities.

These preliminary observations will, it is hoped, provide some sort of background for the control schemes of the 1930's. An experiment with voluntary restriction was tried in 1920, when the price of common tea fell from nearly 16d. per lb in February to 5d. in December. This may have helped somewhat towards the return of prices to a remunerative level during 1921, though bad weather in India, and the recovery of market demand, played the biggest part. Probably, however, more planting had taken place in the immediate post-war years than was estimated. By 1927 production was rising faster than consumption, stocks were accumulating, and a long-term downwards trend in the price started. The onset of the world depression in 1929–30 accentuated this surplus situation, and the price dropped considerably. In 1930 voluntary restriction was tried again, but was found inadequate and was not continued for 1931. By 1932 the average price of all tea sold in London was down to 9½d. as compared with an average of over 18d. from 1926 to 1928, and London stocks represented over six months' supply for the British market. This was probably a record. Sales of Indian and Ceylon teas in Britain were helped by the devaluation of sterling in September 1931, and by the restoration of the preference duty in April 1932; but N.E.I. teas could hardly be sold at all. Consequently it was the Dutch who took the initiative in October 1932, with proposals to the British for an international control agreement to come into force on 1 April 1933 for five years. This was in due course signed by the trade associations concerned, their governments undertaking to back the scheme by passing the requisite legislation to prohibit exports in excess of quotas, and also virtually all new planting. These were the two main forms of control. On the controlling body, the International Tea Committee, voting power was in proportion to standard or basic export quotas (India 38 votes, Ceylon 25, the N.E.I. 17), and on all major matters a unanimous vote was required. Later Britain's East African colonies were brought into the agreement (though with quotas based on liberal estimates of future potential production and not on past exports), and representatives of the British and Dutch governments were added to the I.T.C. The agreement was renewed in substantially the same terms in 1938. It should be noted that export quotas were based on the volume of exports without regard to their quality, and unfilled quotas could not be carried over to the next regulation year. On the other hand export licences were legally transferable and could be sold by one company to others.

The current quota for the first year of the agreement (1933–4) was fixed at 85 % of standard or basic quotas. In the next year this was raised to $87\frac{1}{2}$%, as prices had risen sharply during 1933 for the first time for five years. As there was a decline during 1934, restriction was tightened to $82\frac{1}{2}$% for 1935–6 and 1936–7, and then raised to $87\frac{1}{2}$% for 1937–8 and to $92\frac{1}{2}$% for 1938–9. After the decline during 1934, prices rose a little in 1935, and went on rising until early 1937, and after a decline in 1938 due to the world trade recession, started rising again in 1939 with increased market demand due to fears of war. Nevertheless, there was not much change in the general level of prices over the control period as a whole up to 1938. The average price of all teas sold in London was around 13d. per lb from 1934 to 1936, rose to 15d. in early 1937, and dropped to 14d. in 1938, after which the prospects of war exercised more effect than the agreement. Stocks fluctuated considerably, but with an appreciable downward trend until 1937, and then the rise was only small; and the prohibition of new planting was effective in preventing any increase in capacity for future production. Exports from countries outside the agreement, mainly the green tea producers, tended to increase, but not so as to constitute any serious threat to the trade of the members.

The I.T.C.'s own verdict on the first agreement (1933–4 to 1937–8) was that although the agreement 'has not achieved the full results hoped for, it has certainly not been a failure'. This seems fair enough. There was certainly no attempt to raise prices unduly by excessive restriction, or even for the purpose of rectifying the surplus situation more rapidly. The committee also more or less acknowledged that the raising of the quotas in 1934 was premature and a mistake. On the whole their forecasts were reasonably correct, and the raising of the quota to $92\frac{1}{2}$ % for 1938-9, even if it aroused some criticism at the time, was a shrewd commercial move, for it is unlikely to have been much influenced by anticipations of war or by political pressure. On the whole, the agreement must be adjudged to have been sound and worth while, and to have worked well. Certainly its influence was to the good, even if it was limited. As was said above, regulation of the tea industry is relatively easy, but that is not to say that it is easy. Much might be learned by other industries from the moderation of this tea control in the atmosphere of the 1930's. The only serious criticism of the scheme is that it tended to lower the price of good-quality teas relatively to that of common teas, i.e. that it reduced the premium on quality, and made quantity the major factor in production. But it must be admitted that over five or six years this was not too serious a drawback, whatever it might become over a more extended period. For a more detailed study of these tea agreements, reference may be made to *Tea under International Regulation* by V. D. Wickizer (Stanford University Press, 1944).

Wheat

The international tea agreement was followed some three months later by the first international wheat agreement. The wheat-importing countries had all been endeavouring to counter the great fall in wheat prices by maintaining their internal domestic prices, and so in effect insulating their wheat industries from the rest of the world. The traditionally protectionist countries—France, Germany and Italy—went further, and were successfully expanding their domestic production in order to decrease their need of imported wheat. From the exporters' point of view, it seemed that the lower the price which they accepted for their wheat, despite the costly efforts of some of them, especially the U.S.A., to keep the price at a reasonable level, the greater were the efforts of their customers to avoid buying; or at least to see that prices did not fall, and so bring about the increased demand which the exporters so much desired. For the traditional free-trade importing countries—the U.K., Belgium, Holland and Norway—the protectionist devices into which they were being drawn were as distasteful as they were deemed necessary. All the importing countries were finding the pursuit of their objectives a hard and costly task.

It was this mutually difficult situation which, after the failure of the World Economic Conference, led to the international wheat agreement of August 1933. This was signed by nine exporting countries and thirteen importing countries, including all the most important of both. It was a triumph for international commercial negotiation at that period. The exporters agreed to accept a schedule of export quotas beginning with the season then opening and to reduce their acreage for the 1934–5 crop by 15 %. The importing countries undertook not to increase their wheat acreages further, and to reduce their tariffs when the world price had risen to a certain level. Taken at its face value, the fundamental principles seemed a sound way out of what appeared a permanent impasse, and certainly a move in the right direction, though it is said that many of the signatories made reservations which were never published. In the winter of 1933–4, however, Argentina harvested a bumper crop, and during 1934 deliberately exceeded her export quota. In the summer of 1934 the U.S. and Canadian crops were very small, stocks would clearly be reduced, and prices began to rise. The result was that the agreement was tacitly disregarded by all parties. Thus this agreement accomplished no more than a slight easing of the pressure of exports during the 1933–4 season. But it is important historically as the first commodity control scheme in which importing as well as exporting countries were associated, the first control scheme in which so many governments cooperated, and the first control scheme in which the U.S. government took part. It was a direct forerunner of the international wheat agreement of 1949, and it left as its one permanent legacy a body known as the Wheat Advisory Committee, which was eventually to be of great assistance in preparing the way for that agreement.

Rubber

After the ending of the British restriction scheme in November 1928, the situation in the rubber industry soon went from bad to worse. In 1929 the price averaged 10¼d.: in 1931 3d.: and in 1932 2¼d. World absorption in 1929 just exceeded 800,000 tons. In 1931 and 1932 it was only around 680,000 tons. World production, which was considerably greater than absorption in 1929, fell substantially by 1932 because the output from smallholdings in the Netherlands East Indies was halved under the very low price, and Ceylon's output had also declined; but surplus stocks, over and above the normal stocks of convenience, amounted to over 200,000 tons. Negotiations for an international restriction scheme began in the spring of 1933, but the difficulty of controlling smallholding production in the N.E.I. delayed the signing of an agreement until April 1934. This was an agreement between the British and Dutch governments, and those of Siam and Indo-China, for the regulation of exports, with the usual formula in respect of its objectives (reduction of stocks and 'a fair and equitable price level'). Its administration was to be in the hands of a committee representing all the signatories, together with three representatives of rubber manufacturers, who sat as advisers but had no votes. This last was a completely new development in the organisation of commodity control schemes. The agreement covered all but a few per cent of the world's output, and from that point of view it was a very complete control. Its administration, however, was complicated, since, as well as many hundreds of estates, there were many thousands of smallholders. The practical difficulty of controlling exports from smallholdings in the N.E.I. put a break on the degree of restriction which the controlling committee thought could safely be imposed in the early stages of the scheme's operation. Individual assessments of these producers were not feasible until 1936, up to which time restriction could only be effected by the rough tool of a varying export tax. Thus it was not until the last quarter of 1935 that restriction was tightened to 60%, at which it remained until 65% was allowed for the second half of 1936. The control's task was eased by its relatively late start, for demand was beginning to recover. Such relatively light restriction resulted in the disposal of virtually all surplus stocks, and in raising the price from 3d. in 1933 to a little over 7d. in mid-1936. This was almost certainly reasonably profitable for most estates, and far higher than the price at which the smallholders of the N.E.I., as well as those in Malaya, were prepared to produce their maximum outputs if left free to do so.

So far the relatively cautious policy of the control was achieving satisfactory results. But from mid-1936 onwards demand began to increase rapidly, and the control apparently decided to force prices higher by not removing restriction as much as the situation really justified, despite the protests of the advisory panel of manufacturers. By the end of 1936 the price had risen to 11d., and in March 1937 nearly 14d. was reached. Export quotas were eventually raised to 90% for the second half of 1937, but demand then sharply contracted as the result of the American general recession, and the price was back to 7d. at the end of the year. Restriction was rapidly tightened to 45%

during the second half of 1938, stocks were reduced to a sub-normal level, and the price slowly rose again during 1939. Despite the outbreak of the war, it was decided, probably quite rightly, to continue the control scheme. It was only ended by the Japanese invasions in December 1941 but its wartime history has no general or lasting significance. Suffice it to say that restriction was gradually lifted, though not as quickly as it should have been, at least in the light of events to come. Considerable reserve stocks however were eventually accumulated by the U.S. and British governments as well as merchants and manufacturers, without which the shortage of rubber during the rest of the war would have been still more desperate than it actually was, though that was serious enough.[1]

Copper

A very short note will suffice for the copper control scheme of 1936–9. The Wall Street crash and the world depression not only swept away the international cartel of 1926, Copper Exporters Inc., but led in May 1932 to the imposition by the United States of a tariff on copper of 4 cents per lb. With the current price around 5 cents this was, and was intended to be, prohibitive. Thus the U.S. industry was isolated, and the copper world cut in two, with consequent revolutionary changes in the flows of world trade. In 1933 and 1934, conditions in the industry outside the U.S.A. could only be described as chaotic, but in April 1935 an international conference began negotiations for an agreement to control production, which came into operation with the year 1936. This agreement was signed by producers in Chile and Peru, Rhodesia and the Belgian Congo (Katanga). The U.S. producers agreed to limit exports from the U.S., but Canada and the European producers did not join, nor did Russia or Japan. Thus the agreement covered 70–75 % only of world production outside the U.S.A. Basic quotas for the members were fixed as follows: Chile 262,000 tons, Peru 30,000 tons, Rhodesia 185,000 tons and Katanga 120,000 tons. Apart from the U.S.A., Canada was by far the biggest exporter outside the agreement, averaging 175,000 tons in 1937–8, but much of Canada's copper output is a joint product with nickel, and it is the nickel which sets the pace. From 1936 to 1939 current quotas varied,

---

[1] For more detailed studies of this rubber control, reference may be made to a section by the present author in the *London and Cambridge Economic Service Special Memorandum*, no. 45 (November 1937), p. 29. (This memorandum was also published as *Royal Economic Society Memorandum*, no. 69): or to *The Rubber Industry*, by P. T. Bauer (Longmans, 1948).

but were never less than 75 % of basic quotas, and in 1937, when the price rose above 10 cents per lb, there was no restriction. The costs of production of the members of the agreement at this period were commonly reckoned as between 5 and 8 cents per lb. There was thus no attempt at exploitation, such as Copper Exporters had achieved with a 1929 price of 18 cents. With control of only 75 % of production outside the U.S.A., the members of this 1936 agreement were certainly well advised to exercise little more than a modest regulatory control, and as such the scheme must be adjudged beneficial. It came to an end with the outbreak of war.

13. CONTROL SCHEMES SINCE 1945

World War II brought to an end the commodity control schemes in operation at its outbreak, though the tin and rubber schemes continued in existence until the Japanese invasions at the end of 1941. Direct control by governments then took their place. As the war years went on, thought began to be given to the economic organisation of the post-war world, and as part of this to the proper role of commodity control schemes. Looking backwards over the inter-war period as a whole, and particularly over the 1930's, most observers, whether politicians or civil servants, business leaders or economists, were agreed that the outstanding feature of the world's economy as a whole, and of the economies of primary industries in particular, was a general instability, and perhaps most notably the instability of prices, and especially of commodity prices. Looking backwards, it was difficult to gainsay the view that for producers of primary products business was just a gamble. For the governments of primary producing countries severe internal and external financial difficulties often arose when the gamble went against them. Large price fluctuations were for manufacturers a vexatious nuisance, and an undesired risk in respect of stockholding. Even merchants and merchant speculators found the price fluctuations of the 1930's excessive. For the consumer, though the period was on the whole favourable to his interests as such, yet the extent of the fluctuations in prices created serious counter-balancing problems, such as heavy unemployment in exporting industries, defaults on loans by primary producing countries, foreign exchange difficulties, and so on.

Thus when thought began to be given to the economic reconstruction of the world, the basic idea was that somehow a much greater degree of stability must be secured—stability of consumption, production, prices, costs, incomes and profits. At least in respect of primary products, the emphasis was on stability of prices, in the belief and hope that if prices were stabilised, consumption and production would thereby be steadied together with costs, incomes and profits. Such stabilisation of prices had been at least an underlying objective, even if only rather nominally, in almost all the inter-war schemes of commodity control. Thus the revival and multiplication of such schemes might have seemed one means of securing stability. But to most American politicians and economists these schemes had been highly objectionable, and in other countries there were leaders of thought, such as Lord Keynes in Britain, who took the view that these inter-war schemes, operated as they were by producers and their governments solely in their own interests, were in essence restrictionist and not expansionist: and therefore such schemes should have no place in post-war plans for an ever-expanding world economy, and an ever-expanding volume of international trade.

As Keynes, for example, saw the problem, the really objectionable feature of the inter-war commodity control schemes was the use of quantitative control, which in practice had meant so much restriction of production during the 1930's. Yet he was clear that there must be some form of control in order to achieve the greater stability of the prices of primary products which seemed so obviously an essential requisite for the more generally stable and at the same time expanding world economy which *laissez-faire* under modern conditions had so notoriously failed to secure. He was thus led to advocate buffer stocks as the proper principle for the control of prices, and his elaboration and powerful advocacy of this form of commodity control did much to stimulate thought and discussion on the whole subject of commodity policy in the world of the post-war future. In his view stability of prices did not of course mean fixed prices, but prices which followed reasonably closely the current long-period trend of demand and supply conditions. Stable prices in this sense could not be expected to result in stabilised supply and demand in the short period, for usually prices do not closely govern short-period supply, let alone market demand, in most primary industries, especially agricultural industries. But stable prices could be expected to give greater stability to producers' incomes both in the short and in the long period. This was an essential condition for a steady expansion of the world's economy. The inter-war commodity control schemes had indeed sought stability of prices as a means to greater stability of producers' incomes, but each group had sought to obtain it by restrictive practices at the expense of the consumer or other producers. With a diminishing volume of international trade, restriction therefore assumed a degree of permanency and had to be progressively intensified. It was really a game of beggar-my-neighbour, and as such bound to defeat its own objectives.

It may be said that in 1945 there was broad agreement among those who were studying these problems that commodity policy should have three main aims, which can be formulated as follows:

(1) To develop an expanding world economy with an increasing production and consumption of material wealth.

(2) To preserve a reasonable stability of prices about the current long-period trend.

(3) To establish and preserve reasonably appropriate and stable incomes to primary producers.

Such propositions were commanding general assent on the part of informed opinion in 1945. There was certainly general assent to the conclusion that the economic system, as it had hitherto functioned, had fallen far short of realising these aims. But as to how commodity policy was to achieve these aims, in what forms and by what organisation, mechanism, and means, there was far from any general agreement. Some parties advocated direct government control on the war-time models, others that governments should only play a supporting role. Some pressed the desirability of substantial representation of consumers on the governing bodies as a necessary and effective safeguard against exploitation by producers. Others viewed this as desirable in the interests of producers themselves. Still others had reservations as to its probable efficacy in practice for either purpose. Some pinned their faith on quantitative control of production, others on control by buffer stocks, and still others advocated both. There was almost every shade of opinion on almost every aspect of the problem, and the situation cannot be adequately summarised. Basically, however, this variety of opinion sprang from a fundamental difference of creeds, a difference which has continued to be in evidence, at least in the background, right up to the present time. There was in 1945, and with modifications there still is today, a school of thought which argues that since the economic system, as it has hitherto been known, has so obviously shown itself incapable of realising the aims which have been formulated above, the only alternative must be to establish

ultimately some system of deliberately planned international control. ⑴
This school therefore views the establishment of control schemes
for individual commodities as stepping-stones to planned control
of a much more far-reaching character; thus the organisation and
mechanism of such schemes should be suitable for, and even
conducive to, permanency of operation, and such as will facilitate
co-ordination in an international planned economy. The other school
of thought, which also still continues today, believes that the econ- ⑵
omic system, as it has hitherto been known, has failed simply by force
of outside circumstances, and would work satisfactorily in a more
rationally conducted world; hence commodity control schemes are
to be regarded only as a remedy when things go wrong, as they will
of course continue to do in an imperfect world. Thus this school views
commodity control not as a good thing in itself but as a necessary evil,
in the same sense as medicines may be much better than no medicines,
but are none the less an evil. It therefore considers that resort to a
commodity control scheme is only justifiable under certain circumstances, and that its organisation and mechanism should be such as
will bring about the end of such circumstances as soon as possible,
and therefore its own demise. Such is the fundamental difference of
thought, and therefore attitude, concerning control. As the history
of the last twenty years has shown, neither creed is held consistently
by particular nations, for example, the U.S.A. or the U.K., for political
opportunism plays a large part on actual specific occasions. Nor do
particular classes of persons, for example, civil servants, economists
or business men, all hold one creed. Some in each class hold one
and some the other, though conversions probably tend to be fewer
and more lasting than with governments. Although the importance
of this difference of creeds should not be exaggerated, account must
be taken of its background workings, for otherwise some of the
happenings since the war on the front of the stage will not be fully
intelligible.

Such was the welter of ideas about commodity control at the end
of the war. Out of it was evolved chapter 6 of the draft charter for
an International Trade Organisation, which resulted from the Havana ✓✓
Conference of the United Nations in 1947–8. The essential aims of
the charter were to liberalise world trade, but nations were granted
exemption from certain of its provisions when they acted as members
of intergovernmental commodity agreements which conformed to
the provisions laid down in chapter 6. With the blessing of the

Economic and Social Council of the United Nations, the parts of the charter relevant to commodity agreements were embodied in the General Agreement on Tariffs and Trade, which had been made in 1947 to enable some action to be taken pending the ratification of the charter. Thus these parts of the charter became binding on all the more important nations, despite the ultimate failure to secure ratification of the charter itself. In this way there came to birth an internationally agreed procedure for the establishment of commodity agreements, and also agreed principles to which the agreements must conform. A new era in the development of commodity control had begun.

The agreed procedure and principles may be summarised as follows: International Commodity Agreements are permissible under either of two conditions:

(1) where a 'burdensome surplus', such as would cause serious hardship to the producers, of whom a substantial proportion must be small producers, will not be avoided or prevented from developing by normal market forces, because a substantial reduction in price does not lead to a significant increase in consumption or decrease in production, or

(2) where widespread unemployment or underemployment involving undue hardship to the workers has developed, or is expected to develop, and will not be prevented by normal market forces because of the absence of reactions as above to price reduction, and because there is no alternative employment for the workers involved.

Any member country of G.A.T.T. which considers that one of these conditions is satisfied may ask the United Nations to appoint a study group for the commodity concerned. All members who consider that their country is substantially interested in the production, consumption or trade in that commodity may send a representative to the study group. Non-members may also be invited. On the basis of the recommendations of such a study group, or at the request of members whose interest represents a substantial part of world production or consumption, the United Nations shall convene an intergovernmental conference, which can establish a commodity control scheme subject to the following governing principles. These are:

(1) All members substantially interested in the production, consumption or trade in the commodity shall be invited to participate in the control scheme, and non-members similarly interested may be invited also.

(2) Non-participating members must receive equitable treatment, and that must in no case be less favourable than the treatment accorded to non-members of G.A.T.T. (in other words a sort of most-favoured-nation principle).

(3) An agreement must include consumers as well as producers, and exporters and importers must have equal voting power on the governing body, which is termed a Commodity Council. An escape clause, however, permits unilateral action by exporters in an emergency, but only as a very temporary measure.

(4) There must be full publicity of the terms of the agreement.

(5) Adequate supplies of the commodity to meet the world demand at reasonable prices must be assured, and any expansion of supplies must come from the most efficient producers.

(6) Each participating government must put in hand such internal economic adjustments as should solve the problem within the duration of the agreement.

(7) No agreement or renewal shall be for more than five years.

(8) The United Nations shall make an official investigation and report every three years at most.

(9) The United Nations can call for a revision of the agreement, or its termination, at any time if its operation has failed substantially to conform to the above principles.

This gives an adequate outline of the procedure and principles governing commodity control schemes as agreed in 1947, and which have ruled to the present time. Before studying the results, some observations and comments may be made on this conception of the role of commodity control schemes. It is clearly very different from what it was before the war; and world opinion, as formulated in this agreement by the governments of all the more important countries, had certainly altered very greatly in the intervening period. The approach to the problem was obviously expansionist, and so in line with the main aim and *raison d'être* of the Havana charter as a whole. The general point of view, however, was that commodity control is a necessary evil—a remedy to prevent hardship to small producers and wage-earners when normal market forces cannot be relied upon to do so, and a remedy to be applied for short periods only. Thus little attention was paid to what may be called long-period criteria. For example, there was no heavy emphasis on the need for conformity with long-period trends of costs, prices or incomes, such as would, or at least certainly should, be laid by the school which views control schemes as stepping-stones to a planned international economy. In the relatively short period of five years, the maximum initial duration of any agreement, reliance for due conformity with long-period trends was placed on the equal representation of consumers and producers. On this principle of equal representation there was much and oft-repeated emphasis. It was similarly relied upon to prevent, or speedily stop, any exploitation of temporary advantages to either side, or any action one against the other. How far this reliance on equal representation of consumers and producers as an instrument of economic adjustment is justified, will be considered in the next chapter:[1] there are reasons for doubting its adequacy for the tasks laid upon it. Finally, it should be realised that almost nothing is said about the relative merits of quantitative control and control by buffer stocks: both were in fact treated on the same basis, and any form of control may be used subject to the principle of adequate supplies at reasonable prices— terms which are notoriously vague. Nevertheless, it is at least absolutely clear that commodity agreements which observe the principles laid down in the Havana charter draft will be vitally different from the commodity schemes of the inter-war period; if only because of the absolute insistence on an expansionist approach, on equal representation of consumers and producers, and on a procedure of establishment and general supervision operated by the United Nations.

It seems unnecessary here to describe in detail the staff of gardeners which was in due course appointed to stimulate and supervise the growth of the promising young new fruit tree which had been thus established. The United Nations created an Interim Co-ordinating Committee for International Commodity Agreements, followed in 1954 by a Commission on International Trade; F.A.O. created its own committee on commodity problems in the field of agriculture; and other bodies have taken a hand less directly. What is much more important is the amount and character of the fruit which the tree has borne. The first-fruits were international study groups for tin, rubber and wool; and two existing bodies—the International Cotton Advisory Committee and the International Sugar Council—were grafted in because their work was essentially similar, as was that of the International Wheat Council, which already was very busy drafting an agreement in conformity with the United Nations principles. In more

---

[1] See pages 184–188.

recent years international U.N.[1] study groups have been established
for lead and zinc, cocoa and coffee. These study groups have, however,
resulted in only four commodity control agreements—for wheat,
sugar, tin and coffee. In 1959 an International Olive Oil Agreement
came into force for four years, but as it has no provisions for price
regulation, and is mainly concerned with publicity measures to increase consumption and measures to guard against unfair competition,
it hardly qualifies as a commodity control agreement as ordinarily
understood. On the other hand, the International Tea Agreement of
1950–5 definitely was a commodity control agreement, but one which
did not conform to the United Nations procedure or principles,
although all four signatories—India, Pakistan, Ceylon and Indonesia—were members of G.A.T.T. There was, for example, no actual
or impending 'burdensome surplus' or unemployment, and no provision was made for any consumer representation. This tea agreement
was in fact very like its pre-war predecessor: it operated export quotas,
regulated the acreage under tea, and prohibited the export of tea-
planting material to countries not parties to the agreement. There
was, however, no need to restrict supplies at all drastically, and
presumably for that reason no consumer country challenged the
international legality of the agreement. It was not renewed on its
expiration in 1955, and its intrinsic interest hardly warrants a more
detailed account. Finally, it must be noted that although no commodity agreement has evolved for lead and zinc, yet the International
Study Group's deliberations have resulted in some concerted measures
for the temporary restriction of output, which have had some effect.
In this respect it has been unique amongst study groups.

[In the main, therefore, a study of commodity control since the war
centres on the four international agreements for wheat, sugar, tin and
coffee.]The rest of this chapter will be devoted to the history of each
individually, and some account of their successes and failures, their
individual merits and demerits, and so on. These accounts will not be
more than summaries, and no detailed history will be attempted,
because for the purposes of the present study of commodity control
much, if not most, of the detail is unnecessary, and would indeed be
likely to blur the outlines of the picture as a whole. Moreover, to
trace the detailed history of the five successive wheat agreements since
1949 would demand a book of its own. The full story of the sugar and

---

[1] F.A.O. also has its own study groups and working parties for quite a large number
of commodities.

tin agreements cannot be told shortly, while the fully fledged control agreement for coffee is too recent for final judgements. The accounts which now follow are as condensed as reasonably possible, if they are, as is intended, to prepare the way for the general, mainly theoretical, discussion in the next chapter of the mechanics of commodity control in its post-war forms; and for the broad appraisal of the progress of the movement towards commodity control as a whole, its failures as well as its successes, its changing character, and its future prospects, which will be attempted in the last chapter. Readers who are specially interested in the detailed history of the four post-war international agreements should find the accounts given by Baranyai and Mills in their book *International Commodity Agreements*[1] a convenient and useful sort of compromise between the exhaustive studies which have still to be written, and the summary accounts which are given here. This is not to say that the present author wholly agrees with their observations as to the meaning and implications of the stories which they present.

The International Wheat Agreements

References have been made in chapter 8 to the vicissitudes of the wheat situation during World War II and the immediate post-war years: the surplus of 1939, greatly intensified in the early years of the war though somewhat modified in its later years, the enormous immediate post-war demand culminating in the failure of the western European harvest in 1947 and acute shortage, and the speedy return during 1949 to adequate supplies accompanied by a substantial fall in the price from the level to which it had soared during the shortage. In the breathing space before the upheaval of the Korean War, the International Wheat Agreement of 1949 was successfully concluded. This, however, was no snap agreement. On the contrary, it was the outcome of the most laborious negotiations extending backwards over a very long period. The original predecessor was the Agreement of 1933, of which a brief account was given in the preceding chapter.[2] In 1938 bumper harvests, and the consequently impending surplus, caused work to begin on a new agreement, but this was halted by the outbreak of war. In 1942 a Memorandum of Agreement between Britain and the four big exporters—U.S.A., Canada, Australia, and Argentina—provided for some control of production, and for a relief

[1] Published by the Centro de Estudios Monetarios Latinoamericanos (C.E.M.L.A.), English edition 1963.　　[2] See page 151.

163

pool of stocks to meet the expected needs of Europe when the war ended. It was essentially a war-time measure, but it did establish the International Wheat Council, which in 1946 began to draft a new agreement. This was eventually initialled by the U.S.A., Canada and Australia as exporters, and thirty-three importing countries. Britain refused to ratify on the ground that the proposed maximum price was too high. Negotiations were however resumed, and an agreement was signed and subsequently ratified to come into force in August 1949 for four years. Altogether it took some seven international conferences to produce this agreement, apart from various drafting committees and much negotiation by officials of the Wheat Council. Even then, two important countries stood out—the U.S.S.R. on the ground that its quota was too small, and Argentina on the ground that the proposed prices were too low.

The 1949 agreement is commonly termed a multilateral contract agreement because it concerns marketing only, and provides for no restriction of exports or production, nor any central accumulation of stocks. The essential principles were that quotas were fixed for exporting countries which they must sell at a stated maximum price, and quotas for importing countries which they must buy at a stated minimum price. As long as the price was between the maximum and the minimum, the individual countries were free to negotiate deals under the agreement at whatever prices they mutually agreed. In other words, exporters agreed not to demand a price higher than the maximum, and importers agreed to purchase at not less than the minimum price, both sides up to the quantities laid down as their quotas. The maximum and minimum prices were originally expressed in Canadian dollars, but owing to the devaluation of the Canadian dollar, and the subsequent abolition of any fixed rate of exchange in September 1950, it was agreed that the prices should be in terms of gold, i.e. U.S. dollars. The maximum price was thus 180 U.S. cents per bushel, to which the exporters added a 6 cents storage charge in 1951, making the effective maximum 186 U.S. cents; and the minimum price was 150 cents for 1949–50, falling by annual steps of 10 cents to 120 cents for 1952–3, the last year of the agreement. The quotas under the agreement amounted on the average to about two-thirds of the total world trade in wheat; and the mechanism could therefore be expected to have a definitely restraining effect on major price fluctuations, while still leaving the free market price to operate within reasonably wide limits.

The history of this agreement was dominated by the rise in the price of wheat, in sympathy with the great upsurge of primary product prices generally, which resulted from the outbreak of the Korean War in July 1950. Until then the price of wheat was tending to fall from the August 1949 level of $2.00. For a very short time in the spring of 1950 some transactions under the agreement were made below the maximum price. Then, with the Korean War, the free market price, i.e. for non-I.W.A.-quota wheat, rose well above the agreement's maximum, and remained above it during the rest of the agreement's lifetime. Naturally, importing members were glad to buy as much of their requirements as they could get within the quotas of the exporters, and all I.W.A. transactions were at the maximum price. The exporters would of course have got much higher prices for their wheat if there had been no I.W.A., but they honoured their obligations, and even consented to the admission to the agreement of some eleven more importing countries, which were thus lost customers for 'free' wheat. From a technical point of view the agreement must be adjudged to have worked well; but towards the end, trouble was looming ahead as the result of extremely large crops in the U.S.A., Canada and Argentina, and a declining volume of total world exports. Stocks were about normal when the agreement started, i.e. the equivalent of about six months' exports. In 1951 they rose somewhat, but with a crop failure in Argentina and increased demand from India and Pakistan owing to crop failures there, the surplus disappeared the next year. By August 1953, however, as the result of good harvests almost everywhere, the total carry-over was in excess of 28 million tons, considerably more than the total 1952–3 exports, and represented some six months' surplus. Yet in 1952–3, though supplies were far in excess of requirements, the 'free' price remained well over $2.00.

The explanation largely lies in the working of the U.S. price support policy for wheat, which in the last two years of the I.W.A. was virtually pegging the U.S. 'free' export price at around $2.20. With this price acting as a target, or more realistically as the bull's eye of a target, the Canadian Wheat Board, as single seller of Canadian wheat, naturally sold at a little below the U.S. price, thus, so to speak, securing 'inners', and other exporters tried to do the same though, owing to their weaker marketing situations, they often had to be content with 'outers'. But for all exporters the U.S. 'free' price was the bull's eye, and thus the world 'free' price was really set by one seller, and not by the four large exporters in competition with one another.

On the buyers' side there were some forty countries in active competition. Under these conditions it is not so surprising that, despite more than ample supplies, the 'free' price remained so far above the I.W.A. maximum, and did not fall much more heavily in 1952–3.

Such was the situation in February 1953 when negotiations began for a renewal of the agreement, and proved to be lengthy, largely because of the attitude of Britain. There was little difficulty in agreeing on a new minimum of $1.55, for the current minimum of $1.20 seemed clearly out of touch with reality. But the British delegation started by maintaining that the existing maximum of $1.80 should be continued in the new agreement. Eventually they said that they would accept a new maximum of $2.00 in order to preserve an agreement which had cost so much negotiating in the past, which had worked technically very well, and by sheer luck had been very favourable to importers. The U.S. delegation held out for 5 cents more, presumably with a view to reducing the cost of its domestic support programme, and would not believe that this further rise of a mere 5 cents would be refused, until the British delegation walked out, leaving the other countries to decide that an agreement with a $2.05 maximum, but without Britain, was better than no agreement at all.

During 1953–4, the first year of the second agreement, large crops in exporting countries, and a sharp contraction in exports owing to good crops in most importing countries, resulted in another big rise in the total carry-over to more than 40 million tons, as compared with average world exports at this time of around 30 million tons. The price fell from, say, $2.00 to $1.70. In the next two seasons there was no appreciable change in the situation. Negotiations for a third agreement began in October 1955. British representatives attended, and argued for a radical revision of the terms of the agreement, together with proposals for action by the exporters to check production. The exporters, however, would not face up to this, and eventually the British left the discussions. In the end the agreement of 1956 was essentially on the same lines as that of 1953, though the maximum price was reduced by 5 cents to $2.00, and Argentina joined. In 1956–7 the carry-over was unchanged, but the price drifted downwards to nearly $1.60. In the next year, despite a small fall in the carry-over, there was little change in prices. But in 1958–9 the U.S. produced a record crop, mainly due to an exceptionally high average yield per acre, and though Canada had a small crop, the total world carry-over rose to nearly 55 million tons, about 18 months' export requirements: yet the price actually rose a little! In brief, it was not the international agreements which were controlling the situation, either as regards prices or stocks, but the two largest exporters, the U.S. and Canada. They did the necessary stockholding, and handled their exports so as to prevent any further fall in the price. Moreover, the total of the quotas under the agreement had of course been much reduced by Britain's abstention in 1953. Other importing countries withdrew in 1956, so that the third agreement was directly controlling only about 25 % of world exports as compared with over 60 % under the 1949 agreement. For all practical purposes the international agreement of 1953, and certainly that of 1956, were ineffective, and their absence would probably have made little difference to the course of events.

Negotiations for a fourth agreement started at the beginning of 1959, and were successfully concluded in March. Obviously something had to be done if the agreement was to be a reality, and some useful changes were made, though they did not really amount to much. Three more exporters joined, making the exporters' membership complete except for Russia; and Britain rejoined. The new price maximum was lowered to $1.90, the minimum remaining unchanged at $1.50. The biggest change, however, was in the machinery. Instead of the obligation on exporters to sell quotas at the maximum price, they undertook collectively to supply all the importers' average requirements even when the price was at the maximum, while the importing countries undertook to buy agreed percentages of their average total imports from the exporters as long as the price was between the minimum and the maximum. Thus the exporters got a minimum guaranteed market in return for their pledge to supply all the importers' requirements at a price not exceeding the maximum; and this minimum market was substantial, Britain, for example, undertaking to buy 80 % of her average imports, and West Germany 70 %. Though the change of mechanism will not presumably make much difference so long as conditions of heavy oversupply last, it should in principle make for greater stability under more normal conditions of supply and demand. The new system applies only to ordinary commercial transactions. Special sales to reduce surplus stocks on concessional terms to poor countries in need of wheat, such as sales under the U.S. Public Law 480, are specifically excluded from the terms of the international agreement, which however provides that such sales shall be reported to the Wheat Council.[1] Finally it was agreed that the Wheat Council should publish an annual review of all features of the world wheat situation. This was as far as agreement could be got for tackling the fundamental problem of the oversupply of wheat. Britain in particular had long been pressing for some remedial action by international agreement. This annual review provided an opportunity for such action, but only an opportunity; and so far it has not been taken.

The three-year lifetime of the 1959 agreement saw an appreciable change for the better in the world wheat situation. This, however, did not begin until 1960–1, when world exports jumped from about 36 million tons to 42 million, partly as the result of poor harvests in western Europe and partly owing to large purchases by China from Canada and Australia. Stocks carried over were nevertheless slightly higher, but with the export rise represented only about 15 months' instead of 18 months' supply. In 1961–2 exports rose slightly; and owing to smaller U.S. and Canadian harvests, the former due to some acreage restriction as well as bad weather, the carry-over fell to around 46 million tons, the first decline for nearly ten years, and so represented only about a year's supply. Throughout the 1959 agreement, and indeed since 1956, the price varied by less than 10 cents between $1.68 and $1.77. How much credit the 1959 International Agreement can claim for these results cannot really be determined. It provided a useful framework of regulation and price stabilisation, but it was a framework supported almost entirely by the U.S. and Canada, as had been the case with the two previous agreements: and this is still the position today.

In 1962 a fifth agreement was made, differing little in substance from its predecessor of 1959. The Soviet Union joined as an exporter; Britain and some other western European countries increased the percentages of their requirements which they undertook to purchase from exporting members; and the price range was raised, the minimum being $1.62\frac{1}{2}$ and the maximum $2.02\frac{1}{2}$. In 1962–3 world exports were reduced by about 10% owing to large crops in western Europe, but the carry-over was virtually unchanged, an increase in Canada being roughly balanced by a decrease in the U.S.A. Then in 1963–4 poor crops in Europe, and a virtual failure of the Russian crop, dramatically altered the whole statistical situation, despite good crops

[1] The Council subsequently reported that in 1959–60 these special sales amounted to over 10 million tons as compared with I.W.A. commercial exports of 18·5 million tons. In 1961–2 special sales reached 13·5 million tons. Almost all these special sales were made by the U.S.A.

in the main exporting countries. In the autumn of 1963 the Soviet Union contracted for over 6 million tons from Canada, 4 million from the U.S.A., and smaller quantities from other exporters, and the price rose considerably. The Wheat Council's annual review for the 1963–4 season is not available at the time of writing, but it can be closely estimated that world exports of wheat amounted to at least 56 million tons, as compared with 44 million tons in 1962–3 and the previous record of 47 million tons in 1961–2. The four big exporters—U.S.A., Canada, Australia and Argentina—accounted for over 49 million tons of the 1963–4 world exports, as compared with 33 million tons in 1962–3, and 38 million tons in 1961–2. As a result, the total carry-over of these four big exporters at the end of the season declined from around 47 million tons in 1962 and 1963 to a little under 40 million tons in 1964. This has of course greatly eased the surplus situation, but if exports now return to their level of previous years and their previous rate of growth, the carry-over still represents about ten months' requirements. It seems fairly certain that the harvests of 1964–5 will be well up to normal, and there is no reason to anticipate a repetition of 1964's short crops in Russia and Europe in the near future. Consequently, the fundamental problem of the oversupply of wheat, though temporarily eased, still continues, and it remains to be seen whether the sixth agreement, shortly to be negotiated to follow the present agreement which expires on 31 July 1965, will take any more effective steps towards its solution than its predecessors have done.

The International Tin Agreements

In chapters 8 and 9 brief mention was made of the war and immediate post-war history of tin: the acute shortage in the later years of the war owing to the Japanese invasions of south-east Asia; the rise in price and the recovery of production from 1945–8; and in 1949 the break in price as production got ahead of consumption, the removal of all governmental controls by the U.S.A. and Britain, and the reopening of the London Metal Exchange for dealings in tin. Then came the Korean War, which more than doubled the price in five months. After declining from an average of £1290 a ton in December 1950 to around £950, where it was held during 1952 by the agreement that Britain should supply the U.S.A. with 20,000 tons of tin in return for steel, the price fell during the first half of 1953 to around £600, or roughly to its immediate pre-Korean War level. In 1953 world production was 177,000 tons, and consumption 134,000 tons. Production had been ahead of consumption every year since 1949, but the excess had been mopped up by the U.S. Strategic Stockpile, which in 1953 was nearing its goal. Consumption had been permanently reduced as the result of the substitution of other metals for tin which had been engendered by the war-time and immediate post-war restrictions on the use of tin by the U.S. and British governments; and especially by the spread of a new electrolytic process which nearly halved the amount of tin required for a ton of tinplate. In 1953 the prospects of a further increase in world production seemed much more certain than the prospects of any substantial rise in consumption; while the moment that the U.S. stockpile ceased purchasing, there was the virtual certainty of a catastrophic crisis of overproduction. It is small wonder, therefore, that 1953 saw the urgent resumption of negotiations for a control agreement.

A resumption of negotiations is the correct term, for an International Tin Study Group had been established as far back as 1947 in conformity with the Havana charter–United Nations procedure. After a series of meetings a draft agreement was approved by a majority (the U.S.A. dissenting) for submission to a Commodity Conference. This was held in October 1950, but meantime the Korean War had doubled the price, and the view of the U.S. government that the establishment of any control agreement would be premature was difficult to refute. The Conference adjourned *sine die*, but the Study Group went on meeting until in August 1953 a revised draft agreement was formulated. In November the adjourned Commodity Conference was resumed, and the text settled and sent to governments for signature. By 30 June 1954 all the principal producing countries had signed, and all the major consuming countries except the U.S.A.; so that the minimum conditions for the agreement's operation were fulfilled, despite the fact that the U.S. had been provisionally allotted nearly half the total voting power on the consumers' side. But Indonesia procrastinated over ratification, partly due to her internal political situation, and partly perhaps because the statistical position of tin was changing for the better during 1954–5. Indonesia may have felt that the agreement was now less desirable from the producers' point of view. However, in February 1956 Indonesia ratified; and so this agreement, which had been drafted 18 months previously and signed a year previously, at last became operative as from 1 July 1956.

The objectives of this agreement are stated in the usual sort of terms: prevention of excessive price fluctuations, the achievement of reasonable price stability, and adequate supplies at reasonable prices. The administrative body was to be a council, on which producing and consuming countries were to have equal voting power, the members having voting rights in proportion to their exports and imports. For decisions on the regulation of exports and other important issues a majority of both sides is required, and for the election of the chairman a two-thirds majority of both sides. As in the pre-war agreements, two methods of control were to be established. A buffer stock, equivalent to 25,000 tons, was to be created by compulsory contributions of tin and/or cash in three instalments from producing countries (consuming countries might make voluntary contributions, but none have done so), and was to be under the control of a manager subject to the following regulations. At a minimum or 'floor' price, originally fixed at £640, the manager must offer to buy to the limit of his cash resources; and at a maximum or 'ceiling' price, originally fixed at £880, he must sell to the limit of his tin resources. The range between these limits was divided into thirds: when the price is in the top third (i.e. £800 to £880), he may sell if he wishes, and when the price is in the lower third, he may buy, but if it is in the middle third he may neither buy nor sell. This was the essential framework of the buffer stock, though numerous articles in the agreement were required to provide for various contingencies. The other method of control was to be the regulation of exports, and the Council was subject to no limitations except that there must be at least 10,000 tons of tin in the buffer stock before any restriction is imposed.

On 1 July 1956 when the agreement came into operation, the price was around £750, i.e. in the middle third of the agreed range of prices, and so at a very convenient starting point. Producing countries contributed to the buffer stock as arranged, but since the cash equivalent to a ton of tin had been fixed at the floor limit of £640, contributions were naturally made in cash and not metal. Hence, when the Suez crisis pushed up the price to around £890, the buffer stock was powerless to intervene. By January 1957, however, the price was back to £800, and continued to fall slowly. The Tin Council then decided to raise the floor price from £640 to £730, and to revise the ranges for action by the buffer stock accordingly; and so with the price sliding below £780 in the second quarter, the buffer stock began to make modest purchases. In the second half of 1957 consumption was declining, while production was being well maintained at a figure which proved to be 25,000 tons in excess of demand. In addition the U.S.S.R. greatly increased its exports, which were not included in the recorded statistics. Consequently the price fell rapidly to the new floor level of £730, and was only held there by large buffer stock purchases which were rapidly exhausting its cash resources. At the beginning of December the Tin Council took urgent action to save the situation. It called for the second contribution by producers, amounting to over £3½ million, to be paid in sterling within one week. It arranged with some countries to make their third and final contribution at once, and it imposed a very substantial restriction of exports to come into force immediately. These drastic steps resulted in the maintenance of the price at the new floor level of £730, and by the end of 1957 the big discount on forward delivery contracts was replaced by a small premium. In mid-January 1958, however, the forward price again started falling heavily, presumably due to continued large sales by the U.S.S.R. reinforcing general doubts whether the buffer stock could even now buy all the tin on offer before the restriction of exports could take effect. Faced with this renewal of the crisis, the Council called up the remaining final instalments of contributions to the buffer stock, and asked for further voluntary contributions from the producing countries; and the restriction of exports was tightened. These measures enabled the price to be maintained until September 1958 when the buffer stock, having spent its last available penny, had to stop buying, and the price fell on that same day from £730 to £640. It is said that if the buffer stock had been able to buy only a few hundred tons more, this break in the price would never have occurred. Certainly it was a mere market break, and by the end of the month the price was back to £730. The severe restriction of exports was now taking real effect, and from 1 September quotas had been imposed by Britain, Holland and Denmark on imports from the U.S.S.R. For the rest of 1958 the price continued to rise despite the selling of the special voluntary contributions stock, believed to have been about 5000 tons, and about February 1959 it exceeded £780, so that the buffer stock proper could begin to sell its 23,500 tons. The crisis of excess supplies was over.

During the year 1959 the price held remarkably steady around £780 to £790, export restrictions were gradually eased, the buffer stock was reduced to about 10,000 tons, and as the U.S.S.R. undertook to limit total exports well below the 1957 figure, the import restrictions were consequently removed. In short, the Council was handling the reins of control firmly and successfully. During 1960 much the same conditions prevailed and all export restrictions finally ended in September. World production showed a considerable increase, and so did consumption, which for the third year running exceeded production. The buffer stock was out of the market, and still holding 10,000 tons of tin as well as large cash reserves; the whole situation appeared to be quite satisfactory. But this was only the calm before the next storm. By March 1961 the price was rising rapidly, and the buffer stock was selling hard. On 20 June the price reached the ceiling of £880, and the Council announced that the whole buffer stock was exhausted, and therefore the withdrawal of the buffer stock manager as a seller. With exports already unrestricted, the Council was powerless to stop a further rise, and all control ceased.

All this took place in the last weeks of the 1956 agreement which ended on 30 June 1961. A second international agreement had been negotiated in May–June 1960, and this entered into force provisionally on 1 July 1961, though not definitively until February 1962, for another five years. Membership was much the same, and still did not include the U.S. or the U.S.S.R. The floor and ceiling prices, viz. £730 and £880, were originally left unchanged, but in January 1962 the Council raised them to £790 and £965, with the middle sector, in which the manager may not operate, £850 to £910; and they were raised again in December 1963 to £850 and £1000, in view of the great rise in market prices. The machinery for export control remains, except that it may now be imposed when the buffer stock holds 5000 tons of tin instead of 10,000 tons; but it has of course not yet been started. For though in 1962 the price sagged, and the buffer stock actually bought some 3000 tons, the rise was resumed in 1963, and the stocks were sold out by September, as the price went on its way upwards to reach in October 1964 a peak of £1655. Since 1960 world production and consumption have been virtually unchanged with consumption ahead by some 20,000 tons. With consumers' stocks run down owing to the shortage and the high price, the vital market factor has been the rates of release by the U.S. Strategic Stockpile, which amounted in March 1962 to the huge total of 349,000 tons of which 164,000 tons were surplus to requirements. After apparently abortive negotiations by the Tin Council to persuade the U.S. to co-operate within the terms of the international agreement and its new price ranges, sales from the stockpile began in August 1962, and by September 1964 totalled some 32,000 tons. This did not suffice to check the rising price. For all practical purposes the Council has not been able to exercise any control of the price since the new agreement came into operation in mid-1961, and there is therefore no need to recite events in detail for the purpose of this study of commodity control.

The International Sugar Agreements

Unlike the other three post-World War II commodity agreements, the sugar agreements have covered only part of the world trade in sugar, only that part which is termed the 'free market', i.e. free of tariff preferences and the like. Although in the 1930's there was a 'free market' in the eastern[1] as well as the western hemisphere, in the 1950's the latter only was of any importance, and here the general situation had remained basically the same. This was summarised in chapter 12, but it will be convenient to repeat it here with the statistical proportions appropriate to the 1950's. The two biggest importers are the U.S.A. and Britain, and each has its own 'sugar empire' safeguarded by means of colonial possessions, tariff preferences, etc. The U.S. sugar empire consists of the exports of Hawaii, Puerto Rico and the Philippines, together with a first lien on Cuba's exports for the balance of U.S. requirements (about 3 million tons in the mid-1950's). The British sugar empire covers the exports of colonies and the Commonwealth, but after supplying Canada there is still a substantial deficit (say 600,000 tons) which must be filled from foreign sources. The biggest of such sources were the balance of the Cuban crop which the U.S.A. did not require, and the Dominican Republic, but there were several other exporters such as Brazil and Peru, Taiwan and Indonesia which enjoyed no adequate tariff preferences. It is these exporters who supply the 'free market', and the buyers are Britain, Japan and many of the countries of western Europe. World trade in sugar in the mid-1950's amounted to 12–13 million tons, but the U.S. accounted for over 30% and the British Commonwealth over 20%, leaving only about 45%, or less than 6 million tons, as the free market. Thus the free market supplies only residual needs after the requirements of the two largest importers have been mainly met. It may be observed straightaway that a residual

---

[1] Java was the principal exporter, but her biggest market was much reduced during the 1930's by the increased domestic production of India, and the Japanese invasions during World War II finally extinguished this Dutch-run exporting industry.

market of this character is liable to extreme price fluctuations if supply and/or demand vary appreciably from the expected. Price stabilisation in such a market is *a priori* likely to be an extremely difficult problem.

World sugar production was recovering its pre-war level, and indeed surpassing it, when the Korean War sent the price up to 8 cents a lb. Naturally production was further stimulated, and though physical consumption was increasing year by year, supply ran ahead of demand. By 1953 the price was down to around 3 cents. This led to the negotiation of an International Sugar Agreement, to operate from 1 January 1954 for five years, between all the more important exporters to the free market, except Brazil and Peru, and the principal importing countries. Its objectives were on the usual lines—adequate supplies at 'equitable and stable prices', providing better living conditions in consuming countries, and adequate returns and fair wages in exporting countries, etc. These prices were to be held within a given range by export quota controls. The range was to be between a minimum of 3·25 cents and a maximum of 4·35 cents for the spot price on the New York Sugar Exchange. If the price fell below the minimum for fifteen consecutive days, the Sugar Council, the administrative body, was to reduce the export quotas, but if the amount of the reduction could not be agreed within ten days, quotas were to be automatically reduced by 5%. The opposite procedure was to be followed if the price rose above the maximum, the automatic increase in this case being 7½%. The Council, however, was not permitted to reduce export quotas below 80%, or in the case of very small exporters 90%. The exporting countries also undertook so to regulate production in their countries as to limit carry-over stocks to 20% of their basic tonnages, but to hold minimum stocks of 10%. The Council had limited powers to vary these percentages. On the Council, exporters and importers had equal voting power, and decisions were ordinarily made by a majority of each side. On the importers' side, the U.S.A. and Britain had 245 votes each, Japan 100, Canada 80, West Germany 60, and the rest much smaller voting power. On the exporters' side, Cuba had 245 votes, the U.S.S.R. 100, Dominican Republic 65, Formosa (i.e. Taiwan) 65, Brazil 50, etc. Altogether the agreement, with its 22 articles each with a number of clauses, was a considerable triumph of international negotiation, and it deserved a better fate than has befallen it.

Until November 1956 things went quite well, with prices maintained mostly a little above the minimum with the help of temporary reductions in export quotas. Then the Suez crisis sent prices soaring to 6 cents, and they remained well above the maximum until the end of 1957 despite the removal of all restrictions. During 1957 the price averaged over 5 cents, but in 1958 the situation rapidly changed, for there was a big increase in the world's sugar production. Although consumption continued to increase, there was a sharp rise in stocks both in exporting and importing countries, and the price averaged only 3·5 cents. In the autumn of this year, 1958, a renewal of the international agreement was accomplished, without substantial changes except that Brazil and Peru became members (so that the agreement now covered about 95% of the free market's supplies), and that the basic quotas were fixed for three years only. In 1959 world production again showed a big increase, despite the fact that Cuba's crop, for the first time for several years, dropped below 5 million tons owing to the civil war. The usual increase in world consumption appears to have faltered so that stocks rose considerably. Despite the reduction of export quotas to the permissible limits, the price just failed to average 3 cents (agreement minimum 3·25 cents). This seemed a difficult enough situation, but worse was to come as sugar became a political weapon in the cold war. Early in 1960 the U.S.A. reduced Cuba's preferential import quota by 700,000 tons, which was about 25% of Cuba's basic quota under the international agreement. So far as Cuba was concerned, the U.S.S.R. replaced this lost U.S. market by greatly increasing its purchases. Nor were the free market and the working of the international agreement greatly affected, for the larger amounts purchased by the U.S. from other exporters to make good the reduction in supplies from Cuba were not counted as part of their export quotas, since all sales to the U.S. were outside the terms of the agreement. Nevertheless, the whole sugar situation was disturbed and uncertain when, towards the end of the year, the U.S.A. prohibited all imports from Cuba. The U.S.A. made good its deficiency by increasing domestic beet-sugar production and by larger purchases from Peru and other exporters to the free market, and Cuba largely disposed of its supplies to the U.S.S.R. and China. The price had risen in mid-1960 to around the agreement minimum, but fell again in the autumn, and continued to fall, except for a brief rise in April–May, throughout 1961 until it was slightly below 2 cents at the end of the year. Though export quotas were at the permissible minimum, stocks were very large, and the

1960–1 production was some 5 million tons above the previous season, with an especially good crop in western Europe.

Such was the general situation when, in the autumn of 1961, a conference at Geneva had to fix export quotas for 1962, as the 1959 agreement had only done so for three years. Cuba demanded that the 4·9 million tons of her contracts with the Communist countries should be added to her existing basic quota of 2·4 million tons. The other countries pointed out that this total quota of 7·3 million tons by itself exceeded the combined quotas of all the other exporting members, and maintained that it was anyway far more than Cuba could export. The conference ended in complete deadlock, and so regulation of the free market ended on 31 December 1961. The Sugar Council continues to meet, and to publish reviews of the current situation and prospects; but the 'free' market has been free of any control, and has once again shown how volatile its price can be, for during 1962 it rose rapidly from 2 cents to 4·5 cents, and in 1963 to nearly 12 cents, only to fall again in 1964 below 4 cents. Any stabilisation of the free market price of sugar is, as has been said, a specially difficult problem. The international agreement was soundly conceived so far as it went, and little fault can be found with its administration; but no commodity control scheme can withstand the kind of political upheavals and direct interventions in international trade which sugar experienced in 1959–61. Nevertheless, with consumption rising steadily and faster than with many commodities, the fact remains that the fundamental trouble was excessive production, and export quota regulation alone was bound to be an inadequate remedy. A really effective sugar agreement must provide a more thorough-going mechanism of control, but the prospects for its negotiation are not encouraging.

The International Coffee Agreement 1962

The origins of this agreement go back a very long way. At the end of chapter 11, an account was given of the Brazilian coffee valorisation scheme of the inter-war period, with its prolonged liquidation which was not finally achieved until 1943. World War II, with the disappearance of the European market, and with restrictions on exports to the U.S.A. as the result of the shipping shortage, saw a continuation of the excess supply conditions of the 1930's, though alleviated by the agreement for the sharing of the American market by the fourteen Latin-American exporters. Throughout the war the U.S. government fixed a maximum price of 13.4 cents a lb, which became less attractive to producing countries as the years went on and their general price levels rose. The Brazilian crop, which had averaged 24·5 million bags in the five years ending 1933–4, fell more or less steadily until for the five years ending 1945–6 it only averaged 14·4 million bags. Colombia's crop, however, increased slowly but steadily, and production in the other 'mild' countries was at least maintained, while Africa's production trebled. The net result for the world's production as a whole was a reduction of not more than 7–8 million bags. Nevertheless, demand increased so rapidly and greatly when the war ended that it was soon in excess of world exportable supplies, and all remaining stocks in Brazil had been sold by 1949. Price control in the U.S.A. ended in 1946, and by 1949 the price of Santos 4 had risen to nearly 33 cents a lb. The market then woke up to the fact that for the first time for twenty-five years there was a shortage of coffee, and sent the price rocketing up to over 50 cents. For the next three years supplies proved just enough at that price level, as Brazilian and world production were now expanding again, and demand was checked by a price twice as high as ever previously known. Then in the autumn of 1953 reports of frost damage in Brazil started a market scramble. The price of Santos 4 rose to over 90 cents, and averaged 88 cents for July 1954. That was the peak, and by the end of the year it was down to 70 cents. The frost damage proved to have been much exaggerated; Brazil's 1955–6 crop was forecast as appreciably larger; and more important still U.S. imports in 1954 declined by 4 million bags to only 17·4 million bags. During 1955 the price went on falling to around 57 cents, which level was roughly maintained during 1956 and 1957.

As a result of the rise in price to 50 cents in 1950, new planting had been started in Parana[1] on a considerable scale. With the 1954 boom it reached enormous proportions. New planting was also stimulated on a large scale in Africa, and on a smaller scale in the Central American countries. World production, and particularly Brazil's production, was bound to increase with a jump in four or five years when the new trees would begin bearing, and would continue to increase at an accelerating pace as the new trees approached full bearing capacity. In 1957 Brazil produced an exportable crop of 21 million bags, and the next crop promised to be even bigger, while in 1958 exports were to be only 13 million bags, and the average price was to fall below 50 cents. This in brief was the situation facing Brazil when in October

[1] The state to the south of São Paulo state.

1957 earlier negotiations between the more important Latin-American producing countries were brought to a head by the signing of an export quota agreement for the 1957–8 season at a conference at Mexico City, though in fact Brazil and Colombia shouldered most of the burden of retaining excess supplies. In 1958 this Mexico City agreement was expanded into a Latin-American Coffee Agreement covering fifteen countries, and in 1959 France and Portugal became members on behalf of their African producing territories, and Britain and Belgium promised that their African colonies would restrict exports in accordance with the agreement. In 1960 Britain joined as a full member, and the renewed agreement thus formally covered about 90% of world exportable production. In 1961 the agreement was again renewed, and negotiations began for a new five-year agreement to start in 1962.

Despite these agreements, however, the situation continued to deteriorate, and went from bad to worse. In 1959 the price averaged only 37 cents as compared with over 48 cents in 1958; it was nearly held there during 1960 and 1961, but it sagged to 34 cents in 1962. This, however, was only achieved by the retention of vast stocks in Brazil and substantial stocks in Colombia. Brazil's exportable production in 1958–9 was 26 million bags, 5 million more than in the previous year, but as exports increased by nearly the same amount, only another 8 million bags were added to her retained stocks. Then in 1959–60 the exportable crop amounted to no less than 37 million bags, and with somewhat reduced exports no less than 20 million bags were added to the existing stocks of roughly 16 million bags. In 1960–1, after the strain of the previous bumper crop, the trees were only able to produce 22 million bags, but that was 5 million more than exports; and in 1961–2, 29 million bags were available as against exports of 16·4 million bags. Thus by mid-1962 Brazil had retained some 54 million bags, or more than a year's total world exports of all coffees. Colombia's exportable production increased very little over this period, but by 1962 some 5 million bags had been retained. Africa's production largely increased, but it is doubtful whether surplus stocks there amounted to as much as 2 million bags. Altogether world exportable production in 1962 was some 60 million bags as against world exports of 44 million bags, and there were accumulated stocks amounting to around 60 million bags, of which some 54 were in Brazil, and some 5 million in Colombia.

Such were the broad outlines of the situation when the United

Nations Coffee Conference met in New York in July 1962: 36 exporting countries, 22 importing countries and the representatives of thirteen others. But to the above outlines of the statistical background must be added the vital declarations of the U.S. government, at the Punta del Este meeting of the Inter-American Economic and Social Council of the Organisation of American States in August 1961, that the U.S.A. was willing to join a long-term international coffee agreement, and that the stabilisation of the current price level of coffee was in the U.S. view a desirable objective. These declarations, particularly the latter, opened up possibilities for an agreement of a kind which would suit the views of at least the Latin-American producers much better than their best hopes hitherto. Mention should perhaps already have been made of the creation of an International Coffee Study Group on the usual lines in 1958. Early in 1960 the group decided to initiate a comprehensive survey of the world's coffee industry, together with an outline of a long-term international agreement. Most of the survey—several small books—and the outline agreement were presented at the study group's meeting in Washington in September 1961; but the outline agreement was quietly ignored, mainly because one of its basic principles was a gradual reduction of the price level, a principle which had for all practical purposes been negatived by the U.S. declaration in favour of the maintenance of the price.[1] Instead, a small committee was appointed to design an export and import control scheme which would secure this objective, and after approval by the study group this formed the basis for negotiating the new agreement at the New York Conference.

The main aim of the 1962 agreement, with its lifetime of five years, is to ensure that 'the general level of coffee prices does not decline below the general level of such prices in 1962'. It seeks this objective by establishing a very strong mechanism for regulating the members' exports, and effectively limiting the exports of non-members, in the operation of which the importing countries were to play an important part by requiring certificates of origin, and in other ways. It thus virtually assures the world's coffee farmers of remuneration at least on roughly the 1962 scale, and assures the exporting countries of at

[1] Another principle was the internationalisation of surplus stocks, which was of course wholly unacceptable to Brazil, nor was there much enthusiasm for a proposed buffer stock, or for the proposals designed to give elasticity in respect of production to countries whose coffees proved to be in greatest demand. Nevertheless the principle of declining prices as the main solution for excess production was from the economic point of view absolutely sound, even if it was overridden for political reasons.

least a maintenance of their coffee export earnings, and perhaps an increase. The world's politicians may consider that these are great achievements, but the economist must draw attention to the costs and consequences. The agreement virtually prevents any adjustment of the price level of coffee downwards towards genuine costs of production; and there is no doubt that 1962 prices are far above the level which would reign if demand and supply were in equilibrium. The evidence in support of this assertion is too detailed and complicated to set out here, but at least there can be no doubt that coffee farmers in Brazil have for years been receiving only about half the export price per bag (the other half being required to defray the financial costs of the price defence policy), and that even so the farmers in Parana and the low-cost producers elsewhere have not been faring too badly. Careful investigation[1] suggests that, under what may be termed normal or average weather conditions, Brazil could profitably produce, say, 20 million bags, i.e. more than her recent exports, at an f.o.b. price of 15 cents per lb; and the price of Brazil's coffee undoubtedly determines within broad limits the general world price level. Consumers are therefore to continue to pay prices which heavily subsidise the producing countries. The agreement also virtually prevents any adjustment of sources of supply in accordance with the demand for their particular qualities of coffee, and with their relative production costs. Though chapter 11 of the agreement is headed 'Production Controls', little more than lip service is paid to this vital matter. Little or nothing is done to bring about the elimination of obsolescent high-cost capacity; and the expansion of new low-cost industries, such as the African industry in Kenya, is virtually prevented; while the spread of new techniques which in some countries, notably Colombia, would greatly increase yields must be seriously hindered. The problem of the vast accumulation of stocks is deferred for future consideration. In short, the whole structure of the industry is to be frozen, and artificial prices maintained at the expense of the consumer. The regime solidified by the agreement does not bring the coffee world any nearer to a solution of its problems. It is simply a holding operation, which in five years may with luck make that solution easier, but may easily make it more difficult.

This agreement is, however, admittedly a political move, and to a

[1] See *The World's Coffee* (H.M.S.O., 1963) by the present author, chapter 2 and also chapters 8–9, for a more detailed analysis of the coffee problem and of the 1962 International Coffee Agreement.

large extent a move in the Cold War, and must be judged as such. But the means employed by the U.S. government to bolster up the foreign exchange earnings of the underdeveloped countries of Latin America has set a most dangerous precedent, in that the price of coffee is to be maintained at an artificially high level as a form of aid, in place of direct loans or gifts. Artificially high prices cut right across the basic economic principle that prices should be related to cost of production because, if they are not, resources are being wasted somewhere. This is the economist's real objection to prices artificially maintained well above the costs of production of the supply consumers require, not merely that the consumer is paying more than he should. The politician may argue that the waste of resources which will be engendered or maintained by this coffee agreement is small relatively to the world's wealth, but if this sort of agreement is copied for a wide range of commodities, as politicians in many underdeveloped countries would certainly like it to be, the total will soon be appreciable. In any case even a small waste of human and natural resources is wrong. Further consideration will be given to this matter in the last chapter of this book. Here attention is drawn to it simply as one aspect, and a most unfortunate one, of the international coffee agreement, along with other features which, as noted in the preceding paragraph, are fundamentally objectionable and unsound from the economic point of view, whatever may be the political merits of the agreement as a whole.

The agreement virtually came into force almost at once, though it was not finally ratified until the spring of 1964, owing to delay on the part of the U.S.A. The New York Conference had hardly ended when the price of robustas began to rise sharply, as the result of a rapidly increasing demand and unfavourable weather in several African producing countries, coupled with the effect of the export quotas under the agreement, though these nominally involved only 1 % restriction. In the spring of 1963 the rise appeared for a time to be halted, but it was resumed at an accelerating rate. By October 1963 there was very little difference at around 34 cents between the prices of robustas and Santos 4—a quite unprecedented state of affairs. The prices of Brazils, however, then began to rise steeply as the result of frost damage in Parana, and drought all over the coffee regions, which together were reckoned to reduce the 1964–5 crop to 10 million bags or less. In March 1964 the price of Brazils was around 49 cents, and of robustas 41 cents, despite an increase of about 3 % in export quotas in the previous month, and special concessions to African robusta producers who had accumulated stocks as the result of their export quotas. It might have been supposed that with 50 million bags in store in Brazil, the crop failure would not have advanced the Brazilian price to such a high level; but merchants and roasters were uncertain whether the quality of the stocks would prove satisfactory, and there was a panic rush to secure the limited new crop supplies, while all consuming interests wanted to replenish stocks which had been reduced to a minimum while prices looked like falling rather than rising. Robusta prices rose to their peak because available supplies were small relative to a continued insistent demand, and also in natural sympathy with the rise in Brazils. Mild prices, however, did not rise much, and the normal differential was greatly reduced. From March 1964 onwards there was a considerable decline, especially in robusta prices, but in October Brazils were still around 46 cents and robustas 31 cents.

The second year of the agreement has, as might be supposed, produced considerable strains within the Coffee Council; robusta producers clamouring for increased quotas, while Brazil, and especially Colombia, have favoured the maintenance of the highest possible prices; and consumers have been pressing for increased supplies and lower prices generally. The boom has been only a temporary affair. The drought in Brazil may have weakened the bearing capacity of the trees, especially the older ones, and the frost maimed a considerable proportion of those in Parana. But the coffee tree is tough. Not many trees in Parana have been maimed beyond recovery, and not many of the older trees elsewhere have been abandoned. Already there are estimates of a 1965 crop of 20–25 million bags. It seems clear that Brazil will be producing very large crops again in due course, unless natural hazards play an even more unusual part than in 1963. The problem of excess capacity remains, together with all the resulting problems of prices divorced from costs of production, and of inadequate foreign exchange earnings if prices are adjusted. These problems constitute the world's coffee problem, and they remain unsolved. They cannot be solved unless the international agreement is fundamentally altered, and buttressed by economically sounder forms of aid to the producing countries than artificially high prices.

14. THE MECHANICS OF COMMODITY CONTROL

The Principle of Equal Representation of Producers and Consumers

The outstanding innovation of the United Nations system for commodity control schemes was the equal representation of consumers and producers. This principle is relied upon to secure adjustments of prices and incomes to keep them in conformity with long-period trends of demand and supply. It is also expected to prevent or stop any exploitation of temporary advantages to either side or any action by one against the other's interests. In theory such reliance is broadly justifiable, provided that equally satisfactory representation of the two sides is secured, and that both sides genuinely desire to establish the sort of price stabilisation at the long-period level which should be the general aim and object of commodity control. But how far can such equally satisfactory representation be secured in practice, and how far will the views of the two sides on stabilisation measures in general, and price stabilisation in particular, be wholeheartedly similar? These are questions which deserve careful consideration.

On a commodity council quite a number of different parties should be represented: the actual producers, i.e. the producing industry in each country, secondly the producers' governments, thirdly processors and manufacturers, fourthly the actual final consumers, fifthly the governments of consuming countries, and last but not least the merchants and middlemen, whose interests do not necessarily coincide with those of either the producing or the consuming sides. It is worth while considering the representation and attitude of all these parties in turn, for only so can the answers to the above questions be constructed. Starting with the actual producers, it may be affirmed that in general both large-scale and small-scale producers want to see prices stabilised at a remunerative level, by which they mean a level which will give them returns, either in terms of profits or standard of living, commensurate with their best reasonable expectations. This means of course such a level for the higher-cost producers, and therefore they will always tend to take the lead in pressing for restrictive measures to secure the stabilisation of the price at a level remunerative to them. For the lower-cost producers, this will almost certainly mean profits above their best reasonable expectations even though they have to restrict the output of their existing capacity; and for a time they may be content because of the lure of these high profits, and because they hope that before long the need for restriction may disappear with the normal growth of demand. But if this does not happen, or if in time they come to think that further expansion of capacity would lower their costs—when, in short, they come to the conclusion that it will be still more to their advantage to force some of the higher-cost producers out of business—then they will no longer favour price stabilisation, for they now want price warfare. Nevertheless, though the interests of the low-cost producers thus tend to check the high-price policy of the higher-cost producers, this is a check which may only become powerful, let alone decisive, after a considerable lapse of time. Moreover, the views of the lower-cost producers are only likely to have the backing of their governments if their case appears convincingly strong in the national interest, for all governments are notoriously inclined to leave well alone, and not risk much for something still better in the future, even the near future. The governments of the producing countries usually have many reasons for backing a control scheme which their industries favour, for example, maintenance or improvement of their foreign-exchange earnings, or of their internal budgetary situation. Once committed they will tend to continue their support as long as the scheme seems to be working reasonably well from the national point of view; and therefore they will take the same policy as the higher-cost producers, and if necessary will coerce the lower-cost producers to continue to support the scheme. It is of course for all these reasons that consuming interests should also be parties to a commodity control agreement. It should, however, be appreciated that all the producers or national producing industries may not be unanimous in their views and policies. Even if they are reasonably close together at the start of the control scheme, they are unlikely to remain so over long periods of time.

There is seldom much difficulty today in securing adequate representation of the producers, for even a national industry of small peasant proprietors is fairly certain to be reasonably well organised, and anyway their government will be well aware of their viewpoint. This, however, is most unlikely to be true of the final consumers at the other end of the chain. They are unlikely to be directly represented on a commodity council unless through such limited organisations as consumers' co-operative societies. In fact the final consumers will be represented by manufacturers, merchants and distributors, or by ministers or civil servants who will also be representing their government's point of view. Now manufacturers and distributors, amongst whom must really be reckoned any consumers' co-operative society representatives, want first and foremost the certainty that the price of the commodity will be the same for all their competitors at home or abroad. Secondly, but only secondly, they want price stability. They are only strongly interested in the lowest possible stabilised level of price if the final demand for what they are selling is considerably elastic, and if the primary product forms an appreciable proportion of their total costs. These conditions do not hold good for many raw materials, though they do for some, for example, cotton, wool, and natural rubber. They do not hold good for many staple foodstuffs, since usually the demand is inelastic, at least during short periods. Hence manufacturers and distributors are likely to provide only limited representation of the interests of the final consumers. Ministers and civil servants representing consuming countries will of course realise that the interests of the final consumers must be part of their brief, and therefore that the price must not be stabilised at an unnecessarily high level; they will, indeed, press hard for a lower price under certain circumstances, for example, if their country is short of foreign exchange. It must, however, be observed that most civil servants and their ministers in such a role will be satisfied if they can show that they have obtained some concessions from the producing interests; and further, and a more serious drawback, they are likely to be much influenced by international political considerations, which may well restrain them from insisting on the sort of price level which is in the proper interest of their final consumers, but which seems to be a hard bargain with producers' governments and as such undesirable on political grounds. Thus the representatives of consuming interests may very well not be the ardent advocates of the final consumers which they really need to be in order to balance the leanings of the producing interests towards a high price level. Moreover, they will in particular tend to be strongly averse to breaking up a control scheme which has once come into existence, perhaps as the result of difficult and prolonged negotiations.

Lastly a brief comment may be made on the attitude of merchants. Their representation involves no difficulty as both in exporting and importing countries they will today be effectively organised. In so far as they are speculators, as up to a point they must be, it is often said that they like to see the largest possible fluctuations in the prices of commodities, since that provides them with the greatest opportunity for large profits. But it is also true that large price fluctuations provide the greatest opportunity for staggering losses if they make mistakes. Certainly very many merchants came to regard the magnitude of the risks involved in the price fluctuations of the inter-war period as a deterrent rather than a stimulus. Today merchants are not wholly averse to all measures of price stabilisation, but they are averse to arbitrary intervention to control the price, for that makes their business just a gamble on what the controllers are going to do. If the control is open and within limits automatic, merchants will be prepared to play their part in the making of market prices and the carrying of stocks. If it is not, they will either reduce this part of their activities to the smallest possible extent, and tend to become simply distributors of the product, or they will do their best to bring the control scheme to an end by wrecking tactics. The merchants' point of view coincides neither with the producing nor the consuming interests, but their reactions may well be very important in the practical operation of any control scheme.

These observations on the representation and attitude of the parties interested in a commodity control scheme are not purely theoretical, and most could be substantiated by reference to history. To quote chapter and verse for each would overburden this brief study. They seem to suggest the following broad conclusions. Control schemes operated by producers' interests alone will almost inevitably tend to try and stabilise the price at a level above the long-term equilibrium level, and to keep it there even if that equilibrium level falls. The great check on such controls is the interests of the lower-cost producers; but while the controls last, and that may be several years, they can do much damage to consuming interests, both directly as regards price, and by holding back the expansion of the more efficient sources of production. Most of the inter-war-period controls were run by producers' interests alone, and it was the experience of that period which led to the modern post-war creed that consuming interests must be adequately represented in future control schemes, and that this will be a sufficient economic safeguard. But the truth is that the real interests of the final consumer cannot in practice be fully and properly represented. Moreover, an inter-governmental joint producer-consumer control is very prone to suffer from what can best be described shortly as sheer inertia. Therefore too much reliance ought not to be placed on the principle of 'representation of consuming interests' as a guarantee of the sound economic operation of a control scheme, if only because it is simply not possible to secure it fully and properly. Certainly such consumer representation as can be arranged will be better than none. The price will probably not be stabilised so high as it would be by producers acting alone. There is, however, a probability that it will still err on the high side, and that technical progress by the expansion of low-cost capacity at the maximum rate will be seriously hindered in the alleged interests of stability, simply because adequate representation of the consumers' interests is not practicable. In short, the principle of consumers' representation is an improvement, but it is by no means a panacea.

It is easy to understand why importing countries desired representation on commodity control schemes, but it is not so obvious why producers and producing countries accepted consumer representation with its limitations on the freedom of action which they had in almost all the pre-war schemes. Some brief observations on this matter may therefore be added here. In the first place, some of the pre-war schemes aroused such opposition from consuming countries as to jeopardise the successful operation of control by the producers. This was something to be avoided in the future and, even if it involved some compromise of producers' desires, the price was worth it. Secondly, inter-governmental agreements under the aegis of the United Nations were obviously far more solid, and could be made more comprehensive, than agreements between producing countries on the pre-war pattern. Equally obviously, the former could not be secured in the atmosphere of the immediate post-war world without conceding the principle of partnership with consuming countries. Thirdly, if consuming countries were parties to a control agreement, they might be expected in their own interests to take a hand in enforcing the terms of the agreement on any defaulting members, and even if necessary on non-members: in other words, they could undertake policing measures which were beyond the reach of producing countries. Lastly, the freedom of producing countries to take unilateral action in an emergency was preserved by the inclusion of the escape clause[1] from the draft Havana charter. These are some of the reasons why producing countries reckoned that consumer representation was an acceptable proposition, and indeed an improvement which was well worth any minor drawbacks.

[1] See page 160.

Stockholding versus Restriction of Supplies as remedies for 'Burdensome Surpluses'

Having thus considered the most important new feature of post-war commodity schemes, attention must now be given to methods of control, about which the draft Havana charter had as little to say as it had much about consumer representation. Broadly, there are only two possible methods—some sort of stockholding scheme, and some sort of quantitative regulation of supplies—and their respective functions, and merits and demerits in various situations, are obviously matters of vital importance. The Havana charter envisaged two situations as justifying resort to a commodity control scheme: (*a*) where an actual or potential 'burdensome surplus' is causing, or threatens to cause, hardship to small producers, or (*b*) where widespread unemployment, or underemployment, has developed, or is expected to develop. The two situations are of course really the same, the difference envisaged being between industries which have a substantial number of small producers, and those which are largely capitalistic enterprises employing substantial numbers of wage-earners, for whom unemployment spells the 'hardship' of the small producer. Nothing was said in the charter about the causes of such situations, but since it is obvious that they may be very different, economic analysis must clearly differentiate between them. A 'burdensome surplus' can conceivably arise as the result of a sudden large increase in productive capacity; but this is much more likely to take place only gradually, and it is then essentially a problem of the long period and will be discussed with other such problems in due course. The most common causes of such a surplus are two: (*a*) a contraction of demand, or a failure of demand to expand as much or as rapidly as had been expected and (*b*), in the case of agricultural crops, a sudden increase in the productivity of the existing capacity, i.e. a bumper crop. These are entirely different situations, even if the result in both cases is a surplus; and they merit separate consideration.

Where the surplus has arisen from a failure on the demand side, remedial action may have to be swift if the price is not to fall to an extent which will cause hardship, and if it has already so fallen it must be quickly raised. But in very many primary industries quantitative control over the rate of current output cannot operate with sufficient speed or, if it can, it will create further hardship or unemployment. With annual crops the producers can do little or nothing to reduce their crops within the current crop year; and only if the product concerned is normally grown along with other closely alternative products, as in certain kinds of mixed farming, is any appreciable change-over from one crop to another practicable within two or usually more years, unless governments provide subsidies for land left fallow, and even that may result in unemployment of wage-earners. With other primary products, for example, natural rubber, sisal, and most minerals, it is possible to reduce the rate of production within a few months, but any considerable reduction will result in unemployment or under-employment. Thus, though there may be some partial exceptions, the mechanism for the control of prices in the early stages of the emergency should clearly be some sort of stock-holding; and since in most primary industries the producers will be unable or unwilling to hold back current supplies from the market for any but very short periods without special financing, it must be a collectively organised scheme.

When demand contracts, it is usually impossible to forecast how far it will fall, or when it will recover. It is indeed often impossible to diagnose whether it is a mere temporary fluctuation, or whether it is the beginning of a secular downward trend. Similarly, if the trouble is a failure of the demand to expand as expected, no one can be sure how long it will be before demand catches up with supply. In either case, if the period of excess supply is at all lengthy, the volume of stocks which must be accumulated to prevent a drastic fall in the price may easily become too large to be desirable, or too costly to finance. As the period of excess supply lengthens, control of the price must depend on whether a stockholding scheme can by itself bring about a reduction in current output, and still maintain the price at a reasonable level. Suppose the price has fallen to what is considered the lowest reasonable level, and the control is having to buy heavily in order to hold it there, so that the strain on its resources requires easing by a contraction of current output. It is an elementary proposition of economic theory that no such con-traction can be expected unless and until the price falls below the prime costs of the highest-cost producers, and even then in practice the process may be slow. Now with many, if not most, commodities, prime costs are only a small fraction of total costs, and with some, even in today's conditions, prime costs must not be considered as fixed absolutely even in the short period, but as capable of considerable reduction at the will of the producers if the need arises. The very notion of prime costs in the case of peasant producers is an extremely nebulous conception. In most primary industries the price will usually have to fall a great deal before current output is reduced, hardship will ensue, and the objectives of reasonable price stability and reasonable stability of producers' incomes will be completely lost. Under such circumstances the only remedy is some form of quantitative control. Stockholding schemes by themselves are incapable of reducing current output if reasonable price stability is to be maintained, and therefore unless there is no limit to the size of the stocks and to the requisite finance, they must be buttressed by some measure of quantitative control. Even if the requisite finance is forthcoming, there is of course very great danger in piling up stocks on a scale which may necessitate holding them for several years. The financial, and often the physical, costs of holding large stocks are usually heavy, their liquidation may involve serious financial loss and prolonged dislocation of the market, and in the end they may be redundant, especially if the failure of demand proves to be a secular decline. Meanwhile the control must try and prevent any expansion of low-cost capacity or technical improvements in production, undesirable as this is on general economic grounds. For a very short period, and on a moderate scale, stockholding is a sound because speedy, flexible and relatively painless remedy; but it is of limited application, and must be supplemented by quantitative control of production. Since such quantitative control measures take time to organise, a control scheme will do well to have the necessary mechanism ready, so that it can be put into operation in good time to afford adequate relief to stockholding should that be subject to undue strain. Even if quantitative control proves not to be required, provision for it is likely to increase the effectiveness of the stockholding, because it gives a greater certainty that control will be effectively maintained whatever happens. The two are emphatically not alternative but complementary mechanisms.

This is a conclusion of great importance, for even today there are advocates of one method of control against the other. Quantitative control is not as flexible as control by stockholding, nor as painless to producers, but just as there are close limits to the piling up of stocks, so the very power and efficiency of quantitative control as a remedy for excessive current output mean that its application must not be prolonged. It is often argued that the great drawback to quantitative control is that producers outside the control scheme are stimulated to increase their output, and so restriction of output has to be successively tightened and becomes semi-permanent. This argument can certainly be supported by reference to the history of several control schemes in the past, but today commodity control schemes are most unlikely to be established unless almost all existing producers are included. It therefore usually takes a much longer time for 'outside' capacity to be developed on an appreciable scale, and so to become a cause of undue prolongation of quantitative control. Much more serious today is the freezing of the existing pattern of production. This may take considerable time to show its ill effects in stifling technical progress; but it is a direct cause of the prolongation of quantitative control when the productive capacity of the industry is in excess of the normal demand and the excess is high-cost obsolescent capacity—a common condition when supply has become excessive. When there is such excess capacity, it must be eliminated if equilibrium is to be restored as demand recovers to normal. But both stockholding and quantitative restriction of production hinder this process; and therefore the condition of actual or potential excess of supplies continues indefinitely, and it seems impossible to bring restriction of supplies to an end. Stockholding, by keeping up the price, relieves the pressure on all producers. Quantitative control clearly operates to preserve all existing capacity, for its whole purpose is to effect a reduction of current output, without the need for acute competitive warfare, by allowing all existing producers a share of the available demand, and so to preserve existing capacity, not to destroy it. A restriction-of-output scheme will doubtless increase the pressure on the highest-cost producers by increasing the costs per unit of the output which is allowed; but their elimination by this means is likely to be very tardy and insufficient when much greater pressure in the form of extremely low prices is usually slow to take effect, as history has repeatedly shown. In practice it is only too likely that the price will be raised by further restriction to compensate for the rise in costs due to the restriction. Thus in these circumstances restriction tends to become semi-permanent and indeed to be applied more and more heavily.

Any solution of this problem is extremely difficult. The consuming interests on commodity councils, if they are fully informed of the situation, can argue that the price should be allowed to fall to the lowest reasonable level, and that restriction of output should be eased accordingly. They may hope to be joined in advocating this policy by the lower-cost producers and their governments, but for the reasons given above[1] this hope may not be fulfilled. Even if such a policy were adopted by the control, the pressure on the highest-cost producers may not be sufficient to bring about the elimination of the surplus capacity with any reasonable speed. The only alternative to terminating the control scheme and allowing competitive warfare to run its course is to include in the control agreement specific arrangements for the gradual elimination of the excess capacity. This comes very close to direct international economic planning, and bristles with so many difficulties that the control scheme will certainly be extremely hard to negotiate. Provision may be made in control agreements for periodical revision of quotas in favour of the more efficient producers, but at best lip service will in practice be secured. In the course of time, international collaboration may so improve as to render planned elimination of surplus capacity more feasible, but until that happens the wisest practical course is to end the control scheme and allow competition to eliminate the surplus capacity; and for consuming countries to help by some form of direct aid those producing countries for whom this process means real hardship and serious economic difficulties in adjusting their national economies.

Price Stabilisation by Buffer Stocks and Quantitative Control

So far this discussion has had as its background the conditions of 'burdensome surplus' and hardship which justify resort to commodity control schemes under the United Nations procedure. But in this doctrine the idea of prevention is as important as that of remedy; and the conditions laid down really define a class of industries which are suitable for, as well as in need of, price stabilisation by concerted measures, rather than the exact circumstances in which control schemes are justified. Price stabilisation has been the ultimate objective of all the post-war control schemes, not merely the remedying of desperate situations. The objective has been prevention in the future as well as cure of the present. Thus stockholding schemes as a remedy for temporarily surplus supplies can become a mechanism not merely to prevent prices falling too fast or too far, but to stabilise them at the normal long-period level. The stocks will not all be liquidated when prices have recovered to that level, but at least a part

---

[1] See page 185.

will be held, or new stocks accumulated, against the possibility that the price will rise appreciably above that level as the result of a temporary increase of the demand in the future. Stocks purchased as a remedy for excess supplies thus become a buffer stock—a two-way mechanism of price control, which quantitative control of output cannot of course become, for, once unrestricted production has been resumed, that mechanism ceases to function. It has been argued above that stockholding should have the backing of at least potential quantitative control if it is to remedy surplus supplies. Can a buffer stock by itself remedy a shortage of supplies? Usually a small rise in the price, such as will be consonant with general price stabilisation, will ensure the absolute maximum output from the existing capacity, for the extra costs of working overtime, increasing the labour force, and other such devices, are not usually relatively large. The function of the buffer stock is to prevent the further, often steep, rise in price which will take place under *laissez-faire*, seeing that even *laissez-faire* cannot increase supplies in the short period beyond the absolute maximum of the existing capacity. This the buffer stock can do, provided that it holds sufficient physical stocks of the commodity and not merely money. The size of the stock to be held against a rise in price is as crucial a problem as the financial resources which should be held to meet a fall. Ideally, when the price is stabilised, the buffer stock should be holding adequate stocks against a price rise, and adequate money to buy on a sufficient scale if the price falls, for no one can be sure which way the price will move next. This is of course likely to be quite expensive; yet too small stocks, or too little money, will jeopardise the maintenance of price stability. Moreover, to attain the necessary speed and flexibility of operations, the management of a buffer stock must be in the hands of one man—a committee could only lay down broad policies from time to time—and the manager will require extraordinary, one might almost say superhuman, skill if he is never to make mistakes, if he is always to time his purchases and sales so as to produce maximum effects, if he is eventually to bring his accounts out on the right side, and so on. His integrity must of course be above suspicion, and the same must apply to the members of any supervising committee—a condition which it is not always easy to fulfil. Buffer stock control seems in theory a relatively straightforward and simple device. In practice it is technically very difficult and complicated, and requires far more experience to operate effectively than is so far available. Nevertheless, when backed by quantitative control of production, it is the best mechanism so far devised to stabilise prices when supplies become excessive owing to a temporary contraction of demand. Under these conditions it should be reasonably effective. When supplies run short owing to a temporary increase of demand, its efficiency will be limited by its available stocks of the commodity, but given a reasonable stock it should be able to smooth the rise in price, even if it cannot halt it. The cost of this mechanism, however, should not be underestimated.[1]

The operation of the mechanisms of control, however, will be much affected by the kind of price stability at which the control decides to aim. If it aims to hold the price as close to a predetermined level as possible, its job is likely to be much more difficult than if it is content merely to hold the price within a given range. There are three main kinds of such price-range control schemes. There is the 'automatic' scheme in which the control's maximum and minimum prices are fixed, and within this range the market price finds its own level, as in the International Wheat Agreements. There is the arbitrary scheme in which the control is free to fix the price where it will, and to adjust production or export quotas accordingly, as in the International Coffee Agreement. And, thirdly, a compromise scheme is possible. In this the control is free to act between maximum and minimum prices, but must sell or buy a buffer stock at these prices to the limit of its resources, and adjust production to hold the market price at these limits. The International Tin Agreement will serve as an example. The great advantage of the automatic scheme is that the control operates openly and all concerned know where they are, so that merchants can continue their business in much the ordinary way. It may even be possible to maintain a certain amount of organised speculation with its facilities for hedging. The job of the control is then obviously much easier as long as its resources enable it to hold the price at the fixed limits with absolute certainty. On the other hand, the price is controlled only within a range—the bigger the range, the easier the control, but the less the stability of the price. Under the other two types of scheme, greater stability of the price may be obtainable, for the control can put up the price appreciably to choke a market scramble, or put it down to encourage buying. On the other hand, such arbitrary schemes are likely either to bring ordinary normal

[1] The quality of some commodities deteriorates in time even under the best storage conditions, e.g. coffee and sisal; and the only remedy is to turn the stocks over at regular intervals, which is an expensive addition to the ordinary costs of holding stocks.

merchanting and speculative activities to an end, because it is too
difficult to guess what the control may be going to do next; or, on the
other hand, if doubts as to the control's powers arise, large-scale
speculation may be stimulated and give rise to a situation which the
control may find it very difficult to remedy. The element of secrecy
has its advantages, but it means that the control must be very strong.
Which form is the more desirable, and will be the more successful,
obviously depends on the circumstances of each particular case: there
can be no general conclusion.

So much for the short period. Price stabilisation in the long period
must depend on the ability of the control to increase or decrease the
capacity of the industry. It has already been pointed out that quantitative control is most unlikely to bring about a decrease in capacity,[1]
nor obviously can it bring about an increase. Can either be achieved
by buffer stock control? To stimulate an increase, the control should
obviously revise its estimate of the desirable level of price upwards,
but it can only do so gradually if reasonable price stability is to be
maintained, say for example by five, or at the very most ten, per cent
at annual intervals. If such price rises are continued long enough,
and if the buffer stock can provide sufficient supplies to keep the price
under control, then obviously sooner or later an expansion of capacity
will be forthcoming. But all past history, even if under *laissez-faire*
conditions, shows that when additional capacity was needed in
primary industries, large, sometimes very large, increases in the price
had to be generated before decisions to create new capacity were
forthcoming. Decisions to increase capacity by an appreciable amount
were never forthcoming if the price only rose a little. Substantial investment, whether of capital, or of their working capacity and live-
lihood by small producers, has always waited for a boom in the price.
Judged by past history, the sort of price changes which should take
place under a control scheme whose objective is price stability will
not bring about increases of capacity with any reasonable speed. It is
true that a control scheme, in providing the prospect of more stable
prices, should reduce the risk element to producers and entrepreneurs
as compared with the past; and especially if the range of costs is large,
so that the lowest-cost producers are making handsome profits, they
may well be stimulated to expand their capacity. For this reason,
with a buffer stock scheme in operation, increases in capacity will be

[1] See page 192.

initiated rather more freely and quickly than in the past, but it is
doubtful how far this really changes the picture. A reasonable conclusion might be that in the past under competitive conditions the
initiation of new capacity was usually tardy, though often excessive
in the end because the boom prices created too great a stimulus,
while with a buffer stock control scheme, the initiation of new capacity
is likely at best to be a little less tardy and belated, but will usually be
on an insufficient scale, always lagging behind the true need. And the
converse of this is equally true, and even more definite. Elimination
of capacity is a difficult and too slow a process under *laissez-faire*, even
when prices fall extremely low, and under any control scheme it will
be even more so, unless a planned programme is included in the
scheme. The stimulation of additional capacity on an appreciable
scale is a big problem for commodity control schemes which seek
price stabilisation as, so to say, a permanent objective, and the elimination of surplus or obsolescent capacity is an even bigger problem.
The only solution in both cases involves long-range international
planning of a kind for which international co-operation is not yet
sufficiently developed, nor are the requisite techniques.

This discussion of the means and the extent to which stability of
the price may be secured by a commodity control scheme must not
obscure the problem of deciding at what absolute level, or within
what limited range, the price should be stabilised; nor the probability
that the control will set its sights higher than this, especially if it is of
a semi-permanent nature. From the strictly economic point of view,
the price to be stabilised in the short run is the equilibrium price at
which the current normal demand equals the supply from the existing
capacity working at its ordinary rate of output, and earning normal
profits for the marginal producers. In practice there is likely to be
considerable difference of opinion amongst experts as to what this
price is. Its determination is a difficult technical problem, and, as
likely as not, the necessary data for its solution, especially as to costs
of production, will be incomplete. There is likely to be a still greater
difference of opinion amongst the various producing countries, and
between producers and consumers. In the first section of this chapter,
it was argued that in all probability the price objective of the control
would be fixed on the high side. If the control genuinely desires the
establishment, or re-establishment, of equilibrium conditions in the
industry, experience of the working of control will of course lead to
the modification of the price objective. But there is a great danger in

practice that restriction of output will become semi-permanent in order to try and secure the original price objective; and indeed, as has already been pointed out, this objective may itself be raised in order to compensate producers for the increased costs of restricted output; and thus a sort of vicious circle is created. Meantime the consumer suffers. But if the determination of the price to be stabilised in the short run is difficult, and the proper price unlikely to be exactly achieved in practice, the determination of the proper price in the long run is a far more difficult technical problem, and still less likely to be achieved. In the long run the price should follow the long-period trends of demand and supply, and these may well be very difficult to determine. If they produce a steadily rising price, there will be no great difficulties in practice, though there may be a danger that the control will try and anticipate the increase. But if, as is more likely, technical progress, in the widest use of that term, should result in a declining price trend, and the control ought therefore to lower gradually its stabilised price, there will be great opposition from any high-cost producers who cannot easily modernise their methods of production. The likelihood is either that technical progress will be deliberately stifled by the control, or that the stabilised price will not be reduced, an excess of capacity will develop, and semi-permanent restriction of output will result. Thus the problem of keeping the price stabilised at the truly economic level over long periods is technically very difficult, and even if it is accurately determined, it is unlikely to be acceptable to all concerned. At best a control scheme may avoid serious economic losses. At worst it may create losses so large as in the course of time to overwhelm itself. The level at which the price is to be stabilised, whether in the short or the long run, is a crucial issue for all control schemes, and demands a high degree of enlightened wisdom on the part of producers and consumers.

Price Stabilisation and the Problem of Equalising Crop Variations

The discussion of buffer stocks and the regulation of output started from burdensome surpluses caused by a contraction of demand, or its failure to expand as rapidly as expected, but it has been considerably broadened to cover the problems of price stabilisation in general. No attention, however, has yet been paid to the other principal cause of burdensome surpluses, namely a sudden increase in the productivity of the existing capacity of agricultural crops. Broadened out to become part of the problem of price stabilisation in the short period, this becomes the problem of crop variations and their equalisation. Assuming that demand remains steady on the current trend, and that the average crop equals the demand, i.e. that capacity for production, or in other words the acreage, is in adjustment, then the surplus of a bumper crop should obviously be withheld from the market and carried over as stocks until the corresponding short crop or crops materialise. To some extent this is achieved by merchants under a *laissez-faire* regime. Merchants buy up the whole of the bumper crop at a price below normal, and then hold most of the excess over the normal crop until it is required to make good the deficiency of short crops, and so can be sold at a profit. They have of course to guess how long it will be before the short crops materialise, for this is the basis of their calculations of expected profit. If they have overestimated the interval during which the surplus must be held, they will make more than the expected profit, but if they underestimate, they may lose money. There is thus a risk element, payment for which will be settled by competition between the merchants. But equalisation of crop variations under a merchant speculator regime must necessarily involve relatively large changes in the price of the commodity. If most of the excess of a bumper crop is held until the short crop comes, the total supply offered for sale in the short-crop year may not be much below normal and, if this is the case, the price in that year will not be much above normal. Merchants will only buy the bumper crop at a price so far below the normal price as to provide the whole difference required to cover the expected financial and physical costs of stockholding, and still leave them with a profit commensurate with the risk element. In other words, if the merchants want, say, 20 per cent margin between their buying price and their expected selling price in order to induce the requisite stockholding of the excess of the bumper crop, that will mean not a 10% variation either side of the normal price, i.e. a 10% lower price for the bumper crop and 10% higher price for the short crop, but a 20% lower price for the bumper crop, because the price in the short-crop year will be no higher than the normal or equilibrium price. Actually the situation will not be so extreme as this because the big fall in the price of the bumper crop is bound to stimulate some increase in the actual physical consumption of the commodity. Supplies in the short-crop year will therefore be below, and the price somewhat above, normal. But the elasticity of the physical consumption demand for most primary commodities is usually small over short periods and modifications are not likely to be considerable. The point remains substantially that almost the whole of the margin required by a merchant speculator regime must be found by a fall in the price of the bumper crop. This will be an abrupt and large fall. From the point of view of price stabilisation it will be much worse than a smaller fall in the bumper crop price with a corresponding rise at a later date above the normal price in the short-crop year. The abrupt and large fall of the bumper crop price is also much worse from the producers' point of view. Admittedly it might not mean, probably in most cases would not mean, a large fall in producers' incomes, because for most crops the costs per unit of a bumper crop are much lower, for some very much lower, than the costs per unit of a normal crop. But when the short-crop year comes, producers' incomes will almost certainly fall severely because the price will be only a little above normal, while the costs per unit of that short crop are likely to be much higher, for some very much higher, than normal. Even with peasant production, where 'costs' are mostly family labour, the low price of the bumper crop, because it is large, may not much reduce income, but the short crop will, because its price will be only a little above normal.

Crop equalisation under a merchant speculator regime is thus not consonant with price stabilisation, and necessarily gives rise to instability of producers' incomes. If price is to be kept stabilised in the face of appreciable crop variations, the producers must take over the necessary stockholding. Since few individual farmers can afford to hold back any substantial amounts from the market, the producers must undertake the stockholding collectively, and create an organised scheme which will make it possible to obtain the necessary finance.

Historically, however, crop-equalisation schemes run by producers did not arise on account of the instability of price and of their incomes under a merchant speculator regime. Rather, they were introduced because producers came to the conclusion that in the face of large crop variations their incomes under that regime were absolutely less than they ought to be, or might be—not simply because the price and their incomes fluctuated. From the producers' point of view the trouble seemed to be that the very low price which merchants were prepared to pay for a bumper crop went far to outbalance the reduced unit costs of that bumper crop, and so robbed producers of their seeming good fortune in getting a bumper crop. When the short crop came, there was no such increase above normal in the price as would compensate them for the much higher unit costs of that short crop. As the producers saw these things, the merchant got the best of both good and bad crops, and the producers the worst of both. Thus, for example, the coffee planters of Brazil became convinced that if they cut out the merchants in the business of crop equalisation, and themselves undertook the necessary stockholding, they could obtain for themselves the profit margin which the merchants as a group must normally make, and which the planters reckoned must be very considerable. They argued that by storing surpluses up-country instead of in warehouses at big ports or cities with their consequently high charges, as the merchants did, the heavy physical costs of storage could be much reduced; and also that the heavy costs of financing under a merchant regime could be much reduced, because a collective organisation of producers would be able to borrow more cheaply than individual merchant firms, or more cheaply still by borrowing from or through their government. Reasoning such as this led to the Brazilian coffee valorisation scheme, and the operations of the Canadian wheat pools in the 1920's, and their later successors. Crop-equalisation schemes, organised by producers, can therefore be viewed either as mechanisms benefiting producers in comparison with what happens under a merchant speculator regime; or as necessary pieces of mechanism in plans for dealing with the wider problem of the stabilisation of the prices of crops subject to appreciable annual variations. In both cases the question arises whether such schemes are more or less economic than the results under a merchant speculator regime: in other words, whether the producers' thesis as outlined above is sound, or whether such schemes, necessary as they are for price stabilisation, may nevertheless involve an additional cost in comparison with a merchant speculator regime. These questions can be answered quite definitely, but only by a rather lengthy, close and detailed analysis and argument which would interrupt this general study of crop variations in relation to price stabilisation. It therefore seems better to undertake this task in an appendix to this chapter. The conclusion of this argument is that in common practice, though not in theory, the producers' thesis, as outlined above, is correct for all crops subject to large annual variations; but that for small variations the results are much the same as under a merchant regime. In no case need the results be worse, provided the producers operate their scheme with reasonable efficiency and observe certain cardinal rules. It follows, therefore, that crop equalisation by producers, as a

COMMODITY CONTROL SCHEMES

necessary mechanism in a fully fledged price-stabilisation scheme for
any crop subject to appreciable variations, should not involve an
additional economic cost; and that for crops subject to large variations there will be a positive advantage as compared with the merchant regime, quite apart from the general advantages of price stabilisation as such. Readers who are interested in knowing how these
conclusions are reached, or who doubt their validity, should now
turn to the appendix to this chapter, where the matter is argued in
detail.

A fully fledged price-stabilisation scheme for such crops will, however, have to rely on buffer stocks as its principal means of meeting
fluctuations in the demand, because for all annual crops quantitative
restriction of output can only take the form either of restricting the
amount to be harvested (which is often very difficult to enforce, and
comes very near to the abhorrent resort to destruction of harvested
supplies) or of restricting acreage, i.e. reducing capacity. The latter
again may be difficult to enforce, and anyway there may be difficulty
in expanding acreage again if the land has meantime been put to other
uses. Thus if a price-stabilisation scheme for crops subject to appreciable annual variations is to achieve its objective, there must be buffer
stocks to meet fluctuations in demand, and also at times crop-equalisation stocks. The question therefore arises whether the buffer stock
should also take charge of the business of crop equalisation, making
one international pool of stocks, or whether the two functions should
be kept quite separate.

Though both involve the holding of stocks, the problems of evening
out fluctuations in demand and crop fluctuations are in their very
nature entirely different and require separate treatment. Nothing is
gained by amalgamating these stocks unless as the result of pure
chance. By definition the whole of the excess of a bumper crop will
be required sooner or later to make up the deficiency of a short crop
or crops. If any of the excess is used to meet a sudden increase in the
demand, it will only be by pure chance that the short crop will coincide
with a fall in the demand; and if it does not, there will be a shortage
of supplies. The same is true if a buffer stock is used to make good
the deficiency of a short crop, for it will only be by luck that a bumper
crop will be harvested before the demand recovers, and so refills the
buffer stock. A scheme combining crop equalisation with the evening-
out of fluctuations in demand will not be able to manage with a
smaller total stock over the crop cycle than two separate schemes,

unless there is to be sheer speculation. If such a combined scheme is established, it should keep its crop-equalisation stocks and operations quite separate from its buffer stock, i.e. its demand-equalisation stocks. Crop fluctuations and fluctuations in demand are fundamentally different problems, and pooling of the stocks will obscure both, and jeopardise their successful solution.

If, then, the two stockpiles are to be kept separate, the further question arises whether there is anything to be gained by combining crop equalisation with demand equalisation in an international price-stabilisation scheme. Demand equalisation must be handled by a centralised international scheme, but would it be better for crop equalisation to be handled on a national, or at the most a regional, basis? It is argued in the appendix to this chapter that it is a vital condition for the success of a collective crop-equalisation scheme that the producers must be content with the smallest possible initial cash payment on the bumper crop, because this means the smallest possible borrowing by the controlling organisation, i.e. by the producers themselves. The initial payment should be only just enough to cover the cash or prime costs of the bumper crop incurred by a substantial majority of the producers, but in practice it must cover the cash costs of the highest-cost producers in order to ensure solid support for the scheme. In any single producing country or region, the conditions of production, including the technique of production, are usually roughly similar, and the range of cash costs is relatively small, even though the range of total costs, and often especially total costs plus a normal profit on widely different capitalisations, may be quite large. But as between different countries or regions, the conditions and techniques of production may vary greatly—coffee cultivation in Brazil, Colombia and Kenya: smallholdings and large highly capitalised plantations producing cotton and other crops—and then even cash or prime costs may vary considerably. With an international crop-equalisation scheme, the initial payment will almost inevitably have to be the same for all producers. If it were more for one country than for others, agreement could in practice never be secured initially or, even if it was, there would soon be trouble. Therefore if costs vary appreciably in different producing countries, as is certainly true for many primary industries, an international crop-equalisation scheme cannot work to optimum advantage. It would then be better for crop equalisation to be on a national basis, even though demand equalisation must be handled on a world basis. Moreover, there is a further, and from a long-period point of view a more weighty, objection to international crop-equalisation schemes. With many commodities the degree of crop variation differs widely between some producing countries and others—some are specially prone to large crop variations and others much less so—and a world crop-equalisation scheme would mean that the latter countries would be subsidising the former countries, whose long-period total costs ought to include the cost of the large fluctuations in their crops. This is to say that, if all other costs were equal, their long-period total costs should be higher than those of countries with small crop variations, because crop fluctuations necessarily involve a genuine actual cost. The Canadian wheat crop, for example, is subject to much larger fluctuations than the crops of any of the other big wheat exporters, and a world crop-equalisation scheme for wheat would mean that Canada benefited far more than the other countries. They would be sharing in the costs of crop equalisation beyond their true individual liabilities, and so subsidising the Canadian industry. Thus the case for national or regional crop-equalisation schemes in preference to one international scheme is very strong. National schemes are likely to be less costly because their financing can be related more closely to cash costs of production, and so kept at a minimum. They are also more truly economic because they will not disturb the relative long-period costs of different producing countries. It is true that the extreme variations of national crops are likely to be larger than the extreme variations of the world crop, because not all producing countries are likely to have bumper crops in the same season. Therefore the volume of stocks which a world scheme must hold would probably be smaller than the aggregate stocks of national schemes. But the drawbacks to a world scheme appear to outweigh substantially this advantage.

Crop-equalisation schemes should therefore be on a national, or at most a regional, basis. In a price-stabilisation scheme there must be one centralised buffer stock, and for all commodities which are subject to appreciable crop variations there should be crop-equalisation schemes on a national, or at most a regional, basis. Buffer stock control cannot function effectively unless supply is regularised. A fairly close co-ordination of action between the buffer stock authority and the national crop-equalisation schemes will clearly be necessary, and this may not be an easy administrative problem. Nevertheless, there is no sound short-cut to success by way of establishing grand world schemes to cure the fluctuations of demand and of supply by one mechanism. The sound form of growth for such industries, when they come to desire fully fledged price stabilisation, is to establish crop-equalisation schemes on a national basis; and when these are in operation, to establish a buffer stock scheme on an international basis to remedy short-period fluctuations of demand, backed by quantitative control as a last resort.

Appendix: Crop-equalisation Schemes versus the Merchant Regime

The case for collective stockholding by producers is, as already indicated, not a simple straight issue, but a compound of several issues. First, there is the claim that, given the same conditions, stockholding by a producers' organisation, or for that matter by their government, can be performed as efficiently and cheaply, and by implication more so, as stockholding by merchants. Secondly, there is the claim that with an organised scheme the physical costs of storage can be reduced below those incurred by merchants. Thirdly, there is the claim that the costs of financing stocks can be similarly reduced. These claims obviously demand separate consideration. Taking them in order, it is clear that stockholding by a producers' organisation and stockholding by merchants differ fundamentally, in that with the former the price remains stabilised, whereas with the latter it will fluctuate heavily. Does this make any difference to the relative costs of the two systems, or to the producers' claim that collective stockholding is more advantageous to them than a merchant regime? The answer is that for large crop variations there is a great practical difference, though not much for small variations. Under a merchant regime the margin between the merchants' buying and selling prices which will be required to induce the carrying-over of stocks will be substantial, even if the amount to be carried over is small. On every £100 of financing the merchant will want, say, 10% at least, and the costs of physical storage will be, say, 5%, making a minimum margin of, say, 15%, and very likely it is higher than this. Hence, if the bumper crop is only a little greater than the normal crop, e.g. 10% or perhaps a little higher, the price will fall substantially in order to provide the minimum margin, and the producers' receipts will be reduced. The total costs of producing the crop will be higher than for a normal crop, even if the costs per unit are a little lower. The producers are therefore likely to make a loss on a small bumper crop. If, however, the bumper crop is very much larger than normal, e.g. 30% or more, the margin required by the merchant may increase a little on account of the large volume of financing required, and of some increase in physical storage costs as storage capacity becomes strained, but it will not increase very much, and so the price will not fall much lower than it would for a small bumper crop. On the other hand, especially if fixed costs form a large proportion of total costs, the costs per unit of the large bumper crop will be much reduced, and the reduction may well be greater than the fall in price, with the result that the producers' income will be much larger than normal even though the total costs of producing the very large crop will also be a little larger. Thus the producers make a surplus on a large bumper crop.

In the case of small crop variations, therefore, the producers make a loss in the bumper-crop year; and also in the short-crop year, for then the price will be near normal because of the carry-over from the bumper crop, and the costs per unit of the short crop will be a little above normal. The combined loss represents the cost of the crop variations in comparison with a series of identical crops. In the case of large crop variations, the price in the short-crop year will be normal, but producers' receipts will be very much less than normal, while costs per unit will be very much higher, even if total costs are lower. In the short-crop year, the producers incur a loss which will be larger than the surplus which they made on the large bumper crop—the net deficit representing the cost of these large crop variations. But unless the producers keep and invest the surplus made on the large bumper crop to set against their inevitable coming loss on the short crop, their loss will be staggeringly heavy. Will they do so? The answer without doubt is that the vast majority of agricultural producers, whether large or small, will spend such surpluses on better living, or what is not so spent they will invest in an insufficiently liquid form, probably in extending or improving their farms. Consequently, when the short crop comes along, the producers have nothing to set against their large loss on that short crop. Their net loss on the crop cycle is in practice the whole of the loss on that crop.

Under a producers' collective stockholding scheme, the situation is much the same in the case of small crop variations as under a merchant regime. The price in the bumper-crop year remains unchanged, for the producers sell only the normal quantity, and therefore their receipts remain unchanged; but they have to carry over as stocks the excess of the bumper crop, borrowing the necessary money to enable them just to cover the higher total costs of producing that crop. Thus the producers make a loss on the bumper crop. In the short-crop year their receipts will again be normal, and the total costs of producing the crop will be less than normal, and they will therefore recoup part, though not the whole, of their loss on the bumper crop. The situation will thus work out much the same for small crop variations as under a merchant regime. With large crop variations the same sequence takes place under a collective producers' scheme, only on a larger scale: the producers make a heavy loss in the bumper-crop year, but recoup a large part of it in the short-crop year, when receipts will be normal and total costs less than normal. Their net loss will thus be smaller by the amount of the surplus which producers make on the bumper crop under a merchant regime, and which they will have spent either on consumable or capital goods before the short crop comes. In practice, therefore, a collective stockholding scheme will work out much better for the producers than the merchants' regime when crop variations are large, even though there may not be much difference when crop variations are small. The dividing line between large and small crop variations is the bumper crop for which the proceeds from its sale to merchants just exceed the total costs of producing that crop, for if that is the case, the producers will make a surplus which will not in practice be kept to offset their coming loss on the short crop. The more the proceeds of the sale to merchants of the bumper crop exceeds the total costs of producing that crop, i.e. the larger the producers' surplus on the bumper crop, the more advantageous will a collective stockholding scheme be.

This is the justification of the producers' contention that collective stockholding is more advantageous to them than a merchant regime, though they usually base their claim on arguments which are neither logical or tenable. These arguments often boil down to the allegation that the merchants make large profits, which by a collective scheme the producers could make for themselves. The other claims, that under a collective scheme the physical costs of storage and of financing will be cheaper than under a merchant regime, are much more substantial. Storage up-country certainly should be cheaper than storage at big ports or in large commercial cities, though this admittedly assumes that the physical conditions and general efficiency of storage up-country will be as good as in public warehouses at the ports and cities. Similarly, producers' organisations should be able to borrow more cheaply than individual merchants, and most governments, even of primary producing countries, can almost certainly do so. Much of course will depend on the skill and integrity with which the producers' scheme is operated. Given that this condition is adequately fulfilled, the practical advantages of such schemes are increased by cheaper storage and financing. Thus producers of crops which are subject to large annual fluctuations will be well advised to develop collective crop-equalisation schemes. If price stabilisation is a main objective, such schemes are a necessary mechanism in any fully fledged control scheme for such crops, for only so can the inevitable heavy fluctuations of the price under a merchant stockholding regime be avoided. Even with crops subject to only small fluctuations, stockholding by producers should be at least as economic as stockholding by merchants. But there are two vital conditions for the success of producers' crop-equalisation schemes. First, the price must not be stabilised at a level above the long-period equilibrium, for, if it is, the productive capacity of the industry will tend to increase sooner or later, unless it can be rigidly controlled. Secondly, the producers must be content with the smallest possible initial payments on the bumper crop, because that means the smallest possible borrowing: the higher the initial payments, the less will be the advantage of their scheme over the merchant regime. It was of course the failure of the Brazilian coffee valorisation scheme of the 1920's to observe these conditions, especially the second, which caused its disaster, even though the scheme was fundamentally sound.

Producers of annual crops subject to large variations will therefore be well advised to establish their own collective crop-equalisation schemes as an improvement, from their point of view, on the merchant speculator regime of *laissez-faire*. Only a few crops, however, are subject to large variations over reasonably short periods, i.e. only a few which approach the regularity of the coffee cycle in Brazil, and for which the producers should establish a crop-equalisation scheme on its own merits. But if a fully fledged price-stabilisation scheme is to be established, some form of equalisation scheme is necessary for all crops subject to appreciable annual variations, since under a merchant regime heavy price fluctuations are inevitable in the case of all such crops. In no case should this involve an additional economic cost, while for crops subject to large variations, there should be a positive advantage.

15. THE RECENT PROGRESS AND FUTURE PROSPECTS OF COMMODITY CONTROL

The general conclusion which emerges from the preceding chapter is that within the framework of the United Nations procedure, commodity control schemes, though prone to great dangers and difficulties, which cannot be wholly avoided by the adoption of the principle of equal consumer-producer representation, can play a useful part in stabilising the prices of primary products within a fairly wide though limited range of conditions: and that as such they could represent an important advance in the economic organisation of the primary industries, and so in the world's economy. It is probably true to say that in its early years the new system was expected to produce quite a large crop of successful control schemes, such as would make a considerable contribution to the general stability which was to be the distinctive feature of the new post-war world's economy. Such expectations, however, have not been realised. Since World War II, international control agreements have been concluded for only four[1] commodities. Of these the sugar scheme has been suspended, the tin scheme has lost control more than once, and the coffee agreement of 1962 is, as has been argued above, economically unsound whatever its political merits. None of them has achieved price stability for more than relatively short periods. The record of the wheat agreements is very much better, but this has largely been due to the national stockholding policies of the two biggest exporters and their consequent behind-the-scenes control of prices. Cocoa recently reached the stage of a negotiating conference, but agreement could not be reached between the two sides on the minimum level at which the price was to be maintained. In short, to those who believe in the merits of commodity control as an instrument of stability, the situation could hardly be much more depressing.

Those who view control schemes simply as remedies for 'burdensome surpluses' may claim that such surpluses have only appeared in the case of a few commodities, e.g. wheat and coffee; that the tin scheme should have been wound up after surplus conditions had been remedied at the end of 1959, that the sugar scheme and the proposed cocoa scheme were really unnecessary, and that control schemes for rubber and other commodities have rightly been rejected on the same

[1] The International Agreement for olive oil does not provide for any regulation of price or supplies. See page 162.

grounds. In other words they may claim that there has so far been no need for quicker or more widespread development. All the same, the 'burdensome surplus' school, as well as the would-be price stabilisers, must feel somewhat dismayed by the enormous difficulties, as shown by experience, in negotiating international commodity agreements even when there is a fairly general feeling that an agreement is desirable. Burdensome surpluses usually require speedy remedial action, while fully fledged price-stabilisation schemes are even more difficult to negotiate. Commodity agreements are formidable documents. The original wheat agreement had 23 articles, each with a number of clauses and sub-clauses; the sugar agreement 40 articles; the tin agreement 22 articles; and the recent coffee agreement no less than 72 articles. The sheer mechanical difficulties of getting agreement in such detail by often quite a large number of parties are very much greater than the architects of the Havana charter can have envisaged. Producers, when acting alone as in the inter-war period, found any sort of control scheme difficult enough to establish, especially when the state of supply and demand, and therefore prices, was altering rapidly. How much more difficult is the establishment of a control scheme which satisfies the Havana charter–United Nations procedure! The mechanical difficulties are, of course, reinforced by the varied and varying national interests of the different countries concerned; even when each has been clearly defined beforehand by usually prolonged national consideration of all the different aspects of this or that policy, not always, however, with adequate knowledge of conditions in other countries. It has not been the case that some particular important country has been consistently pursuing a policy unfavourable to the spread of commodity agreements. The attitude of the United States, for example, has never been wholly averse to commodity control, even though the Randall Commission in effect condemned it in any shape or form. The U.S.A. was an original member of the wheat agreement, and has probably always been desirous of a cotton agreement if an effective one could only be devised and generally agreed. Recently the U.S.A. took the initiative in promoting the International Coffee Agreement. Similarly the British Commonwealth Prime Ministers' Conference had only just declared in favour of the principles of commodity control and of its extension when Britain refused to join the international wheat agreement of 1953. It is the mixture of interests—interests as producers of this commodity and as consumers of that commodity—which has resulted in the varied attitude and policy of some of the leading nations of the world towards the making of agreements for particular commodities, and has therefore hindered general progress in the development of commodity control.

This mixture of interests, and the history of commodity control negotiations in the 1950's, led some of those who believe in the merits of commodity control to argue that progress would be faster if, instead of a commodity-by-commodity approach, i.e. by separate negotiations for each commodity, there was a general approach, i.e. an international conference to consider control schemes for, say, six to ten commodities at the same time. It is argued that countries would then bargain as they do over tariffs at the G.A.T.T. conferences, yielding here in order to gain elsewhere. Thus the U.S.A. might agree to participate in agreements for rubber and tin if this facilitated an agreement on cotton, while Britain might have continued membership of the wheat agreements in 1953 and 1956 if this had facilitated agreements for rubber and tin. From the point of view of practical politics there may be something to be said for this idea, provided one condition is satisfied, namely that there is among the nations a genuine fundamental desire to bring about general and widespread commodity control. At least until very recently it could not be said that this condition was satisfied, if only because of its absence in U.S. policy. Unless it is satisfied, any such general approach is doomed to failure, just as G.A.T.T. would never have made much progress had there not been a general fundamental desire among the nations to lower tariffs, if on balance this could advantageously be achieved. From an economic point of view, however, there are obviously great dangers if bargaining over membership were to lead, as it probably would do, to bargaining over the terms of the agreements, and especially over the level at which prices were to be stabilised. The results might well be the regulation of industries on an artificial basis divorced from costs of production, which would lead in due course to serious economic disadvantages and losses, both to producers and consumers. Moreover, the individual commodity-by-commodity approach has the great advantage that it provides experience of the working of controls without serious cost to the world's economy as a whole. The accumulation of such experience is most desirable, for there is so far little enough to go on, especially in respect of buffer stock and crop-equalisation mechanisms. It may be doubted whether a general approach has much more to commend it now than in the past.

Despite much consideration by a variety of international organisations and committees, and despite the many studies and reports which have appeared in considerable profusion, the record of actual control schemes which have been in operation since World War II does not suggest that the prospects for any widespread development of commodity control in the near future are at all promising. This was certainly so until, say, 1960. Since then there has been a very important change in ideas as to the nature and functions of commodity control, which requires careful and critical study. Before embarking on this, however, mention must be made of one brighter part of the general picture, namely the achievements of most, if not all, of the international study groups which have come into existence under the Havana charter–United Nations procedure. The formation of these study groups was originally planned as a first preliminary step towards the making of an international agreement for the commodity concerned, and the four international agreements were all prepared by such bodies.[1] But in addition study groups have been set up for a number of other commodities, of which some of the more important are cotton, wool, rubber, lead and zinc; while F.A.O. has similar groups for several foodstuffs, including cocoa, coconut products, grains, rice, bananas and citrus fruit. Most, if not indeed all, of these study groups have greatly improved the available statistics concerning their commodities, and some have initiated annual or periodical reviews of recent history, present position and prospects, for example, the rubber study group. Only in the case of cocoa has the study group got as far as actually drafting a control agreement, but the other groups have done much to bring about a generally collaborative attitude among the parties, and to initiate some degree of more or less informal consultation. This role has appeared most definitely in the case of the lead and zinc study group, which in recent years has more than once brought about effective restriction of production extending over most of the industries, even though on an entirely voluntary basis and without any formal written agreements. There can be no doubt that by and large these study groups have been a most useful addition to the international organisation of the industries concerned, even if they have only led on to formal commodity control agreements in a few cases.

[1] The International Wheat Council and the International Sugar Council were in effect grafted into the system in so far as their work was similar to that of study groups constituted by the U.N., as in the cases of tin and coffee.

Against this background, attention must now be given to the change of ideas as to the nature and functions of commodity control which, as already mentioned, has been taking place during recent years, and is still in progress. Since about 1960 the whole vast problem of aid to 'underdeveloped' countries has come much to the fore in international relations. In about 1960 it was realised that the prolonged downward slide of the prices of most primary products during the 1950's was neutralising a large part of the financial aid which the developed or richer countries were giving to the underdeveloped or poorer countries; and that heavy fluctuations in primary product prices,which resulted in large fluctuations of total national export earnings, were jeopardising the long-term development programmes which the financial aid was meant to support. Here the focus was on the national economies of the underdeveloped countries, and only on the problems of their important primary industries in so far as they affected the national economy of the country concerned. Consequently, so far as commodity control is concerned, the emphasis has shifted from price stabilisation as a benefit to the commodity's producers and consumers, i.e. to the particular primary industry, to price stabilisation as a benefit to the national economies of the producing countries. And if commodity control to secure price stabilisation, why not commodity control to raise the stabilised price to a level which would give the producing countries larger export earnings? In other words, commodity control schemes should be instruments for stabilising prices at the highest possible level, as a form of direct and most effective aid from the richer consuming countries to the poorer primary producing countries, by providing them with larger and steadier foreign incomes.

Commodity control has thus been caught up into the toils of aid to underdeveloped countries. As such, it has become a political as much as, or more than, an economic instrument. Political considerations which tend to be based on short-term views have become more important than economic considerations, which are often of a longer-term character. The 1962 International Coffee Agreement was the first example of these developments, and a glaring example at that. This agreement has already been subjected to scrutiny above,[1] but the reader may be reminded that its primary objective was to prevent any decline of coffee prices in general below the 1962 level; a level which was roughly double the price at which Brazil, by far the largest

[1] See pages 180–2.

producer, could profitably supply more than her export quota under the agreement. The United States undoubtedly took the main initiative in bringing about this agreement, partly as a political move in the Cold War and to promote Pan-American solidarity, but also on the basis of President Kennedy's dictum that a fall of one cent a lb in green coffee prices cost Latin-American producers 'enough seriously to under-cut what we are seeking to accomplish by the Alliance for Progress'. In short, a commodity control scheme was used for political ends, and without regard to economic considerations and economic consequences, which are not of course confined to the results of divorcing prices from costs, vitally important as that link is.

Further evidence of a new conception of the role of commodity agreements was supplied by the abortive cocoa conference in October 1963. The producing and consuming sides proved to be wide apart in their proposals for the 'floor price' at which restrictive quotas would be put into operation. As *The Economist* commented,[1] 'the producers' demands were pitched unrealistically high because they saw the agreement as part of a programme of aid for underdeveloped countries. The consumers were anxious to fix the floor price at a level that keeps the operations of the agreement to a minimum for commercial reasons.' The negotiations made it quite clear, moreover, that the floor price was simply and solely a matter of hard bargaining, and was to be fixed by reference to no economic criteria. The producers are said to have started at 248s. per cwt, and to have come down to about 200s. The consumers raised their original proposal slightly to about 160s. In this case, unlike that of coffee, the consuming side appears not to have been much influenced by political considerations, or by the need for aid to the producing countries; and so no agreement was reached, and the conference broke down; but the episode illustrates the way in which the wind was blowing.

This wind further increased in force at the United Nations Trade and Development Conference in Geneva in the summer of 1964. The underdeveloped countries, which are mostly of course dependent on exports of primary products, made it quite clear that in their view the most suitable and desirable form of aid is prices for their exports stabilised at as high a level as reasonably possible, i.e. that the richer nations, which are the main importers, should in effect subsidise the prices of primary products instead of giving financial aid in the form of gifts and loans. 'Trade, not aid' was the slogan, and one which

[1] Issue of 2 November 1963.

seems, on the face of it, much more suitable and dignified than mere charity. But if 'trade' means trade at high prices divorced from any relationship with costs of production—prices as high as the richer nations can be coerced into paying by political and any other pressures—then this is really only charity in disguise.

If commodity control is to be used in this way to stabilise prices at an artifically high level, the results will be disastrous to the world's economy and to the growth of the world's wealth at the maximum rate. It is a fundamental economic principle that prices should be related to cost of production.[1] If they are not, resources are being wasted somewhere. Demand, supply and price are always altering, and cost of production is the only true measuring rod by which the world's resources can be continually and correctly adjusted to the world's needs. Restriction of production in order to maintain artificially high prices inevitably means restriction of the world's wealth, because resources of land, labour, and capital are either left unused or being misapplied. Moreover, the productivity of different sources of supply is continually changing, as are the consumer's preferences for different qualities and different amounts of individual products, and the regulators are relative costs and prices. But if the existing structure of an industry is frozen by a control scheme, no such adjustments will take place—capacity which is or becomes high-cost and obsolescent feels no compulsion or incentive to close down, and the entry of new producers is prevented or at least delayed. Unless the measuring rod of cost is continually in active use, the world will produce too little of some things from the wrong sources. Then either resources will not be fully utilised or, as is probable, they will be transferred to the production of too much of other goods. Thus the production of wealth will be smaller than it need and should be. In short, artificially high prices mean restriction of production, and restriction cannot result in expansion. The lessons of control schemes in the inter-war period should not be forgotten.

If the politicians of consuming countries accept this doctrine of trade at artificially high prices as preached by the politicians of underdeveloped countries for their primary products, then economists everywhere should shout, and for once can do so with one voice, that this policy is bound to lead to the waste and misuse of the

[1] Cost of production should be taken to mean the cost of an average crop, or of full normal output (including a normal profit and full allowance for depreciation) to efficient producers working under normal conditions.

world's limited resources, and cannot maximise the world's wealth. If the supply of primary products is restricted below what the world should have, as shown by the measuring rod of cost, the whole economic system of the world becomes twisted and warped, and cannot function with maximum efficiency. Admittedly some countries may succeed for a time in snatching a temporary advantage, but that can only be at the expense of others. The use and adaptation of commodity control schemes deliberately to secure artificially high prices is a throwback to the worst examples of controls in the inter-war period, such as the British rubber restriction scheme and Copper Exporters Inc.; it is the negation of the ideas and doctrines on which the Havana charter–United Nations conception of the proper uses of commodity control schemes was built; it amounts to the prostitution of control schemes as instruments for the proper stabilisation of prices. These are hard words, but the present trend of political thought, not only in the underdeveloped countries but also, for example, in the United States as witness the International Coffee Agreement, calls for plain unvarnished speaking and teaching concerning its economic drawbacks and consequences.

All this, however, is not to say that commodity control schemes have no part to play in solving the vast, many-sided and intricate problem of aid to underdeveloped countries. On the contrary, they can, if properly used, contribute substantially to its solution. In respect of their external or international situation, underdeveloped primary producing countries today have two main specific problems: fluctuating foreign earnings, and inadequate foreign earnings—inadequate, that is, in relation to their need and plans for rapid development. Now the first problem—fluctuating foreign earnings—can be largely solved by commodity control agreements of one kind or another if properly operated, and should be so solved. But commodity control must not be used to solve the second problem— inadequate foreign earnings—for it has no powers to increase productivity, and it cannot raise prices artificially without distorting the world's economy, and thereby reducing its potential wealth. This is not to deny that restriction of supply can raise prices artificially, or that with an inelastic demand this will raise the foreign earnings of the exporting countries; but history shows that this is unlikely to continue for long, and even if this policy is applied to only a few primary products it is none the less objectionable and unsound from the point of view of the world's economy as a whole.

Commodity control, then, has a definite part to play in the solution of the problems of underdeveloped countries, but it is a limited part confined to helping to even out fluctuations in foreign earnings. The raising of inadequate foreign earnings, and all the other facets of promoting the development of the poorer countries at the maximum rate, are outside the proper domain of commodity control, and therefore outside the scope of this book. Nevertheless, the role of commodity control in helping the development of primary producing countries, so many of which are underdeveloped countries, should not be underestimated. Fluctuations in the foreign earnings of a primary commodity which forms a large proportion of an underdeveloped country's total exports are a real evil. The service of foreign loans, both short and long, is jeopardised, and this makes such loans more difficult to obtain; the fear of restrictions on the transfer of funds abroad inhibits capital investment by foreign firms; domestic savings and investment are deterred or become irregular; and planning for development becomes generally difficult and hazardous. As has been argued at length in this and the preceding chapter, commodity control, properly and skilfully operated, can provide most valuable remedial treatment, which will undoubtedly be of great benefit to such countries. By stabilising the price, in the proper sense of the term, commodity control schemes of one kind or another can go far towards stabilising the export earnings of such producing countries, as well as the incomes of the actual individual producers.

As has been stressed in this study, however, control schemes in practice have various dangers and drawbacks, which are not likely to be wholly avoided. This has led to proposals for international compensation schemes.[1] In essence these provide for the creation of a central fund by contributions from exporting and importing countries, from which compensation would be paid to countries whose export earnings fell below an agreed average or trend. In some versions of such schemes, the contributions of the richer importing countries would be larger than those of the poorer exporting countries, and there are other provisions which can make the scheme a channel for aid to underdeveloped countries. But even if the scheme is confined to its simplest form of evening out fluctuations in national export earnings, it is the governments of the exporting countries which would receive the compensation payments, not the actual producers

---

[1] See the U.N. publication *International Compensation for Fluctuations in Commodity Trade* (1961).

of the commodities exported. Such a scheme is intended to prevent the repercussions on the national economies of countries whose export earnings from all sources are subject to large fluctuations, and the compensation is meant to be used accordingly. It is not a scheme to stabilise the incomes of the actual producers of the exports. But it follows that a compensation scheme of this character and commodity control schemes can both operate together. A compensation scheme does not produce the same results as commodity control: the two are not alternatives, nor mutually exclusive, and they can well be complementary: indeed commodity control should make a compensation agreement easier to negotiate, and should facilitate its operation. Compensation schemes, however, are really concerned with the problem of aid to underdeveloped countries; they have only been mentioned here in order to make the point that they are not an alternative to commodity control; and nothing more will be said about them except to remark that they have their drawbacks and dangers just as has commodity control.

Surveying the prospects for the extension and development of commodity control in the foreseeable future, it seems clear that much will depend on whether it will be misused for political purposes. There is a real danger at the present time that it will be so misused in connection with aid to underdeveloped countries; and this is all the more frightening because it may bring to an end the whole Havana charter–United Nations conception of commodity control as a partnership between exporting and importing countries. Importing countries which try to secure price stabilisation at an economic level may well find that they cannot persuade the underdeveloped primary producing countries of the errors of their high-price policy; and unless they resort to extreme measures, such as the cutting off of all aid or its considerable reduction, all they can do is to walk out of the conference room. But that may not be the end. After the failure of the cocoa conference of 1963, the producing countries promptly set about establishing a control scheme of their own, with artificially high prices as its almost certain objective.[1] If this example is widely followed, commodity control will be back in the inter-war period, with all the dangers and drawbacks of schemes run by producers only. Yet not all primary producers are, to use a vernacular idiom, 'price drunk',

---

[1] This did not meet with much success: in March 1965 the price was down to 130s. (compare p. 214). In December 1964 the Ghana Cocoa Marketing Board publicly burned 500 tons of stocks with the avowed object of raising the price.

in the way in which cocoa and coffee producers seem to be, and also producers of some other mainly tropical and sub-tropical agricultural commodities. Producers of copper have been trying to hold its price by informal agreements at a level far below the so-called free market level of the London Metal Exchange, simply because they are convinced that higher prices will result in the widespread use of substitutes, notably aluminium.[1] Zinc producers in July 1964 adopted the same policy for the same reason, and lead producers were fully conscious that the rise in price had gone too far for their industry's well-being in the long run. Producers of sisal were said to be very nervous of the high price level ruling in 1963–4, again because of its encouragement to the development of substitutes and the general effects on demand. Natural rubber producers ever since the war have of course had to watch most closely the competitive position of synthetic rubber; and cotton and wool producers cannot afford to be indifferent to the competition of artificial fibres. In short, some primary industries have learned the dangers of excessively high prices from past experience, reinforced by the current threat of new as well as existing substitutes; but others have no such inhibitions. It therefore seems probable that in the foreseeable future commodity control will present a very varied picture. There will be some schemes which have been established on a sound basis and are operating to secure price stabilisation at a genuine economic level: the non-ferrous metals, rubber, sisal, tea, perhaps wheat and sugar, and even cotton and wool seem likely or at least possible candidates. There will be other schemes which are designed and operated to raise prices artificially high in order to serve political interests, whether in connection with cold wars or aid to underdeveloped countries: coffee may well continue to be the outstanding, but not the only, example. And if the present example of the producers of cocoa is copied, as it may well be, there will be schemes run by producers only in order to secure the highest possible prices, irrespective of the risks involved. The results will consequently also present a varied picture of good and evil, of political gains and economic losses. On the whole, it seems likely that commodity control will be extended and developed in this varying fashion, but how soon and how quickly is guesswork. It must never be forgotten how difficult and complicated a business it is to negotiate a commodity control agreement, let alone operate it to secure its objectives, whether these be economically sound or unsound.

[1] For a somewhat fuller account, see chapter 9, p. 108.

Excessive price fluctuations are a running sore in the world's economy. They are like an illness of the human body which does not kill but greatly impairs its efficiency. Commodity control is like a drug which can largely neutralise such ills if administered correctly, but which can produce extremely dangerous results if the right dosage is exceeded, or if it is administered in wrong ways. The trouble is that the world has as yet only vague ideas as to how it should be administered correctly, especially as dosage of a certain order can produce results of a kind which seem for a time to be beneficial, though ultimately making the patient worse. To give up experimenting with such a drug is a counsel of despair. There is enough, if only just enough, experience of how it should, and should not, be used to support a prima-facie case that it can be a most efficacious remedy. This prima facie case has been set out here both in theory and with the backing of commodity control's history to date. It may be hoped that this study will at least help to prevent the repetition of past mistakes which might otherwise recur, and that it will indicate the lines on which future experimental treatment should be conducted. For the correct administration of commodity control can only be learned by experiment. The world may find this a lengthy and perhaps costly process, but it should be well worth while in the end.

INDEX

aid, economic, 99, 213–15, 217–18
Algeria: imports, 30–1; zinc export, 12, 118
arbitrage, 45, 56
Argentina: export policy, 97–8; exports, 7–9, 11, 113–16; government selling, 54; imports, 30–1; relation to wheat agreements, 164–6; wheat, maize and meat industries, 18–19
Australia: exports, 7, 9–10, 12–13, 113–15, 118–19; government selling, 54; imports, 30–1

barter terms of trade, 83, 88
Bolivia, tin export, 12, 117
Brazil: coffee industry, 22–3; coffee valorisation scheme, 81, 89, 133–6; cotton industry, 23–4; exports, 8–9, 11–12, 113–14, 116–18; imports, 30–1; retention of coffee stocks, 179
British West Indies, sugar export, 10
Bulgaria, tobacco export, 11, 116
bulk trading, 52–3, 55; appraisal of, 62–3; comparison with private merchanting, 63–6
Burma, rice export, 11, 116

Canada: control of wheat prices, 81, 89, 130–1, 166–7; exports, 7, 9, 12–13, 113, 115, 118–19; government selling, 54; imports, 30–1
capacity for production, changes of, 75, 196–7
Ceylon, exports, 8, 10–11, 114, 116–17
Chadbourne countries, 145–7
Chile, copper export, 9, 115
China, exports, 8, 12, 114, 117
coal, regional export, 3, 28–9
cocoa, 110, 112; abortive conference, 214; export, 5, 11, 117; import of, 31; price fluctuations, 67, 102
coffee, 110, 111; Brazilian valorisation scheme, 81, 89, 122, 124–5, 133–6, 201; export of, 5, 9, 114; import of, 30; international agreement, 177–83, 209; price fluctuations, 67, 102; production of, 22–3; Uganda, 34–5
collection of products, 34–7
Colombia: coffee export, 9, 114; coffee production, 23; retention of crop, 179
commodity control, see control schemes
companies, holding, 16
companies, joint-stock, 13, 19, 37; nonferrous metals, 15–18; petroleum, 14–

15; rubber, 25–6; sisal, 21; sugar, 25; tea, 20
compensation schemes, 217–18
Congo, exports, 8–10, 12, 114–15, 117–18
consumer representation, 138, 152, 160, 184–8
consumers; principal, 29–31; regional, 28–9
consumption, post-war increase in U.S.A., 97
contracts: long-term, 65; standardised, 48
control schemes, 81, 89, 90, 105; aims and methods of, 157–60; changed function of, 213; history of, 127–9, 136–55, 155–83; prospects of, 211–20; working of, 184–208, 209–11
co-operative societies: consumers', 185–6; producers', 19, 20, 34, 35–6, 55, 56
copper, 110, 111; control scheme, 90–1, 154–5; export of, 5, 9, 115; Exporters Inc., 125–6; import of, 31; price fluctuations, 67, 102, 108; production of, 17–18; restriction of output, 81, 124
costs, see production and stockholding
cotton, 110, 111; American, 2, 132; British insurance scheme, 66; export of, 5, 8, 114; import of, 30; price of, 102; production of, 23–4
crops: destruction of, 135–6; equalisation of, 198–205, 205–8
Cuba: exports, 10, 11, 115; sugar, 81, 125, 145–6, 176–7
Cuban crisis, 67

dairy products: export of, 5, 10, 116; import of, 31
demand: final, 73–4, 148; market, 69–70, 85, 129, 189
Denmark, export of dairy produce, 10
depression, world, 87–8, 127
distribution of products, 38–9
Dominican Republic, sugar export, 10, 115

Europe, export of primary commodities, 5, 12, 13; western, imports, 30–1
export of primary commodities: see tables I, 5; II, 7–13; V, 113–19

farms: family, 21; mixed, 19
fats and oils, 110, 111; export of, 5, 8, 114; import of, 30
fibres, hard: export of, 5, 12, 118; import of, 31

221

fluctuations: of crops, 202–3; of demand, 202–3; of price, 67, 155, 213, 219 (longer-term, 73–5; short-term, 68–73)
foodstuffs: export of, 2; production of, 79
foreign earnings of underdeveloped countries, 216
foreign exchange, post-war difficulties, 155; in Latin America, 182; in U.K., 53–5
Formosa (Taiwan), sugar export, 10, 115; import, 30
France, 77
future delivery, 46
futures markets, 47–52, 54, 55

G.A.T.T., 159
Germany, 77; inflation in, 78
Ghana: cocoa export, 11, 117; marketing-board, 34–5
gold standard, abandonment of, 85, 149
government interventions, 54, 89–90, 137; by direct control, 155; see also prices
Greece, tobacco export, 11, 116
groundnuts, 22

hedging, 50–2

import of primary commodities, see table III, 30–1
India: exports, 11, 114, 116–17; imports, 30–1
Indonesia: exports, 8, 10–12, 110, 114–15, 117; imports, 31; political changes, 97; relation to tin agreement, 170
integration: horizontal, 16–18; vertical, 14, 16–18
Iran: export, 7; import, 31; petroleum industry, 15
Iraq: export, 7; import, 31; petroleum industry, 15
iron ore, regional trade, 3–4, 28–9
Italy, 77

Japan: imports, 30–1; invasions of Asia, 95, 154
Java, sugar industry, 25, 145–6
jute: export of, 5, 12, 118; import of, 31; price of, 102

Keynes, Lord, 60–1, 156
Korean War, 101–2, 169–70; see especially table IV, 102
Kuwait, petroleum export, 7

Labour government, 53

lead, 110, 112; export of, 5, 13, 119; import of, 31; price of, 102
Liverpool, 39, 42, 47; reopening of markets, 54

London, 36, 37, 42, 47; commercial pre-eminence, 39; post-war auctions and markets, 54–5

maize, 110, 112; export of, 5, 11, 116; import of, 31
Malaya, exports, 8, 10, 12, 116–17; imports, 31
Manilla (fibre), 110; export of, 12, 118; import of, 31; price fluctuations, 67
manufacturers, 186
marketing, 33; collection, 34–7; distribution, 38–9; shipment, 37–8; stock-holding, 39–42
Marketing boards, 34–5
markets: port, 38–9; satellite, 39, 43
Mauritius, sugar export, 10
meat, 111; export of, 5, 7, 113; import of, 30
mechanisation, 84
merchants, 186–7; in distribution, 38–9; in price-making, 45, 69–71; itinerant, 37; local, 34, 43
metals, non-ferrous: price fluctuations, 67; production of, 15–18
Mexico, exports, 8–9, 12–13, 114, 118–19
Middle East, petroleum export, 7; petroleum industry, 14–15
middlemen, 37, 184
minerals, metallic: mining of, 68–9; sale by description, 37
monopoly, 47, 53; in control schemes, 121, 137
Morocco: exports, 12–13, 118–19; import, 31
Munich agreement, 89, 91

Netherlands, export of dairy produce, 10
New York, 37, 39, 42, 47, 55
New Zealand: exports, 7, 9–10, 113, 115; imports, 30–1
Nigeria: exports, 8, 10–12, 117; marketing boards, 34–5

oils, see fats and oils
oils, vegetable, 8, 30 n.

Pakistan: jute export, 12, 118; rice import, 31
Peru, exports, 8–10, 12–13, 114–15, 118–19
petroleum, 110; export of, 5, 7, 113; import of, 30; production of, 14–15
Philippines, exports, 8, 10, 12, 114–15
planned economy, 158, 193
plantation estates, 20–1, 22–4
political factors, 62–3, 176–7, 181–2, 214
population, increase of, 86, 107
ports, 33
price-range control, types of, 195

prices, 43–76 *passim*; control policy in 1930's, 138–9; government control of, 52–3, 62–3, 103, 132; indexes of, 78, 80; making of, 37, 41; manipulation of, 59–60; movements of in late 1920's, 83, 85, 130; movements of since 1939, 91–109 *passim*; speculative control of, 56–62; stabilisation of, 76, 156, 193–8, 198–205, 208, 217; support policy in U.S.A., 165; world, 44–5, 57, 66, 99

primary industries: definition of, 1–2; value of exports, 2

processors, 1, 37, 184

producers' representation: direct, 184–5; governmental, 185

production, 86–7, 95, 100; conditions of, 13–26; costs of, 83, 128, 155, 215; freezing of pattern of, 192, 215; scale of, 26–7

productivity, rise in, 83, 128, 189, 198

quantitative control, 189–93, 193–8

quotas: export, 146–54 *passim*, 175; import, 172

raw materials, export of, 2

regional trade, 28–9, 34

Rhodesia, exports, 9, 11, 115–16

rice, 109, 111; export of, 5, 11, 116; import of, 31

rubber, 111; export of, 5, 10, 116; international agreement, 152–4; import of, 31; price fluctuations, 102; production of, 25–6; restriction schemes, 81, 123–4, 126; war-time shortage of, 94

Russia, *see* U.S.S.R.

Saudi-Arabia: petroleum export, 7; petroleum industry, 15

shipment of commodities, 32–4, 37–8; war difficulties, 77, 92, 95

Singapore, 42; tin market, 47

sisal, 110, 112; export of, 12, 118; import of, 31; price of, 74, 102, production of, 21; sale of, 36

smallholders, 13, 34–5, 153; industries of, 21–2, 22–4, 25–6

South Africa: exports, 9–11, 115–16; imports, 30–1

speculation: organised (appraisal of), 56–62 (compared with bulk trading), 63–6; second-degree, 60–1

speculators: function of, 45–7, 52; in relation to crop-equalisation schemes, 199–200, 205–6; *see also* merchants

'spot' markets, 48–50, 52, 55

stockholding, 38; collective, 206–8; contrasted with supply restriction, 189–93; costs of, 42, 72–3; described 39–42

stockpiling: in 1939–40, 92; post-war, 97, 99, 101–3, 170

stocks, 40–1; buffer, 139, 143–4, 156 (in relation to price control, 193–8); changes in, 81–2, 86

study groups, 120; U.N., 159, 161, 212

subsidies, 87

Sudan: cotton export, 8, 114; cotton production, 23–4

Suez crisis, 105, 171

sugar, 110, 111; export of, 5, 10, 115; import of, 31; international agreements (in 1930's), 90, 144–8, (post-war), 174–7, 209; price of, 67, 102; supplies of, 78

supply and demand, 82–3, 87, 96, 99; relation to price, 66–7, 68–9, 75

supply: market, 70–1, 74–5; restriction of, 189–93; shortages, 94–6; sources, 109–12; surpluses, 93–4

Tanganyika, 36; sisal export, 12, 118

tariffs, 87, 211; on copper, 154

tea, 110, 112; export of, 5, 11, 117; import of, 31; international agreement, 90, 148–51; production of, 20–1

technical progress, 128

Thailand, exports, 10–12, 116–17

timber, regional export, 3, 28

tin, 2, 109; control schemes, 90, 140–4, 169–74, 209; export of, 5, 12, 117; import of, 31; price fluctuations, 102; war-time shortage, 73, 94

tobacco, 110, 111; export of, 5, 11, 116; import of, 31; production of, 21

Turkey, exports, 8, 11, 114, 116

Uganda: exports, 8, 9, 114; marketing boards, 34–5

underdeveloped countries, 214–15, 216

unemployment, 159, 189–90

United Arab Republic, cotton export, 8, 114

United Kingdom, 5, 33, 77, 166; imports, 30–1; wartime controls, 52–4

United Nations, 160

Uruguay, exports, 7, 9, 113–15

U.S.A. (United States of America), 77, 210; coffee, 180; controls, 52–4, 131–2; copper industry, 17; cotton, 23–4, 132; exports, 7–8, 11–13, 113–14, 116; home consumption, 2; imports, 30–1; petroleum industry, 14–15; price-support policy, 165; rice, 22 n., 110; sugar, 174; wheat and maize, 18–19

U.S.S.R. (Union of Soviet Socialist Republics), 28, 78, 80; tin, 172–3; wheat, 168–9

Venezuela: petroleum export, 7, 113; petroleum industry, 15

volume of exports (primary commodities), 5, 109–19

wages and incomes, 83, 107, 156–7

Wall Street crash, 85, 127, 129

war, 91; Korean, 101–2; World I, 77, 122; World II, 52–3, 55, 73, 155, 177

waste of resources, 182, 215–16

wheat, 77, 78, 110, 111; Canadian pools, 81, 89, 130–1, 201; export of, 5, 7, 113; government selling, 54; import of, 30; international agreements, 90, 151–2, 163–9, 209; measures in U.S.A., 131–2; price of, 102; structure of industry, 18

wool, 37, 110, 111, 122; export of, 5, 9, 115; import of, 31; price fluctuations, 67, 102

zinc, 110, 112; export of, 5, 12, 118; import of, 31; price of, 102